"LUXURY" FLEET

"Luxury" Fleet:

The Imperial German Navy 1888–1918

HOLGER H. HERWIG

London

GEORGE ALLEN & UNWIN

Boston   Sydney

First published in 1980

GEORGE ALLEN & UNWIN LTD
40 Museum Street, London WCIA ILU

© Holger H. Herwig, 1980

British Library Cataloguing in Publication Data

Herwig, Holger Heinrich
  'Luxury' fleet.
  1. Germany – Kriegsmarine – History
  I. Title
  359'.00943   DD106

  ISBN 0–04–943023–8

Typeset in 11 on 12 point Baskerville by Watford Typesetters Ltd
and printed in Great Britain
by Unwin Brothers Limited, Old Woking, Surrey

In Memory of My Grandfather,
Hermann Strauss

Contents

List of Illustrations

PLATES

The illustrations listed above are reproduced from the Collection of
the Imperial War Museum, by permission. The cartoon "Sweeping the
North Sea", however, is reproduced by permission of The Proprietors
of *Punch*.

"The German Emperor is ageing me; he is like a battleship with steam up and screws going, but with no rudder, and he will run into something some day and cause a catastrophe."

— Sir Edward Grey

Abbreviations and Conversions

mm	......	1 millimetre (0.039 inches)
cm	......	1 centimetre (0.39 inches)
m	......	1 metre (1.09 yards; 3.28 feet)
km	......	1 kilometre (0.6 miles; 1,093.6 yards)
kg	......	1 kilogram (2.2 pounds)
t	......	1 tonne (0.984 British long tons)
sm	......	1 seemeile, 1 nautical mile (1.85 kilometre; 6,080 feet)
kn	......	1 knot per hour (6,080 feet p.h.; 1.15 miles p.h.; 1.85 kilometre p.h.)
GM	......	1 Goldmark (6.146 grains of gold, 900 fine, or British standard gold in the value of 11.747 *d*, of £0.0489; US $ 28.8 cents)

in	......	1 inch (2.5 centimetres)
ft	......	1 foot (0.3 metres)
yd	......	1 yard (0.9 metres)
mile	......	1 mile (1.6 kilometres)
lb	......	1 pound avoirdupois (0.4536 kilograms; 453.6 grams)
ton	......	1 British long ton (2,240 pounds; 1.016 tonne)
£	......	1 pound sterling (20.40 Goldmarks; $4.85)
hp	......	1 horse power (550 foot-pounds per second; power required to lift 75 kilograms one metre high)

Introduction

On 27 June 1897 the Royal Navy flaunted its maritime supremacy at Spithead before the assembled leaders of the Empire who had come to celebrate Queen Victoria's Diamond Jubilee. Six mighty columns, each of five miles length, paraded an awesome array of 165 British warships. *The Times* was barely able to maintain its reserve: "It is at once the most powerful and far-reaching weapon which the world has ever seen." Since 1805, when Britain crushed the combined fleets of France and Spain off Cape Trafalgar, there had occurred no major naval challenge. Her traditional enemies, France and Russia, were scarcely in a position to threaten her at sea and the emergence of two new navies, those of the United States and Japan, posed no menace at the turn of the century. Britannia did, indeed, rule the waves. Her naval ship designs were eagerly copied everywhere, her training missions visited foreign lands from Turkey to Japan, her shipyards were purveyors to the nations of every continent, the dress of her officers and ratings had become universal, and – also importantly – her proud naval tradition and history commanded respect from those who were eye-witnesses of the review.

But storm clouds were already ominously gathering on the horizon. In the same year as the Diamond Jubilee Germany announced her intention to create a sizeable battle fleet, one that, as it was soon realized in London, would be concentrated primarily in the North Sea. Britain, on the other hand, did not maintain a single first-class naval station along her eastern coastline. In the Navy Bills of 1898 and 1900, augmented by Supplementary Bills in 1906, 1908 and 1912, the Reich proposed to create a modern battle fleet of 41 battleships, 20 large cruisers and 40 light cruisers. Such a force, expected to be second only to that of Great Britain, would complement the most efficient army certainly in Europe and possibly in the world.

Germany already possessed by 1900 the nucleus of a colonial empire. Under Chancellor Otto v. Bismarck she had acquired in the 1880s German South–West Africa, Togoland, the Cameroons, German East Africa, German New Guinea, and the Marshall

Islands. To be added to this later were Kiaochow, the Caroline, Palau and Mariana islands, and parts of Samoa. German merchant lines such as the Hamburg–America Line and the North German Lloyd were opening up new trade routes from the Orinoco to the Yangtze rivers. Her industry flooded world markets with efficient and dynamic salesmen, and pressure groups at home clamoured incessantly for new overseas possessions. Nor was the academic community immune to this development: in the years between 1897 and 1906, no less than 270 so-called "fleet professors" actively worked on behalf of the navy in raising support among the German people and government for the construction of a mighty battle fleet.

Behind this feverish activity stood the influence and power of German business and industry. Friedrich Krupp, Albert Ballin, Arthur Gwinner, and Adolf Woermann were just a few who underwrote the fleet propaganda. German production since 1871 had been spectacular. Her coal output had risen from 38,000,000 tons in 1871 to 179,000,000 tons in 1913, and by 1910 she produced annually 13,000,000 tons of steel – some 5,000,000 tons more than Great Britain and second only to the United States. Her population by 1914 had increased to 67,000,000 people, a 60 per cent rise since the end of the wars of unification in 1871 (41,000,000), and along with a healthy birthrate of 1 per cent per annum, the depressing flow of emigration had ebbed from a high in 1881 of 221,000 to slightly more than 30,000 per year by the turn of the century. The population flow from country to city trebled the number of major cities and doubled the urban population by 1900 (30,000,000). The upshot of rapid industrialization, combined with this demographic shift, was that the working class increased from one-fifth of the German *Volk* in 1870 to one-third in 1907. The Reich's merchant fleet (ships over 100 t) grew meteorically from 82,000 tons in 1872 to 5,134,000 tons by 1914. Other branches of industry, such as textiles, electricity, chemical products, and machine making, among others, witnessed equal or even greater growth. And her four major private banks (Deutsche, Dresdner, Diskonto, and Darmstädter) financed railway construction, especially in Turkey and Venezuela.

These impersonal statistics take on meaning if one thinks of them in terms of blast furnaces, rolling mills, rail networks, factory chimneys, and generators producing the steel, energy and tools necessary to construct a modern battle fleet, as well as to meet the demands of the world's major markets. Moreover, there burst upon the scene in June 1888 the last of the Hohenzollerns: Wilhelm II, German Emperor and King of Prussia, as he believed, by the Grace of God. Dynamic, impetuous, aggressive, yet at the same time insecure, nervous, hesitant, Wilhelm quickly gathered around him an entourage of advisors who catered to his every whim while at the same time taking advantage of his weaknesses. With the appointment in June 1897 of Alfred Tirpitz to the Navy Office (Reichs–Marine–Amt) and Bernard v. Bülow to the Foreign Office, a "New Course" was clearly charted.

In terms of national psychology, the time was also opportune. A generation had grown to adulthood since the wars of unification and had tired of the endless *Bierhalle* discussions concerning the daring deeds of their fathers in Bismarck's campaigns against Denmark (1864), Austria (1866–7) and France (1870–1), and of the Iron Chancellor's "satiated" Reich. The movement from farm to city had become a veritable flood and the vision of a rustic Germany ruled by country *Junker* had long ceased to correspond to reality. Through organizations such as the Colonial League and the Navy League, young Germans expressed a desire to expand beyond the Continent.

Wilhelm II became the spokesman for this age. Much more than the Iron Chancellor in the Sachsenwald at Friedrichsruh, he represented the dreams as well as the potential might of this new generation. His blustering speeches, his sabre-rattling, but also his support of modern technology, education and industry, typified post-Bismarckian Germany. The restraint and moderation imposed upon Germany's foreign policy after 1871 by Bismarck were cast aside; the new slogans centred around a future on the seas, around *Weltmacht* and *Weltpolitik*. And while many aspirations could be realized through preying on what were considered "dying" colonial powers – Spain, Portugal, the Netherlands, Denmark – there constantly remained the ultimate challenge: Great Britain. The Reich's extremely unfavourable maritime geographical position denied her free access to the shipping lanes of the Atlantic Ocean and beyond, and this disadvantage Tirpitz sought to overcome by concentrating in the North Sea an armada of superior German battleships "in the form of a sharp knife, held gleaming and ready only a few inches away from the jugular vein of Germany's most likely enemy" (Paul M. Kennedy).

Germany's calculated risk in challenging unilaterally the British

naval supremacy in the North Sea in order thereby to wring from
London colonial concessions and possibly an alliance, stampeded
the major powers into a naval arms race that has found its equal
only in the recent Soviet–American arms race. By August 1914,
Britain had 20 Dreadnought battleships in commission with a
further 14 either under construction or planned for completion
by 1916; she also possessed 9 battle-cruisers operational. Germany,
on the other hand, had 15 Dreadnoughts in service in August 1914
and an additional 4 scheduled for operations by 1916; 6 battle-
cruisers were either operational or near completion, with a further
2 due for sea duty by 1917.

But war came for Germany in 1914 some eight years too early.
Naval construction was 8 battleships, 7 large and 6 light cruisers
behind schedule, while the fleet of 60 capital ships envisaged in
Tirpitz's master plan would be ready to challenge the Royal Navy
only in 1922, or thereafter. Moreover, one of the most poignant
ironies must surely be that these vast naval squadrons did not
engage in a single decisive encounter in the North Sea between
1914 and 1918. The chance meeting of the fleets on the last day
of May 1916 off Jutland was broken off before either side could
land a telling blow, and has accordingly become the object of
impassioned debate and bitter acrimony. The war at sea was to be
fought most intensely by submarines and escort craft – to the dismay
of flag-officers on both sides. And the end came with a whimper
in the form of the surrender of the Imperial German Navy in
November 1918 in the wake of rebellion and revolution, and the
decision to scuttle the fleet during internment at Scapa Flow in
June 1919.

It is necessary, then, to analyse the "Tirpitz" fleet in terms of
matériel and manpower in its European setting, and also to place
it within the German situation in general between 1888 and 1918.
This is not first and foremost a work of new research, rather it
strives instead to present the general reader with an overview of
recent historical investigation by Volker R. Berghahn, Wilhelm
Deist, Friedrich Forstmeier, Eckart Kehr, Paul M. Kennedy, and
many others. I have also incorporated into the book my earlier
researches dealing with the naval officer corps and various aspects
of German naval history : *The German Naval Officer Corps: A
Social and Political History 1890–1918* (Oxford, 1973); *Politics of
Frustration: The United States in German Naval Planning, 1888–
1941* (Boston, 1976). Much of the documentation has been gleaned

from the German Federal–Military Archives – see Reference Literature, p. 258 – while supporting material is listed separately; translations from the German are my own and have been made as far as possible to conform to ordinary English usage. German names are left as in the original. Many issues, designs, battles, strategies, and events will either be glossed over or entirely omitted; it is hoped, however, that those treated will afford the reader a clearer perception of the role that the "luxury" fleet, as Winston Churchill as First Lord of the Admiralty in February 1912 termed it, played in German and especially in European affairs in this exciting and fateful period.

Nashville, Tennessee   H.H.H.
November 1978

Part One

I

Modest Beginnings

The Prussian/German Naval
Tradition to 1888

Germany did not possess a strong, continuous naval tradition. Becoming a nation only in January 1871, Germany lacked the experience of Spain, Portugal, France, the Netherlands, or Great Britain. The approximately 360 states that comprised the Holy Roman Empire in the eighteenth century did not have either the will or the potential for naval enterprise. After all, what could one expect of Anhalt-Zerbst, Schaumburg-Lippe, Baden, Bavaria, or even Prussia, especially at a time when the Continent was engrossed in a 200–year struggle to prevent French hegemony? No less a German naval enthusiast than Alfred Tirpitz noted upon entering the Prussian Navy in 1865 that there was little enthusiasm for this force among the German people.

This notwithstanding, some German naval officers and historians later attempted to trace the genesis of a modern German battle fleet through the ages. Hugo v. Waldeyer-Hartz dated the concept of a German navy back to the Vikings, and Rear-Admiral Adolf v. Trotha to the Hanseatic League of the thirteenth century or, at the latest, to the Great Elector's plans for Prussian colonial expansion in the seventeenth century. But there was no continuity, no strong naval tradition in Prussia. The Hanseatic League had declined precipitously by the end of the thirteenth century. And the ambitious schemes of Friedrich Wilhelm, the Great Elector (1640–88), to found a Prussian colony in West Africa and a modest merchant marine and navy with the aid of the Dutchman Benjamin Raule came to naught. There existed in Prussia no wealthy group of merchants willing to invest in the Elector's plans and the Court quickly tired of being coerced to invest in the project; the Dutch

swept Raule's forces off the seas as soon as they constituted a
nuisance to them. Moreover, King Friedrich Wilhelm I (1713–40)
abolished the nascent Brandenburg–African Company in 1711 and
sold what little remained of both the merchant fleet and the navy
at bargain prices.

Nor did Friedrich II (1740–86) share the Great Elector's dreams
of overseas empire. In fact, for much of the eighteenth century
Prussia and Austria were locked in a mortal struggle for supremacy
in Central Europe, a course of events that allowed little time for
naval development. Joseph II of Austria alone made an effort to
enhance Austria's naval presence in the Adriatic Sea in the 1780s,
while Friedrich II under his policy of *rétablissement* poured vast
sums of money into rebuilding his war-ravaged territories.

The French Revolution and the Napoleonic era stifled any
attempt to increase the Prussian fleet. In the wake of the humiliating
defeats at Jena and Auerstädt in 1806, Prussia was forced to adhere
to Napoleon Bonaparte's Continental System, with the result that
Great Britain seized some 300 Prussian barges and coastal vessels
and thereby virtually ended all Prussian sea traffic. Moreover, the
Wars of Liberation were fought between 1813 and 1815 by a
Prussian Army whose officer corps was totally dominated by the
landed gentry (*Junker*). Field Marshal Gebhard v. Blücher's victory
at Waterloo and subsequent occupation of Paris further enhanced
Prussia's role as a dominant land power; Nelson's decisive victories
at Aboukir and Trafalgar were not generally appreciated or understood in assessing Napoleon's defeat.

The Congress of Vienna rekindled a flicker of naval enthusiasm
in Prussia by awarding that country the last remnants of Swedish
territory, including the island of Rügen in the Baltic Sea as well as
six Swedish gunsloops. Between October and December 1815, these
ships were organized into the newly-formed "Royal Prussian Navy"
and two Swedish officers became the first – and until 1848 the
only – naval officers of Prussia. To be sure, it was a modest
beginning. Several prominent Germans advocated that this force
be enlarged; they included Prince Adalbert of Prussia, nephew of
King Friedrich Wilhelm III (1798–1840), Friedrich List the
economist and founder of the *Zollverein,* or customs union, and
Professor Jakob Grimm of Göttingen University, the famous
philologist and mythologist. In December 1841 Prussia joined
Great Britain, Russia, France, and Austria in suppressing the slave
trade in the Atlantic Ocean, but throughout the 1840s Prussian

leaders still regarded the Netherlands as a sort of German "admiralty state" that could protect the "German" interests on the high seas. Yet the greatest impetus for navalism lay just round the corner, in the liberal *Bürger* who sat in the Frankfurt National Assembly in 1848–9.

This national parliament, which had been convened after the outbreak of revolution in order to draft a constitution and to bring about German unification, found itself powerless to oppose the Danish Navy in the struggle over the disputed duchies of Schleswig and Holstein, and thus turned to the idea of building a German navy. A national fleet, the argument went, would spur on the German people toward unification; it would overcome the purely particularist influence of the various German armies. In June 1848 the parliamentary deputies appointed Archduke Johann of Austria Imperial Administrator (*Reichsverweser*); in November they created a "Naval Commission" under Prince Adalbert to supervise the proposed naval construction. The assembly "granted" 6 million thalers – slightly less than £1 million sterling – for naval expenditure. Prince Adalbert proposed to build a fleet consisting of 20 ships of the line and 20 large and 10 small cruising ships. Officers and men for the fleet were to be recruited in Great Britain, France, the Netherlands, Denmark, and the United States, because German states lacked experienced naval personnel.

The National Assembly was not destined to realize this ambitious programme. The few ships that were built or purchased were eventually taken over by Prussia in 1852 (*Barbarossa, Eckernförde*) and became the nucleus under Prince Adalbert for the navy of the North German Confederation (1867–70), and subsequently of the German Empire. The remaining 9 warships and 27 smaller craft were sold to bidders at bargain prices. Only the dream of the Frankfurt liberals of building a German navy survived and transcended the narrow bounds of particularism, notably among the bourgeois intellectual and industrial elite. But the black-red-gold ensign was not to be broken on a German warship for another 104 years.

The embryonic Prussian Navy was to carry on the dream of a grand German fleet. In November 1853 the naval administration was taken out of the Prussian War Ministry, and an independent Admiralty under Prince Adalbert was created; in March 1854 Adalbert received the cumbersome title of "Admiral of the Prussian Coasts" after King Friedrich Wilhelm IV (1840–61) had ruled out "Fleet Admiral" because "we do not have a fleet". More importantly, in November 1854 Prussia acquired from Oldenburg the Jade river area, the future site of her major North Sea naval station (Wilhelmshaven, founded in 1869). In terms of administration, it was an uneasy and indecisive period. The Prussian Admiralty in March 1859 was transformed into the Supreme Command of the Navy and the Naval Administration; the latter, in turn, gave way in April 1861 to the Ministry of Marine under General Albrecht v. Roon. Naval construction was severely limited during this era. Paddle-wheelers and sailships were slowly giving way to steam, and wood was yielding to steel. Germany, with insufficient naval technical personnel and almost no modern shipyards, was unable to make the transition. Her small fleet became more outdated year by year.

Otto v. Bismarck's unification "from above", by virtue of Prussia's successive military victories over Denmark, Austria and France rather than by popular election or consent, ultimately resolved the burning issue of Germany's quest for nationhood, but not the quest for a navy. The Austro–Prussian war with Denmark in 1864 marked the first time since the days of the Great Elector that Prussian warships operated in foreign waters, but the Army quickly subdued the Danes and thereby again asserted its primacy in Prussian affairs. In addition, Prussia still lacked shipyards and had to rely on foreign builders: in August 1864 the first Prussian armour-clad, and hence first non-sail vessel, *Arminius,* was launched in London; and in July 1867 she bought her first twin-screw armour-clad *(Friedrich Carl)* from France. Of major consequence, however, was the fact that in March 1865 Prussia acquired Kiel, destined to become her major naval station in the Baltic Sea and in November 1866 the site of her Navy School.

However, in 1865, the year that Tirpitz entered the Navy, the Prussian Landtag (regional parliament) rejected the government's request for twenty armoured ships and an annual budget of 5 million thalers. The armour-clad *König Wilhelm,* launched in April 1868, was to remain Germany's largest warship, with 9,754 tons displacement, until 1891. This dismal picture was brightened only by the official opening of Wilhelmshaven harbour in June 1869 by King Wilhelm I (1861–88).

The Franco–Prussian War (1870–1) completed the unification of Germany and laid the permanent basis for the glory of her Army and especially her *Generalstab* under Field-Marshal Helmuth v.

Moltke. The war at sea was conspicuous by its absence. Already in the struggle with Austria in 1866 the Navy had contributed no significant deeds, and the seizure of Hanover's fortifications on the Elbe and Weser rivers by Prussian monitors had not affected the outcome of the war in the least. In 1870 a French fleet under Vice-Admiral Bouët-Willaumez quickly seized about forty German merchant ships, while another fleet under Vice-Admiral Fourichon blockaded the North Sea coast and particularly the new installations at Wilhelmshaven. There was, in fact, to be so little action at sea that the French crews were eventually put on shore for the defence of Paris. The creation of the German Empire on 18 January 1871 in the Hall of Mirrors at Versailles was largely the work of the Prussian Army, reinforced by various German regional armies.

Article 53 of the constitution of both the North German Confederation in 1867 and the German Empire in 1871 recognized the independent status of the Navy; in 1871 the Navy was granted imperial status.

Perhaps because its role in the wars of German unification had been only minimal, the Navy from 1872 until 1888 was commanded by Army officers. The first of these, Albrechtorn Stosch, instilled the junior service with Prussian military *esprit de corps*, and transferred to it the drill and regulations of the Prussian Army. The general assigned the Navy primarily coastal defence functions, once describing it as a "living coastal defence". His tactics for war at sea were the same as for infantry, with the principal opponent being France, and later a possible Franco–Russian combination. Stosch hoped that his force could prevent an enemy landing on German soil and, if possible, safeguard German coastal cities from enemy shelling. There were, on the positive side, several reforms and innovations launched by Stosch that were to have a permanent effect. In 1872 he transformed the Ministry of Marine into the Imperial Admiralty, and three years later he partly camouflaged his Army origins by receiving the rank of admiral. In March 1872 Stosch created the Navy Academy at Kiel for the future intellectual development of especially able officers. This was followed in May 1872 by the formation of a "Machine Engineer Corps" and in February 1873 by the grant to the Medical Corps of Officers of equal status with Army and Navy officers. In July 1879 Stosch introduced the "Torpedo Engineer Corps" entrusted with the maintenance and operation of torpedoes and mines.

Stosch's tenure of office also witnessed a large-scale revamping

of the antiquated Royal Prussian Navy – now the Imperial German
Navy. In May 1872 he laid down a ten-year building plan calling
for the construction of 8 armoured frigates, 6 armoured corvettes,
7 monitors, 2 floating batteries, 20 light corvettes, 6 avisos, 18
gunboats, and 28 torpedo-boats – at a projected cost of 218,437,500
Goldmarks (GM).* It was a major building programme and surprisingly received approval in the Reichstag, perhaps because a
quarter of the money was provided from the French indemnity of
1870–1.

Between 1874 and 1876, the four ships of the *Sachsen* class were
laid down : *Bayern, Baden, Sachsen,* and *Württemberg.* They were
7,500-ton armoured frigates with six 26 cm, six 8.7 cm and eight
8.8 cm steel guns; in 1886 they received three 35 cm torpedo tubes.
A smaller vessel, *Oldenburg,* was ordered in 1883.

When Stosch left office in 1883 – according to Tirpitz, because
of his inability to get along with Bismarck – he left behind a fleet
consisting of 7 armoured frigates and 4 armoured corvettes, the
first tactically unified group of German warships, and personnel
consisting of 423 officers and 5,062 ratings.

His successor, Leo Graf v. Caprivi, was an Army general obsessed
with the notion of a war on two fronts, against France and Russia,
and he spent his term in office developing elaborate coastal defence
plans. These centred especially upon the deployment of shallow-
draught monitors as well as torpedoes and mines. The German Navy
had in 1882 purchased several Whitehead torpedoes; this special
weapon was later to be developed in the Reich by the Schwartzkopf
firm in Berlin. General v. Caprivi's penchant for torpedoes led, in
turn, to the development of torpedo-boats (and not destroyers),
which had first been built in Germany in the autumn of 1871.
Caprivi hoped that these relatively inexpensive and yet purely
aggressive vessels might accord a second-rate naval power a chance
against superior surface fleets. In order to oversee the development
of the torpedo-boats, Caprivi in March 1886 created a special
"Inspection of Torpedo Development" in Kiel; in October 1887 he
followed this up with the formation of the First Torpedo Division
in Wilhelmshaven and the Second Torpedo Division in Kiel. Only
in 1887 did Caprivi ask for the construction of ten armoured
frigates, wishing to conserve "every man and every penny" for the
expected land war. Finally, Caprivi also had a hand in expanding

*One pound sterling was worth about 20 GM. See Abbreviations and
Conversions, p. xiv.

German canal facilities: in June 1887 he attended the cornerstone laying for the projected North Sea–Baltic Sea (Kaiser-Wilhelm) Canal by Kaiser Wilhelm I, completed in June 1895. Caprivi left the Navy in 1888 with a complement of 534 executive officers (*Seeoffiziere*) and a total strength of 15,480 men. The fleet consisted of 18 armour-clads, and 8 large and 10 small cruising ships.

But the Caprivi years had raised a troublesome issue that was not resolved until 1898. Europe's reliance upon ships of the line was severely challenged in the 1870s and 1880s by the writings of the French *jeune école* (young school) of Admiral Théophile Aube. The latter argued rather forcefully and convincingly at first that torpedo-boats were the main weapon with which secondary naval powers could hope to neutralize the British battleship superiority. Aube later refined his thought along the lines of *guerre de course,* that is, of the need to build cruisers with which to interdict Britain's immense merchant fleet and thereby to deprive her of the requisite imports. At a still later point the submarine was to become a major weapon in the arsenal of minor naval powers against first-class maritime nations. Alfred Tirpitz ironically was initially (1877–88) an ardent advocate of torpedo-boats, of the "black host" as his T-boats came to be known.

The counter-argument of *la vieille école* (the old school) revolved round the battleship as the locus of the battle fleet, and in 1890 it received a tremendous boost with the publication of Alfred Thayer Mahan's *The Influence of Sea Power upon History.* Mahan argued that a concentration of naval force in battle fleets decided control of vital sea lanes; that large-scale blockades and not cruiser warfare were decisive; that overseas colonies were vital to a nation's prosperity; that naval bases (*Stützpunkte*) were more valuable than control of large land areas; and that sea power alone guaranteed the rise of a nation to world stature.

These great debates were carried out in Germany in theory only, by a small handful of naval officers, owing to her lack of sea power. Moreover, throughout the 1880s and 1890s no central organization to direct naval enthusiasm into official channels existed. The Conservatives and Socialists, though for very different reasons, steadfastly opposed costly naval expenditure, and the Catholic Centre Party remained indifferent to the idea.

Bismarck, despite his brief flirtation with colonial – and hence naval – matters in 1884 at the zenith of his *rapprochement* attempts with France, wanted Germany to remain "a sea power of the

second rank", and especially among Army officers there existed
little enthusiasm for the Navy, pejoratively referred to as "the
Army's satellite". Field-Marshal Freiherr v. Manteuffel in 1883
summed up the prevailing attitude in Prussian Army circles in a
letter to the Chief of the Military Cabinet, General v. Albedyll:
"I, too, belong to the uncultured supporters of the politics of King
F[riedrich] W[ilhelm] I, who sold his last warship in order to
create one more battalion." This situation was to change dramatic-
ally on 15 June 1888 when Wilhelm II became German Emperor
and King of Prussia after the sudden death of his father Friedrich
III, Kaiser and King for only ninety-nine days.

II

Kaiser Wilhelm II

*The Years of Hope
and Misdirection, 1888—1898*

The last of the Hohenzollerns brought to the throne an active interest in naval affairs. Youthful memories of Kiel and Portsmouth, readings in naval history, recollections of British naval reviews, visits to the regattas at Cowes, and Mahan's *The Influence of Sea Power upon History,* which he read in 1894 and wanted to memorize, helped shape the young Kaiser's outlook. In 1895 he proudly exhibited his painting "Sea Battle", depicting the attack of a torpedo-boat flotilla upon a squadron of ironclads. When he dismissed Bismarck in March 1890, Wilhelm cabled the Grand Duke of Sachsen-Weimar : "The position of Officer of the Watch of the Ship of State has come to me. . . . Full steam ahead." On 1 January 1900, in an address to the officers of the Berlin garrison commemorating the dawn of a new century, Wilhelm gave perhaps the clearest indication of the role that naval affairs were to assume during his reign :

And as My grandfather [did] for the Army, so I will, for My Navy, carry on unerringly and in similar manner the work of reorganization so that it may also stand on an equal footing with My armed forces on land and so that through it the German Empire may also be in a position abroad to attain that place which it has not yet reached.

Wilhelm was constantly concerned about the historical image that he hoped to realize. He informed Chancellor Chlodwig Fürst zu Hohenlohe-Schillingsfürst in 1899 concerning naval expansion : "In this question there is for Me no turning back, just as [it had been] for My honourable grandfather in the question of the Army reorganization." There could hardly be a clearer exposition of this preconceived historical parallel : Wilhelm I had raised Prussia/ Germany to great-power status with an army that was responsible solely to him; Wilhelm II desired to raise Germany to world-power status (*Weltmacht*, a term that he first used publicly on 18 January 1896) with a navy completely dependent upon him.

The Kaiser was so carried away with his maritime mission that history was often the victim of gross misconceptions. The Hanseatic League and the Great Elector were singled out for repeated praise; Charlemagne and the Emperor Heinrich VI (1189–97) were depicted as great "universal monarchs" on land as well as at sea; and in February 1897, in perhaps his single most damning domestic speech, Wilhelm claimed that Bismarck and Moltke ("pygmies") had merely been "tools" (*Handlanger*) in the hands of his grandfather, now constantly referred to and celebrated as "Wilhelm the Great", "who in the Middle Ages would have been beatified".

Such nonsense, when it went without correction, merely encouraged Wilhelm's vision of his role as German Emperor and King of Prussia "by Grace of God". His public utterances soon became an embarrassment to the government. Phrases such as "We are the salt of the earth", "the trident belongs in our fist", "I am the *arbiter mundi*", and "the German empire has become a world empire", among many others, quickly made their way into the world press. Wilhelm soon came to be known as the "Fleet Kaiser".

In July 1900, at the launching of the battleship *Wittelsbach,* he advised the world : "No great decision may now be made without the German Empire and the German Emperor." Already as Crown Prince, Wilhelm had candidly informed his mother, the Empress Frederick, the former princess royal of Great Britain, that his rule would usher in a "New Course" in terms of kingship :

> The Crown sends its rays through "Grace of God" into palaces as well as huts and – pardon me, if I dare say so – Europe and the world listens intently in order to hear "what says and thinks the German Emperor?," and not, what is the will of his chancellor! . . . For ever and ever there will only be one true Emperor in the world, and that is the German Kaiser, without regard for his person or his traits, alone by right of a thousand-year tradition and his chancellor has to obey!

1. The Kaiser instructs his workmen at Kiel during the First World War.
Wilhelm II is in the centre of the picture; his royal brother Admiral
Prince Heinrich is on the far right

2a. A rare glimpse of Admiral Prince Heinrich (second from left) and Admiral v. Tirpitz (third from left) in civilian dress at the Royal Yacht Club, Queenstown, *c.* 1900

2b. Germany's naval leaders in the First World War. Front row, from left to right: Admiral Reinhard Scheer, fleet commander, Kaiser Wilhelm II, Admiral Henning v. Holtzendorff, Chief of the Admiralty Staff, and Admiral Georg Alexander v. Müller, Chief of the Navy Cabinet

Random comments such as these prompted King Edward VII in 1901 to label his egregious nephew "the most brilliant failure in history".

Wilhelm, for his part, believed that a new reapportionment of the globe was about to take place. "Old empires pass away and new ones are in the process of being formed." Although he firmly believed that the British Empire was in decline, his most immediate thoughts were with territories of "dying" colonial powers, specifically, Spain, Portugal, Denmark and the Netherlands. Others agreed with the Kaiser. Bernhard v. Bülow in December 1899 lamented that "the world is already partitioned", yet took hope in the thought : "In the coming century, Germany will either be the hammer or the anvil." In that same year the Chief of the Navy Cabinet (Senden-Bibran) acknowledged that "a new reapportionment of the world is constantly under way and one can say that it has now just begun anew". Admiral Tirpitz was of similar mind : "We are now standing only at the beginning of . . . a new division of the globe. The great decisions will come only in the approaching century." For the time being, the immediate need, as Wilhelm succinctly expressed it, was simply "fleet, fleet, fleet". Only a fleet could accord Germany her proper "place in the sun". "After twenty years, when it is ready, I will adopt a different tone."

One outward expression of Wilhelm's affinity for "his" navy was his love of titles and uniforms. In addition to being the first Grand Admiral of the Imperial German Navy, he was also an Admiral of the Imperial Russian Navy and of the Royal Navies of Great Britain, Sweden, Norway, and Denmark, and an honorary Admiral of the Royal Greek Navy. Conversely, in 1914 the Emperors of Russia and India as well as the Kings of Great Britain, Spain, Norway, Sweden, and Denmark were officers *à la suite* of the Imperial German Navy. And Wilhelm jealously guarded his privilege of being the only ruling prince in Germany to wear the naval executive officer's uniform. It was only in 1911, after years of begging by his friends, that the Grand Duke of Oldenburg, a skilled seaman and an ardent naval supporter, was also granted this privilege. Robert Graf Zedlitz-Trützschler recalled that the Kaiser went so far as to receive the British ambassador in the uniform of a British Admiral of the Fleet; the Kaiser even attended Wagner's *The Flying Dutchman* in a naval uniform. In short, a man of elegant superficiality.

The Kaiser's vanities must appear to the modern reader both

amusing and pathetic. His participation in gaudy fleet reviews and his love of naval garb often evoked the cry "parvenu" from old-line aristocrats, and sarcastic barbs from prominent officers. On one such occasion, Wilhelm appeared in 1903 in naval uniform before the Leibgarde Husaren, whom he had until recently commanded. This brought a smirk from a personal friend. When questioned on this by the monarch, the friend, a prince, replied: "I suppose that [Your] Majesty comes from the Berlin Aquarium?"

Imperial preference for naval affairs did not fail to affect Army officers. Three successive chiefs of the Prussian General Staff, Waldersee, Schlieffen and the younger Moltke, opposed the basic concept of the battle fleet, but none dared to intervene. The reason for this is perhaps best summed up by Graf v. Waldersee: "The Kaiser is unswervingly following his goal of enlarging the Navy, but without letting this be known, which is probably clever as the extent of his plans would arouse anxiety." Yet not even Waldersee could fully endorse the new era: "We are supposed to pursue *Weltpolitik.* If one only knew what that is supposed to be."

Initially, Wilhelm II had been a disciple of the *jeune école*. Cruisers could best defend German interests in far-flung colonies and in time of war might keep even the most formidable naval power off-balance. The Kaiser shared Mahan's Darwinistic analysis of the influence of sea power, but he also realized that the Reichstag would more readily agree to the construction of cruisers than it would to the creation of a battle fleet. The monarch was primarily interested in obtaining "more ships", but once Tirpitz had displayed his ability to wring money from the Reichstag for naval building, he proved willing to abandon his own concepts in favour of Tirpitz's battle-fleet programme. This did not, however, prevent Wilhelm from dabbling in naval construction policies – much to the chagrin of Tirpitz and his aides. The Kaiser actively participated in matters concerning technical design of coastal forts, ships, houses, motors, and the like; he submitted sketches of warships to the Navy Office, frequently attempting to combine the battleship and the cruiser into one "fast capital ship", his pet project. He decided to adorn German overseas vessels with multiple smoke-stacks in order to create an impression of power.

On the domestic scene, Wilhelm's enthusiasm for naval affairs often proved an embarrassment to naval planners. In 1899 he made his famous 'We have dire need of a strong fleet" speech in Hamburg, demanding an immediate increase in the size of the fleet and even threatening to dissolve the Reichstag if it opposed this measure, which completely surprised Tirpitz in its timing and forced him to accelerate plans for naval expansion. It is fair to state that the monarch's role was, from the start, a nominal rather than a decision-making one, but, as one observer at Court aptly put it, Wilhelm was truly the creator of the fleet by associating it with his person and prestige. "As the sum total of all observations . . . I would like to say that the Navy draws great advantages from the lively interest that prevails for it at the Highest Place, yes, that without this it could hardly move forward, [that] the Kaiser is thus really the creator of our fleet." Wilhelm's famous naval tables giving the size of the German fleet, prominently displayed in the rotunda of the Reichstag, were also not without effect.

The monarch's role with regard to the Navy was defined in Article 53 of the Constitution of 1871 : "The Navy of the Empire is united under the supreme command of the Kaiser. The organization and structure of the same is within the jurisdiction of the Kaiser, who appoints the officers and civil servants of the Navy, and receives a direct oath of allegiance. . . ." One of the young ruler's first acts on assuming leadership was to reorganize all his military entourage into a *maison militaire*. Wilhelm stressed his role of "Supreme War Lord" and sought to maintain the fiction of the commander-in-chief. Moreover, on 28 March 1889 he created a Navy Cabinet (*Marine-Kabinett*) as a counterpart of the very significant Military Cabinet, which until then had discharged duties for the Navy. The chief of this new office was responsible for the transmission of all imperial orders concerning naval affairs within home waters to the responsible authorities, promotions and appointments for all naval personnel, decorations for foreign naval visitors, duty assignments, the Kaiser's naval correspondence, and a host of other related matters. During the period under discussion, Gustav Freiherr v. Senden-Bibran headed the Navy Office from 1889 to 1906, when he was replaced by Georg Alexander v. Müller, who held the post until November 1918.

On 30 March 1889 Wilhelm dissolved the Imperial Admiralty and placed strategic command into the hands of a new Chief of the High Command of the Navy (*Oberkommando*), with the corresponding rank of commanding general in the Army, who was responsible for the deployment of ships, military tactics and strategy, and ships in foreign waters. Administrative control was given to a State Secretary of the Imperial Navy Office (*Reichs-Marine-Amt*) nominally serving under the chancellor. The head of the Navy Office was responsible first and foremost for the construction and maintenance of all naval units and, at least in theory, possessed no direct connection with the performance and deployment of the fleet. His sphere of operations, however, was so vast that he appeared to do everything; he actually seemed to many to be the commander of the Navy. The Navy Office in time developed into a sizeable operation with no less than ten major departments: Central (M), Shipyards (B), Administration (C), Armaments (W), Medical (G), News (N), General Navy (A), Construction (K), Nautical (H), and Legal (J). (The letters in parentheses are code names for the departments.)

Wilhelm II on 14 March 1899 replaced the High Command of the Navy with an Admiralty Staff (*Admiralstab*), ultimately composed of about thirty-five officers, with rather limited functions pertaining to naval strategy and tactics. During peacetime this new organization acted purely on an advisory basis, preparing strategic plans for the fleet, training officers for staff duties, conducting naval intelligence, and drafting sailing orders for German warships in foreign waters. In wartime it was to conduct all naval operations – with the Kaiser's approval. Generally speaking, it had the same function, but not nearly the power, of the Prussian General Staff. Actual leadership of the fleet rested between 1900 and 1903 with the Chief of the First Squadron, between 1903 and 1907 with the Chief of the Active Battle Fleet, and thereafter with the Chief of the High Sea Fleet (*Hochseeflotte*). (Table 1).

The main drawback of Wilhelm's naval reorganization schemes was that they all broke away from the unified command principle established in 1871. But a centralized, responsible Ministry of Marine could never be created as long as the monarch maintained the fiction of his personal "supreme command". The fragmentation of the naval hierarchy was driven forward when in March 1899 Wilhelm appointed himself Supreme Commander of the Navy and, apart from the three naval commands already discussed, set up several other connective links with the naval establishment: the chiefs of the Baltic and North Sea naval stations, the Inspector of the Navy's Education Department (until 1907, when it was placed within the Navy Office), the Inspector-General of the Navy, the Chief of the First Battle Squadron (replaced in February 1907 by the Chief of the High Sea Fleet), and the Chief of the Cruiser Squadron in East Asia. Power rested with the heads of these nine, later eight, commands; the officers were responsible to the Kaiser alone and thus had the right to an imperial audience (*Immediatstellung*). At least in theory, the naval reorganization of 1899, which Tirpitz had helped to bring about with the promise that "Your Majesty can now be your own Admiral" and which remained in effect until August 1918, left the Kaiser firmly established as the active head of the combined naval command.

The fragmented command-structure successfully fulfilled Tirpitz's aim to eliminate the rival influence of the Admiralty Staff, and to prevent its development as a parallel to the powerful, independent Army staff of the elder Moltke. It is safe to conclude that Tirpitz intended to allow this system to continue until a time of national emergency, when he could, according to his plan, create a new centralized naval command around himself. However, Tirpitz was to learn in March 1916 that final power in the Prussian/German constitutional system rested solely with the Kaiser.

One may well ask to what degree Wilhelm II managed to live up to the central commanding role that he had assigned to himself in naval affairs. It should be remembered that the monarch did not possess the capacity for concentrated long-term work. "He is not faithful to duty," Admiral v. Müller later stated, "or else he would devote more of his free time to the serious problems of his occupation." According to one source, Wilhelm spent more than one-third of his reign on board the royal yacht *Hohenzollern,* at times as much as 200 days of the year. In addition, he did not have the proper sense of proportion towards his many duties. He insisted on carrying out his obligation to sign every promotion for naval officers beginning with the rank of lieutenant, and he gauged his growing importance and industry by counting the annual sum of signatures given. He even reserved the right to decide, down to the last petty detail, the winter fleet manoeuvres, but when faced with the arduous task of planning such an extravaganza, exploded :

> I am tired of these discussions. I simply command and that is that. I am always supposed to ask Tom, Dick and Harry [Hinz und Kunz] and only sign what the Republic Navy decides is good. I am finally tired of this. To hell with it ! I am the Supreme War Lord. I do not decide. I command.

This inability to execute a self-designated role greatly troubled Germany's military leaders. The Army's reaction perhaps came out best in 1912, during a general discussion concerning the role of the supreme commander (Wilhelm) in a future war. Major Erich Ludendorff informed the younger Moltke of the most convenient manner in which to avoid the technical and constitutional difficulties of the issue : "The emperor will not even be asked in case of war." The Navy could not afford such overt impertinence. Tirpitz, clever politician, public relations expert and forerunner of the modern professional manager, merely assumed many of the Kaiser's functions and duties indirectly. Every summer the state secretary retired, along with his most trusted aides, to his country home in St Blasien in the Black Forest to prepare and plan every aspect of forthcoming naval discussions. In the autumn, Tirpitz would appear first in Rominten, then in Berlin, with meticulously prepared briefs designed to overcome any possible opposition from the Kaiser or the Reichstag. Wilhelm was no match for this tactic. He succumbed to Tirpitz's wishes on most important points, and even allowed him to create a tight network of naval attachés who reported directly to Tirpitz rather than to the chancellor.

But Tirpitz arrived on the scene only in mid-1897. Given Wilhelm's anxiety for a fleet, his fervent belief in an approaching struggle for reapportionment of the globe, and his domineering position within the German political and especially military structure (particularly after "dropping the pilot" Bismarck in March 1890), one may well ask what Wilhelm was able to accomplish during his first decade of rule (1888–1898).

When Wilhelm II came to the throne he found under construction the armoured frigates *Siegfried, Beowulf, Frithjof, Heimdall,* and *Hagen*. In addition, two armoured corvettes, *Odin* and *Ägir*, were designed in 1892 and completed four years later.

On 5 July 1888 Wilhelm had appointed the first naval officer, Vice-Admiral Alexander Graf v. Monts, the son of a Prussian Army general, to head the Admiralty. Monts at once went to work on new designs, and during the winter of 1888–9 managed to wring from the Reichstag the first four battleships of the *Brandenburg* class. Designed to replace the antiquated 3,500-ton armour-clads, the new ships displaced 10,000 tons, attained a best speed of sixteen knots, and had a cruising range of 4,500 sea miles at ten knots. Six 28 cm guns comprised the main battery, while eight each 10.5 cm and 8.8 cm guns and six 45 cm torpedo tubes formed the secondary armament. All cannons were manufactured by Krupp. The four vessels of this class, *Brandenburg, Kurfürst Friedrich Wilhelm, Weissenburg,* and *Wörth,* were launched between June 1891 and August 1892, and completed by 1894 at a cost of 15,832,000 GM each.

With the *Brandenburg* class, German naval designers for the first time turned away from foreign models and laid the foundations for the later concept of a "High Sea Fleet". *Wörth* and *Brandenburg* were protected by so-called "compound" plates, introduced in 1877 and formed of steel-clad wrought-iron plates alternating with layers of wood and an inner skin of two layers of sheet iron. However, special British Harvey nickel-steel alloy plates, with top layers enriched by carbon, were fitted to *Weissenburg* and *Kurfürst Friedrich Wilhelm.* Yet these ships – as well as the later *Kaiser* class – retained the French belt armour system first introduced in the 1870s, while the *Wittelsbach* class later (1900) adopted the newer "citadel belt armour". First tried in 1890 on the French cruiser *Dupuy de Lôme* and refined for battleships in the British *Royal Sovereign* class in 1891–2, the "citadel belt armour" extended to the bow and stern as well as to the upper deck. The lighter nickel-steel plates permitted this extension of armour protection without substantially increasing the ship's weight.

The new plates were developed by Harvey in Great Britain, Krupp in Germany and Simpson in the United States. They allowed a gradual reduction in armour belts from 400 mm in the *Brandenburg* class to 225 mm in the *Wittelsbach* class. Krupp engineers later added chromium and manganese to the carburized nickel-steel, and by heating the carbon-packed face of the plates only while they were buried in clay, managed to increase the hardness of the plates as well as the elasticity of their backs. This method was quickly adopted by all major naval powers as Krupp cemented (KC) armour.

Vice-Admiral v. Monts did not witness completion of the *Brandenburg* class. He died in January 1889. The Kaiser's creation of two rival naval commands (High Command and Navy Office) to take the place of the Imperial Admiralty destroyed the unity of planning and command; construction programmes hereafter seemed to come in spurts and without a master plan, causing one Reichstag critic of the Navy (Eugen Richter) to speak of "limitless fleet plans". In June of that same year Wilhelm II ceremoniously opened the 100-kilometre-long Kaiser-Wilhelm Canal. Built at a cost of 150 million GM, it was twenty-two metres wide and had a normal depth of nine metres. Funds were also made available in 1895 for the construction of an additional five battleships.

The *Kaiser Friedrich III* class, comprised of *Kaiser Wilhelm der Grosse, Kaiser Friedrich III, Kaiser Barbarossa, Kaiser Karl der Grosse,* and *Kaiser Wilhelm II,* was launched between July 1896 and April 1900, and completed by 1902. These ships displaced 11,500 tons and cost 21,472,000 GM each. This class brought forth a development well in advance of other navies. The first chief designer of the Imperial Navy, Professor Alfred Dietrich, following British experimentation in the 1870s and Italian in the 1880s, designed intricate underwater protection by a close system of watertight compartments, later refined for further stability by counter-flooding apparatus. Solid compartmentation was designed to localize flooding from shell damage. The propulsion plant was protected by fore-and-aft bulkheads made of ordinary sheet metal; coal bunkers were situated on the sides in order to absorb any explosion before it reached the inside.

In addition, the replacement around 1885 of highly volatile nitro-cellulose, or nitro-glycerine, with so-called "smokeless" powders, that is, slow-burning and stable "cordite", permitted a muzzle velocity of 800 metres per second. The upper limit of naval armament in the 1890s was represented by the 30.5 cm breech-loading gun with a barrel length of forty calibres, which became the standard weapon of most powers, except Germany. In addition, strides were also made in developing armour-piercing shells. It was found that by placing soft chrome "caps" over steel projectiles, the "caps" softened the armour on impact, allowing the explosive part of the shell to break through inside where it could do the most damage. War was, indeed, becoming a scientific endeavour.

The *Kaiser Friedrich III* class constituted a setback in terms of armament development. The *Brandenburg* class main battery of six 28 cm guns in twin turrets was unique in its day, and has been depicted as the forerunner of the later "all big gun one calibre battleships". The *Kaiser Friedrich III* class, as well as the following *Wittelsbach* class, however, carried a smaller main armament of four 24 cm guns in accordance with the then prevalent tactical "hail of fire" principle, that is, to spray the enemy with a constant fire. Moreover, the 24 cm gun at that time was the largest to which the quick-loading system could be applied. These were the first German battleships with triple screws. (Table 2).

The years immediately prior to Tirpitz's appointment as State Secretary of the Navy Office also witnessed the construction of the last class of large, protected cruisers and the change-over to production of armoured cruisers that was eventually to lead to the battle-cruiser class. The large cruiser was designed for reconnaissance, to fight in the line if need be, to destroy enemy stragglers after a sea battle, and to protect her own damaged vessels after such an encounter. The large cruiser *Kaiserin Augusta,* launched in January 1892 by Germania in Kiel, was the first triple-screw unit of the Imperial Navy. Her successor, the *Hertha* class, represented the last five large cruisers in Germany : *Freya, Hansa, Hertha, Victoria Louise,* and *Vineta.* The ships could be classified as "overseas" cruisers as they were without belt armour and hardly larger than contemporary British light cruisers.

The need to build large, protected cruisers for the fleet as well as small, protected cruisers to fight enemy torpedo-carrying craft that threatened one's heavy units caused a severe strain on naval budgets. This was compounded for Germany by the need for light cruisers to serve overseas in the colonies. Ideally, one would need large, protected cruisers for service with the fleet; still faster large cruisers for possible commerce-raiding functions overseas; light cruisers with belt armour to act as "scouts" and to protect the fleet from torpedo craft; and light cruisers for colonial service. But Britain alone was able to develop these various classes of cruising ships; for lack of funds, the Reich had to perfect a uniform class of light cruisers as well as large cruisers that could serve equally well with the fleet and overseas.

The latter task proved to be most difficult. Germany initially followed French designs, preferring to classify "armoured cruisers" simply as large cruisers. However, it quickly became apparent that the armoured cruisers with their heavy protective plates and large guns were not able to generate the speed requisite for surface *guerre de course* and were, by the turn of the century, more and more restricted and adapted for use with the main battle fleet.

The *Fürst Bismarck,* built between 1896 and 1900 at nearly double the cost of the *Hertha* (18,945,000 GM), inaugurated Germany's development of armoured cruisers, designed for the fleet. As such, *Fürst Bismarck* represented a link in the genesis of large cruising ships from the armoured corvettes of the 1860s via the avisos of the 1880s (*Blitz* and *Pfeil*) to the battle-cruisers of the *Invincible* class (1907).

The need for greater speed also brought minor changes with the *Prinz Heinrich* (named for the Kaiser's brother), constructed between 1898 and 1902. Four additional ships, *Friedrich Carl, Prinz Adalbert, Roon,* and *Yorck,* were added between 1900 and 1906. A reduction in displacement and in armour increased best speed to twenty knots. The armament for this class was reduced by two 24 cm and two 15 cm guns; two side underwater torpedo tubes were also removed. The *Prinz Heinrich* class ships cost considerably less (16,588,000 GM) than the *Fürst Bismarck*. The prototype on 30 December 1902 by imperial decree became the flagship of the newly created Commander of Scouting Forces, Rear-Admiral Ludwig Borckenhagen.

Owing to restrictions imposed upon armoured cruiser construction by the limited size of her docks and harbours, the Reich was never able to develop fully the armoured cruiser type on a level with France, Great Britain and Russia. It was only in 1906 that Germany was to build ships approximately equal to their British counterparts with the *Scharnhorst* class (p. 44). (Table 3).

German efforts with light cruiser construction were much more successful. The immediate pre-Tirpitz period brought a fundamental decision : the old division between "overseas" and "fleet" light cruisers was abandoned in favour of a uniform model designed for service with the fleet as well as abroad. The *Gazelle* class of light cruisers, planned in 1896 and built over the next eight years at a unit cost of 4.6 million GM, represented the initial synthesis of the "fleet cruiser" with the "overseas cruiser". The class included the *Amazone, Arcona, Ariadne, Frauenlob, Gazelle, Medusa, Niobe, Nymphe, Thetis,* and *Undine.* The finished ships were attached first to the fleet as a protective screen against enemy torpedo craft and, as soon as they could be replaced by more modern vessels, released for overseas service with the Cruiser Squadron. Subsequent classes of light cruisers down to 1918 brought few fundamental changes, mainly technological refinements. (Table 4).

Torpedo-boat development also flourished during this period. Between 1890 and 1896 the Friedrich Schichau Company at Elbing (today Elblag) near Danzig (Gdansk) had attained a monopoly of torpedo-boat construction, having in 1885 won the Admiralty's competition for these vessels from German as well as foreign bidders. Germania in 1897 and Vulcan in 1907 also entered the field; Blohm & Voss in Hamburg and Howaldt in Kiel added only a few units later on. For the sake of simplicity, the torpedo-boat series will simply be referred to as "T" vessels, sacrificing shipyard identity for clarity.

The first units built for General v. Caprivi had a displacement of 80–90 tons and a speed of 15–17 knots, and were armed with one 5 cm gun and three torpedo tubes. Between 1890 and 1897, Schichau laid down the *T42–T81* series of 110–150-ton boats with a best speed of twenty-two knots. Armament remained one 5 cm gun and two deck torpedo tubes as well as one bow tube. The next major series, the *T90–T136* vessels, was built between 1898 and 1907. These were larger boats of 360 tons, with a best speed of twenty-eight knots. Two 5 cm guns were added in this series; all three stern 45 cm torpedo tubes were now up on deck. Schichau also launched in 1899 the large *S90* series of 310–394-ton boats, designed for service with the battle fleet. Three-cycle triple-expansion engines developed 5,900 hp and a best speed of twenty-six knots. The armament remained the same as in the *T90–T136* series.

One group of torpedo-boats, however, did not live up to expectations. In 1887 so-called "Division Boats" of 230 tons, twice the then normal size, were introduced. By the turn of the century, there existed a refined class of ten "D" boats, displacing 350 tons and armed with three guns and three tubes. They were roughly equal to British "A" and "D" destroyers. However, the German boats proved to be slow and unwieldy, and by 1914 were detailed for experimental or minor supervisory roles.

The Reich also brought out modern gunboats in the pre-Tirpitz era. The famous "predator" class, consisting of *Eber, Iltis, Jaguar, Luchs, Panther,* and *Tiger,* was built between 1897 and 1904 for service overseas. They were armed with two 10.5 cm guns which proved to be inadequate – as witnessed by the *Panther* in January 1903 in attempting to subdue the ancient stone citadel, Fort San Carlos, in Maracaibo, Venezuela. This class had a best speed of only fourteen knots.

The first German submarine (*U 1*) was not completed until 1906, and the development of airships (Zeppelins) likewise commenced in that year with *Z 1*.

In general terms, all Imperial Navy warships had grey hulls with light grey superstructures. Water lines were painted dark grey, and funnels showed a narrow black top edge. During the Great War, the turret tops displayed a broad white ring on a black background for aerial identification. The ships carried their coats of arms on the bow as well as a large eagle on the stern until 1918.

Wilhelm I had presented the Navy with its war flag on 4 July 1867 : a white cloth with black cross-bars; the black-white-red ensign with the Iron Cross of 1813 superimposed, in the upper left-hand corner of the flag; and the Prussian eagle planted at the intersection of the cross-bars. This flag was specifically designed on the King's orders to stress the Prussian character of the North German Confederation and, thereafter, of the Empire. In November 1892, Kaiser Wilhelm II could not resist making minor alterations in the Prussian heraldic eagle as well as broadening the black cross-bars in order to avoid confusion with the Royal Navy's ensign. It should be noted that the Prussian Army received the black-white-red cockade only in March 1897.

The Navy also maintained a rigid scale of gun salutes : 33 for the Kaiser and his wife; 21 for the Crown Prince and his wife, members of other German ruling houses, and the imperial couple on their birthdays; 19 for a grand admiral; 17 for an admiral, the State Secretary of the Navy Office, and the Inspector-General of the Navy; 15 for a vice-admiral; 13 for a rear-admiral; and 11 for a commodore. This salute order was strictly maintained. When in 1901 Prince Heinrich's squadron bound for China was not saluted by a British fishery patrol boat, Wilhelm's brother dispatched a cruiser to investigate this breach of naval etiquette. The logical reply by the British captain that he did not have a salute cannon on board was deemed inadequate, and the matter was followed up through diplomatic channels.

The Kaiser was ushered on board warships to the strains of the ancient Prussian "Heil Dir im Sieger Kranz" (1796), and in January 1901 Wilhelm gave the Navy the "Holländischer Ehrenmarsch" as its formal march in honour of the 225th anniversary of Admiral Michael de Ruyter's death – an officer most closely associated with the Second Dutch War and specifically with the destruction of British warships in the Medway in May 1667. Hoffman v. Fallersleben's "Deutschland über Alles" (1841) was not adopted as the official national anthem until 1922 under the Weimar Republic. In terms of nautical nomenclature, Wilhelm II in 1889 had ordered that large naval units be given the names of German princes, states or famous battles; that smaller craft receive masculine names from German mythology; and that light cruisers be christened for famous females of German royal houses or German mythology. After 1903 light cruisers carried the names of German cities. Finally, in 1899 the Kaiser ordered that French military terms be "Germanized".

Purveyors of naval equipment now emerged. The Friedrich Krupp AG in Essen took the lion's share of the market, providing all armour plates and naval guns. It is estimated that this monopoly allowed the company to realize a profit of 1.2 million GM on every capital ship costing 20 million GM. And when Krupp in 1905 agreed to reduce the cost of armour plate from 2,320 to 1,860 GM per ton, the *quid pro quo* was a monopoly of all naval purchases over the next three years. The Germania yard in Kiel, which Krupp joined in 1896 and bought out in 1902, also realized a tidy slice of the naval pie : between 1901 and 1905 alone, the shipyard built four battleships at a cost of 97.3 million GM and eleven torpedo-boats at 12.5 million GM. The Navy Office calculated in 1912–13 that its business accounted for 12 per cent of the total Krupp production, or 53 million GM on which Krupp turned a net profit of 4,396,200 GM (8.3 per cent). Naval engines and heavy electrical supplies were furnished by Siemens & Schuckert, Siemens & Halske, AEG (Allgemeine Elektrizitäts-Gesellschaft), and MAN (Maschinenfabrik Augsburg-Nürnberg).

By 1898, then, naval construction in Germany, although still far removed from that of Great Britain, had made significant strides, Tirpitz's statement concerning the "lost" decade between 1888 and 1897 notwithstanding. Imperial yards at Wilhelmshaven, Kiel and Danzig built German warships, as did private installations in Hamburg, Bremen, Kiel, Danzig, Stettin, and Elbing. Vast strides had been made in naval ordnance, armour plates, hull compartmentation, and torpedo development. A Navy School at Mürwik, a Navy Academy at Kiel and Engineer and Deck Officer Schools at Kiel and Wilhelmshaven had been established – a far cry from an earlier time when material on nautical engineering had to be sought abroad. The opening of the Kaiser-Wilhelm Canal had virtually doubled the effectiveness of the German fleet, and had eliminated Denmark as a potential naval threat by providing the Reich with a direct sea link between the Baltic and North Seas through territory that it occupied. The acquisition of Helgoland island in August 1890 provided a forward naval outpost to protect the estuaries of the Weser, Ems, Elbe, and Jade rivers, and thus Hamburg, Bremen and Wilhelmshaven – along with the western outlet of the Kaiser-Wilhelm Canal at Brunsbüttelkoog. The potential of this rock in the North Sea was not appreciated in 1890, however, and German colonial enthusiasts denounced the surrender of the "three kingdoms of Witu, Uganda and Zanzibar" for the "bathtub" Helgoland.

In terms of *matériel,* the 8 available battleships were in 1897 organized into a squadron; there were also on hand 8 armoured coastal-defence ships, 10 large and 22 light cruisers, 13 gunboats, 110 torpedo-boats, and a host of small craft. Lacking, on the other hand, were a unified command-structure and an officer able to provide consistency and a master naval construction programme. The latter was remedied on 18 June 1897 with the appointment of Rear-Admiral Alfred Tirpitz as State Secretary of the Navy Office – a post that he was to hold for the next nineteen years.

III

The "New Course"

Alfred v. Tirpitz, Architect of the
Battle Fleet, 1897-1905

Rear-Admiral Alfred v. Tirpitz around 1900 was the very epitome of what one would expect in appearance from an irascible sea dog. A long, powerful face with a prominent nose was further delineated by two dominant physical features, one natural, the other carefully cultivated: sharp, round piercing eyes and the famous "two-pronged" beard. A trim, erect frame fully enhanced the smart dark-blue uniform, with its thick, loose gold epaulettes and bright gold sleeve stripes. A sword, dangling apparently nonchalantly from the left hip, was held in place at just the proper jaunty angle by a firm left hand. With but a little imagination, one could easily envisage this man swaying with a rolling deck, feet firmly planted, telescope clenched in a fist, the beard sprayed by salty brine, bellowing orders above the screaming North Sea gales.

But this image is deceptive, and not only because the passing years were to soften the features, whiten the beard and expand the midriff. Tirpitz was, in fact, anything but a simple sea dog. He had earned a reputation in the 1880s with the torpedo service, and between 1892 and 1896 as Chief of Staff of the High Command; but he last set foot on a German warship as Chief of the Cruiser Squadron in East Asia in 1897. He never commanded a modern battleship – much less a squadron or fleet of capital ships. The nineteen years as State Secretary of the Navy Office were spent primarily behind a massive wooden desk at the Leipzigerplatz in Berlin, or at his summer house in St Blasien. Stag hunts in Rominten or fox hunts in Donaueschingen in time became more familiar venues for him than the North Sea or the Atlantic Ocean. In 1898 he became a voting member of the Prussian Ministry of State, thereby achieving that special union of imperial with royal functions that Bismarck had initially designed only for himself. And two years later, Tirpitz was raised into the hereditary Prussian nobility.

Nor were historians to cast him in the role of the salty sea dog. Some attributed to Tirpitz a penchant for thinly disguised falsehoods, while others depicted him as being one-sided, with the fanaticism of a true believer; another group found him "crafty", too much the disciple of sheer power politics as well as the narrow specialist; some have laid at his feet the charge of having been a dangerous anti-parliamentarian. Most have described Tirpitz as being ruthless, clever, domineering, patriotic, indefatigable, aggressive yet conciliatory, pressing yet patient, and stronger in character and drive than the three chancellors and seven heads of the Foreign Office who were destined to be his co-actors on the political stage. To be sure, he was all of these things, but above all he was a manipulator of men and ideas, the forerunner of the modern professional manager, an expert parliamentary tactician, a capable organizer, and the forerunner of the twentieth-century propaganda specialist. His naval policy has been evaluated by various scholars as a "gruesome error" and a "monstrous mistake". His place in Wilhelmian Germany, however, remains pivotal.

Born the son of a county court judge in Küstrin, Brandenburg, on 19 March 1849, Tirpitz entered the Navy in 1865 and was commissioned four years later – at a time when, by his own admission, the Navy was hardly a popular institution. During his tenure in office, however, the Navy was to attain equal social status with the Army cavalry or *Garde* regiments and, for a time, to assume a dominant role in German politics. No less an authority than Chancellor v. Bülow later commented that the Reich's foreign policy during the Tirpitz years had, "to a degree, stood in the service of our armaments policy".

Ten years older than Wilhelm II, Tirpitz had witnessed the wars of unification as a midshipman and then an ensign in the Royal Prussian Navy. He therefore belonged in the 1890s to a generation that was not content to rest on the old Bismarckian laurels, but was already seeking a further stage of development – from *Grossmacht* to *Weltmacht*. When he last visited the Iron Chancellor in the Sachsenwald in 1897, Tirpitz felt that Bismarck still lived in the Germany of 1871, or the England of 1864. But times had changed. Industry was booming. It was an era of industrial concentration of capital, cartel formations, banking syndicates, and revolutionary technical innovations such as the telegraph, telephone, daily news-papers, and the like. And the world's trade of 150 billion GM between 1890 and 1910, Germany with 16 billion GM ranked second only to Great Britain.

These statistics, in turn, caused many to become dissatisfied with the physical dimensions of Bismarck's Reich. Great Britain and France had their empires in Africa and Asia. The United States had a western frontier. Germany seemed stifled and hemmed in by France and Russia. Her meagre colonial empire, a disparate collection of unwanted African real estate and far-flung Pacific islands, offered little consolation. But many Germans in leading positions believed that a new division of the world was at hand. In his initial speech in parliament on behalf of the First Navy Bill on 6 December 1897, Tirpitz stated than the Navy had become "a question of survival" for Germany. In February 1899 he opined that in the coming century power shifts in Asia and South America would require strong German sea power in the service of "our entire foreign policy". If at that time the Reich was not ready to take advantage of the expected power shifts with a mighty battle fleet, she "would sink back to the status of a poor farming country".

Vast ship-building contracts would also act as a pump-primer for German industry. Especially, regular placements of contracts would help to overcome the vicissitudes of the capitalist business cycle, and bring added prosperity to the German proletariat. Tirpitz's description of the fleet as "a strong palliative against Social Democrats" expressed his hopes for its effect in settling domestic social rifts.

Tirpitz was not, however, about to conjure up 1848 visions of a "parliamentary" fleet. What he had in mind was a weapon solely in the hands of the Supreme War Lord. The Second Navy Bill of 1900 and the Supplementary Bill of 1908 established that battle-ships would be built, and would be automatically replaced after twenty years of service, regardless of the costs involved. Funds for the maintenance of the ships, docks, training centres, and personnel were calculated according to the number of ships in service, and were to be made available automatically. In February 1898 Tirpitz promised his sovereign that he would "remove the disturbing influence of the Reichstag upon Your Majesty's intentions concerning the development of the Navy". He proved to be as good as his word.

There was no question that the fleet was built first and foremost

against Great Britain. Already in his first month in office, Tirpitz
had informed the Kaiser : "For Germany the most dangerous naval
enemy at present is England." The naval race inaugurated unilaterally by Germany in 1898–1900 was to prove the superiority of
the Prussian/German system over the British parliamentary system
with its civilian control over the fleet. In a sense, then, the fleet was
to be built against *two* parliaments.

But Tirpitz also put forth strategic and tactical reasons why the
fleet had ultimately to be able to challenge the Royal Navy. The
British, he argued, could never concentrate their entire sea power
in the North Sea, where the German fleet could "unfold its greatest
military potential between Helgoland and the Thames". Given his
unbending belief in the effectiveness of massed torpedo-boat attacks
against battle fleets, Tirpitz calculated that any attacking fleet
would require at least 33 per cent numerical superiority. The Navy
Office estimated in 1899 that with a battleship ratio of 2 : 3, Germany
would possess a genuine chance of victory "even against the Royal
Navy", owing to the higher quality of German ships, superior
tactics, better-trained officers and ratings, first-rate leadership, and
the centralized command-structure headed by the Kaiser – which,
of course, was a fiction. Tirpitz viewed as his ultimate goal a navy
of 60 capital ships and 40 light cruisers. Accordingly, under the
aegis of the 2 : 3 formula, Britain would have to build 90 ships by
1918–20. Even if this were possible, Germany, by virtue of the fact
that she maintained two-thirds of the High Sea Fleet on active duty
at all times while the Royal Navy kept only one-half in service,
would be able to concentrate a greater force in the North Sea
immediately upon the outbreak of war.

Tirpitz probably did not intend to attack Great Britain and
counted instead on British recognition of the danger posed by the
German fleet concentrated in the North Sea. This recognition, in
turn, would allow the emperor "to conduct a great overseas policy"
(1899). Herein lies the quintessence of the so-called "risk theory"
(*Risikogedanke*) : the ultimate strength of the fleet would deter any
eventual opponent from risking an all-out naval encounter with
Germany because even if he emerged victorious from battle, such
an enemy might then find himself at the mercy of a third strong
naval power, or even coalition (France/Russia). In addition, Tirpitz
explained, the fleet would enhance Germany's value as an ally
(*Bündnisfähigkeit*), especially in the eyes of relatively minor sea
powers equally in search of a "place in the sun". The "risk theory"

foresaw the period of greatest danger to the Reich while the fleet of sixty capital ships was under construction. Tirpitz calculated that "the danger period would be past" by 1914–15. Until that time, there existed the danger that Britain, angered by and envious of the German fleet, might decide to "Copenhagen" it in German ports, a reference to Admiral James Gambier's seizure of the neutral Danish fleet in 1807 in order to prevent it from joining France, either voluntarily or by coercion. Arthur Lee, the Civil Lord, in 1905 at Eastleigh had indirectly warned Germany that in case of war "the Royal Navy would get its blow in first, before the other side had time even to read in the papers that war had been declared". Admiral C. C. P. Fitzgerald also called for war before the "Tirpitz-fleet" was completed, but when Sir John Fisher in 1904 and again in 1908 suggested the "Copenhagen" route to the king, the latter replied in shock: "My God, Fisher, you must be mad!"

Tirpitz could not, of course, demand at a single stroke a fleet equal in size to that of Britain, even if in 1914 he finally admitted: "We must have a fleet equal in strength to that of England." Hence for tactical reasons, he decided to create his fleet by stages (*Etappenplan*). As Bülow once put it, "we must operate so carefully, like the caterpillar before it has grown into the butterfly". Tirpitz later described his programme as "the patient laying of brick upon brick". Concerning the ultimate size and disposition of the fleet, he confided that this revolved round thoughts "which one can certainly think, at times must [think], but which really cannot be written down". In December 1899 Tirpitz informed the Saxon military representative in Berlin: "For political reasons the government cannot be as specific as the Reichstag would like it to be; one cannot directly say that the naval expansion is aimed primarily against England."

There were also financial reasons at the root of this *Etappenplan*. The Reich's principal source of income lay in customs receipts and indirect sales taxes; the individual states alone had the right to tax their citizens. To be sure, state governments could be called upon to cover deficits in the federal budgets through special grants, but this usually proved to be a trying and lengthy process. Hence the navy had to be financed by increasing indirect levies on the "little man", that is, on sugar, salt, beer, brandy, railway tickets, stamps, candles, and so on. The introduction of an inheritance tax or federal income tax, on the other hand, would have brought the tax-

privileged Prussian nobility to the barricades. The stage-by-stage
plan was thus a ruse designed not only for the German parliament
and the Royal Navy, but also to avoid much-needed tax reform that
would have entailed social reforms.

   The anti-British nature of Tirpitz's – and indeed of Germany's –
policy at the turn of the century is clearly documented. H. Wickham
Steed, then a newspaper correspondent in Germany, found that no
fewer than nine out of every ten German papers revelled in anglophobia. Joseph Chamberlain's feelers in May 1898 in Birmingham
and in November 1899 in Leicester for " a new Triple Alliance
between the Teutonic race and the two great branches of the Anglo-
Saxon race" were made because isolation had ceased to be splendid.
They were rejected in Berlin. Instead, the Reich burst in on Anglo-
Portuguese discussions in the summer of 1898 in a heavy-handed
attempt to share in the spoils of the "dying" Portuguese empire.

   Another *idée fixe* nurtured by Tirpitz was his obsession with
battleships. In his famous "Memorandum IX" of 1894, as well as
in earlier tracts of 1888 and 1891, Tirpitz had called for a fleet of
battleships concentrated in home waters. In 1896 and again in 1897
he bombarded Wilhelm II with studies detailing sea battles against
Great Britain in the North Sea. Only in this manner, he argued,
could colonial concessions be wrung from Britain. "The bear skin",
he slyly suggested, could not be divided up "before the bear is
killed". In accordance with Mahan's "blue water" school, Tirpitz
banked all on a decisive naval battle (*Entscheidungsschlacht*)
in the southern or central North Sea in order to "kill the
bear". "Memorandum IX" had clearly posed the alternative
"Entscheidungsschlacht on the high sea" or "inactivity, that is,
moral self-destruction". Cruisers, according to Tirpitz, could resolve
colonial disputes and quell native rebellions; they could never protect German merchant ships against the Royal Navy.

   Opponents of battleship construction were not tolerated at the
Leipzigerplatz. Tirpitz viciously attacked proponents of cruiser warfare such as Admiral Hollmann, Admiral v. Koester, Admiral
Oldekop, Vice-Admiral Valois, and Captain v. Maltzahn, denouncing them to Admiral v. Müller as "dangerous to the Navy".
Nor was the Supreme War Lord spared : Tirpitz opposed Wilhelm's
blueprint for the "fast capital ship", a combination of cruiser and
battleship. And in 1904 the state secretary denounced submarines
as only local and secondary weapons, and refused to create what he
termed a "museum of experiments". Lieutenant-Commander Franz

Rust in 1904, Vice-Admiral Karl Galster in 1907, 1908 and 1909, Captain Lothar Persius between 1908 and 1914, and Vice-Admiral v. Schleinitz in 1908 all felt Tirpitz's wrath for supporting submarine warfare (*Kleinkrieg*). Young officers who associated too closely with cruiser or submarine tactics could be assured of short careers in the Imperial Navy.

In conclusion, Tirpitz came to the Navy Office with a well thought out, comprehensive naval construction programme. The creation of a mammoth battle fleet would provide the power basis for a great overseas policy. This, in turn, would mean large building contracts and hence prosperity for German industry and proletariat alike. Boom and profits would buttress at home the dominant political and social position of the ruling elements and, it was hoped, arrest demands for further parliamentarization on the part of the Social Democrats and Liberals, and at the same time would turn the energies and ambitions of Germany's middle classes towards overseas expansion.

Wilhelm II readily accepted the domestic aspects of Tirpitz's naval programme. The Navy offered the fascinating appeal of becoming a force relatively independent of parliamentary control and thus more directly a part of his "personal regime". In speaking of the new Navy Bill with which he had "completely tricked the Reichstag", Wilhelm expressed his certainty that the parliamentary deputies "were absolutely unaware of the extensible consequences" of this bill, which provided for automatic replacement of antiquated ships. He intended that "the dogs shall pay until they turn blue".

The ruler also understood the salient points of the programme in terms of foreign policy. Both his admiration for the Royal Navy and his hatred of "perfidious Albion", this "hateful, mendacious, unscrupulous nation of shopkeepers", moved him in this direction. As the Empress Frederick noted: "Wilhelm's one idea is to have a Navy which shall be larger and stronger than the British Navy." The Kaiser discarded from the outset Bismarck's erstwhile policy of consolidating Germany's continental position by trying to direct conflicts of other European powers to the continental periphery or to overseas areas. Such a policy would allow Germany's neighbours to increase their political and economic influence while the Reich stood still. Wilhelm proposed instead to consolidate and expand Germany's position in Europe while *simultaneously* laying the foundations for her future expansion overseas.

It was one thing to develop a theoretical naval programme, how-

ever comprehensive or well thought out it might be, but quite
another to realize it. It was precisely in this area that Tirpitz made
perhaps his greatest contribution. Hailed by many as the "Roon of
the Navy", in obvious reference to the Prussian parallel of 1862,
he started out, however, not by opposing parliament, but by
popularizing the idea of a German Navy with the masses in order
to persuade the Reichstag to grant the necessary funds for naval
construction. Tirpitz changed the *Marine-Rundschau* from a technical journal into a popular magazine. The naval annual *Nauticus*
was founded and a special News Bureau within the Navy Office
influenced the press. Orders were placed for Mahan's *Influence of
Sea Power* to be translated into German. The "bible of the Navy"
was serialized in German journals, copies were placed on board
every warship, and some 8,000 free copies were distributed by the
Navy Office. Mass rallies in favour of naval expansion were
organized throughout Germany. Political and industrial leaders
were invited to attend naval reviews, officers courted the favour of
Reichstag deputies, popular journals and books glorified naval
history, and naval uniforms became the vogue for children, including the Kaiser's six sons. In fact, Wilhelm's brother, Prince
Heinrich, entered the Navy in 1877, and his third son, Adalbert,
followed in 1901. The German academic community also lent support to the naval initiative as outstanding scholars such as Hans
Delbrück, Erich Marcks, Hermann Oncken, Gustav Schmoller, and
Max Weber – among roughly 270 "fleet" professors – provided the
theoretical underpinnings for "navalism" and *Weltpolitik*.

Various political pressure groups in the Reich were also asked to
endorse the naval programme. The Colonial League, with 20,000
members in 1897, distributed in one year alone 250,000 brochures
and 7 million pamphlets on behalf of it. The Pan-German League
also became a propaganda auxiliary. And in 1898 Alfried Krupp
and Prince Wied founded the German Navy League (*Flottenverein*)
in order to "emancipate large sections of the community from the
spell of the political parties by arousing their enthusiasm for this
one great national issue". The Navy League financed its own newspaper, *Die Flotte*, which soon had a circulation of 750,000. Its
membership rose from 78,652 in 1898 to 1,108,106 in 1914. Krupp
had earlier aided the naval cause by publishing a book entitled
What has Parliament done for the Navy? – it contained numerous
blank pages. The "Central Union of German Industrialists", federal
princes, provincial governors, church organizations, and national

women's groups carried Tirpitz's message to the remote corners of the land.

Wilhelm, in addition to donning naval uniform and clothing his sons in sailor's suits, stressed the naval crusade. His lavish sea pilgrimages to Norway during the summer and later to Corfu during the spring resembled a small armada. In fact, the monarch maintained a small flotilla of ships. In 1891 he purchased the British *Thistle* (renamed *Meteor*); later on, a second *Meteor* (former *Comet*) and even a third *Meteor*, a former American schooner, were bought. His old paddle-steamer *Hohenzollern* was retired in 1893 as *Kaiseradler*, and replaced in April by a new *Hohenzollern*, with gold plating from bow to stern. This royal yacht between 1893 and 1914 spent about 1,600 days, or four and a half years, at sea with Wilhelm on board. The empress also maintained her private yacht, the *Iduna*. Vast sums were spent on the *Meteor* in order to defeat Krupp's entry in the famous regattas sanctioned by the Imperial Yacht Club in Kiel and the North German Yacht Club on the Elbe river. Krupp, not to be outdone, in 1912 spent 90,000 GM to rebuild his *Germania* in order to defeat the *Meteor* – at a time when the monthly income of one of his industrial workers was about 10 GM. The "Kieler-Woche" became a renowned international event and was frequented by kings, presidents and millionaires from around the globe.

But Tirpitz remained the master of what he termed "spiritual massage". Only the Social Democrats and Richter's Left Liberals remained immune to his charms. Tirpitz visited federal princes to gain their favour; he travelled to Friedrichsruh to court Bismarck; he received Reichstag deputies in his office and let them into armaments secrets; he dispatched officers to influence shipping and industrial magnates; and he invited the latter to dine in officers' *Kasinos* (messes) and to undertake cruises aboard new warships. Moreover, he gathered around him a coterie of aides who were loyal to him and who spent their summers in St Blasien preparing the annual naval budgets: Capelle, Dähnhardt, Fischel, Hopman, Heeringen, Büchsel, Coerper, Ingenohl, Scheer, and Trotha, all officers destined to climb the ladder of naval command.

These tactics were not without result. National Liberals, Free Conservatives, Agrarian, and Centre delegates were all too easily seduced by this propaganda. The Conservatives, who had first rallied under Bismarck in 1879 under the slogan "rye and iron" in order to stem the mounting tide of Socialism, united now with the bourgeoisie under Johannes v. Miquel's *Sammlungspolitik* (politics of concentration). Aristocrats and *Bürger* were again asked to join forces in a loose Reichstag coalition ranging from the National Liberals to the Conservatives, in which the latter would agree to drop their opposition to the "hated fleet" and vote for naval construction in return for higher tariffs against foreign grain. The alliance proved workable: the Navy received Conservative support in 1898 and 1900; the Agrarians, in turn, received higher customs dues in 1902.

On 10 April 1898 the Reichstag passed the First Navy Bill calling for the construction of 19 battleships, 8 armoured cruisers, 12 large and 30 light cruisers by 1 April 1904. The heavy units were to be replaced automatically every twenty-five years, light cruisers every fifteen years. Building costs were not to exceed 408,900,000 GM while recurrent naval outlays were limited to 5 million GM. The Navy Bill was to include the existing 12 battleships, 10 large and 23 light cruisers, and therefore would entail new construction of only 7 battleships, 2 large and 7 light cruisers over the next six years. Such a fleet was regarded as strong enough for limited offensives against France and Russia. It was not a serious threat to Britain's naval position.

On 14 June 1900, further influenced by the Boer War and the Boxer rebellion in China, the Reichstag passed the Second Navy Bill. This called for nothing less than a doubling of the fleet to 38 battleships, 20 armoured cruisers and 38 light cruisers. The ships were to be apportioned as follows: 2 fleet flagships, 4 squadrons of 8 battleships each, 8 large and 24 light cruisers for the main fleet; a reserve of 4 battleships, 3 large and 4 light cruisers; and an overseas flotilla of 3 large and 10 light cruisers. In sharp contrast to the First Navy Bill, the Second Navy Bill set no cost limit for construction. A large portion of the naval expenses had, in the end, to be covered by national notes (*Reichsanleihen*) and hence deferred to future generations. Moreover, as Paul Kennedy has shown in his superb study of the Second Navy Bill in the *Militärgeschichtliche Mitteilungen* (1970), Tirpitz regarded this force of 38 battleships as only an interim stage, and had already in September 1899 spoken to Wilhelm of 45 battleships in addition to heavy cruisers. Indeed, in 1900 the Navy Office had even discussed at length the possibility of wringing from parliament a "third double-squadron", that is, a fleet of 48 battleships (Table 5).

The Navy Bill of 1900 – Walther Hubatsch's claim that it caused "absolutely no reaction" in Great Britain notwithstanding – was tantamount to a unilateral German declaration of "cold war" against Britannia. The concentration of so many battleships in the North Sea reaffirmed Tirpitz's belief that "overseas conflicts with European nations with greater naval strength will be settled in Europe" – the "dagger at the throat "strategy, according to Kennedy. The overall policy could no longer be camouflaged. The Navy now brazenly commented : "If we wish to promote a powerful overseas policy and to secure worthwhile colonies, we must be prepared first and foremost for a clash with England or America."

The Navy Bills of 1898 and 1900 gave the green light for German naval building. No less than twelve battleships were laid down and completed between 1900 and 1905, and British Admiralty officers calculated that Germany would be the second naval power in the world by 1906.

The first class of battleships laid down under Tirpitz was the *Wittelsbach* series : *Wittelsbach, Schwaben, Mecklenburg, Wettin,* and *Zähringen.* Launched in 1900–1, they were completed between 1899 and 1904 at a cost of 22.7 million GM per ship. The *Wittelsbach* vessels were the first to be protected by the new "citadel belt armour". They carried the same armament as their predecessors (*Kaiser Friedrich III* class), adding one 45 cm underwater stern torpedo tube.

The subsequent *Braunschweig* class (*Braunschweig, Elsass, Hessen, Preussen, Lothringen*), named after German states, came under the Second Navy Bill. The ships were launched in 1902–3 and completed by 1906 at a cost of 24 million GM each. Changes in gunnery were introduced under Chief Designer Rudloff : it had proved possible to extend the rapid-fire principle to the 28 cm gun, and hence the *Braunschweig* vessels received four of these guns arranged in two twin turrets fore and aft.

Of greater consequence was the fact that the running distance of torpedoes, around 900 m in 1898, had been doubled by the invention of heat engines. The gyroscope, adapted for torpedo use by the Austrian Ludwig Obry, further enhanced torpedo efficiency and accuracy to the level of naval guns up to a range of 1,800 m. Still further mechanical improvements by 1905 provided accurate firing up to a range of nearly 2,700 m. This, in turn, ushered in not only new developments in destroyer construction, medium-range rapid-fire weapons and machine-guns, but also prompted German designers to opt for an increase in the secondary armaments of battleships. With torpedoes travelling faster and farther, and because the maximum muzzle velocities of the 15 cm guns could not be stepped up owing to barrel wear, it was decided to raise the number and the calibre of the medium guns. The *Wittelsbach* accordingly received fourteen 17 cm and eighteen 8.8 cm guns (Table 6).

Between 1903 and 1908 Germany built the last series of pre-Dreadnought battleships, the *Deutschland* class. The *Deutschland, Schlesien, Schleswig-Holstein, Hannover,* and *Pommern* were launched in 1904–6 at a cost of 24.5 million GM per ship. Guns and torpedo armament were not altered from the *Braunschweig* class – apart from adding two 8.8 cm guns – but armour was once again increased.

German development of armoured cruisers followed British production in terms of speed, protection and displacement. Lord Fisher was an enthusiastic advocate of the fastest armoured cruisers with the heaviest possible armaments, to be used as scouts with the main battle fleet. The ships were intended to force their way through the enemy's screen of light cruisers, to monitor an opponent's flight, to report his position and available strength to the battle fleet; in short, to be able to crush any cruiser afloat as well as to hunt down armed merchant raiders – including the German trans-Atlantic liners with their best speed of twenty-five knots, should the latter ever be converted to armed auxiliary cruisers. At best, the battle-cruisers were to be able to hunt down, pursue and destroy a crippled enemy fleet after a victorious battle. Initially referred to as simply large armoured cruisers or even "fast battleships", they were in 1911 officially termed "battleship-cruisers" and the following year "battle-cruisers". With his favourite slogan, "speed is armour", Fisher launched project HMS *Unapproachable* under the guidance of W. H. Gard, building three such battle-cruisers in 1907. The *Invincible* class, as they were known, will be dealt with in the next chapter.

Germany answered between 1904 and 1908 with the *Scharnhorst* and *Gneisenau*. These twin ships were built at a cost of 20.3 million GM; armour was sacrificed for greater speed. The two ships, named after famous early nineteenth-century Prussian Army reformers, carried eight 21 cm, six 15 cm and eighteen 8.8 cm guns. They were designed for service with the battle fleet.

A final pre-Dreadnought armoured-cruiser was the *Blücher,* built between 1907 and 1909 at the enormous cost of 28.5 million GM. Admiral v. Tirpitz had opposed the impending "super" armoured-cruiser construction race because he viewed these ships as purely reconnaissance vessels. The British were thus able to surprise him in 1907 by leaking news that the *Invincible* was to be armed with 23.8 cm (9.2 in) guns, whereas, in reality, the *Invincible, Inflexible* and *Indomitable* received eight 30.5 cm (12 in) guns. As it was too late to alter *Blücher's* ordnance, she was outfitted only with twelve 21 cm guns arranged in six twin turrets, one fore, one aft, and two on each side (hexagonal mounting). She was, of course, named after the victor of Laon and Waterloo. *Blücher* was usually counted in later years as a battle-cruiser (Table 7).

The fleet of the 1898 Navy Bill was organized into the First Squadron, composed of four ships of the *Brandenburg* class as well as four of the earlier *Sachsen* class. By 1901-2 the ships of the *Kaiser Friedrich III* class neared completion and allowed the First Squadron to be composed of eight modern battleships. In mid-1903, the First Squadron, commanded by Admiral Hans v. Koester, contained only *Kaiser Friedrich III* and the latest *Wittelsbach* vessels; the *Brandenburg* class underwent rebuilding in 1904-5. The available ships were reconstituted in 1903 into the "Active Battle Fleet". The fleet set forth in the Second Navy Bill of 1900 was realized only in 1907, when the Second Squadron of *Braunschweig* and *Deutschland* battleships was created. This allowed Wilhelm II in February 1907 to establish the "High Sea Fleet" (*Hochseeflotte*), which it remained until November 1918. The Kaiser's brother, Admiral Prince Heinrich of Prussia, became its first chief (1907-9), raising his flag on the *Deutschland* (fleet flagship since 1906).

German shipyards also continued development of the uniform type of light cruisers inaugurated with the *Gazelle* class in the 1890s. The *Bremen* series (*Bremen, Berlin, Danzig, Hamburg, Königsberg, Leipzig, Lübeck,* and *München*) was built between 1902 and 1907 and, in accordance with the imperial directive of 1903, given the names of German cities. The cruisers mounted ten 10.5 cm guns, and showed triple smoke-stacks as well as the old-fashioned-looking "extended ram" bows. It is worthy of note that the *Lübeck,* launched in March 1904, was the first turbine-driven cruiser in the Imperial Navy; Vulcan in Stettin outfitted her with 14,000 hp Parsons steam turbines.

Triple expansion engines, it turned out, were unable to maintain best speed for battleships (13,500 hp in the *Kaiser Friedrich III*

class) for as long as eight hours without suffering breakdowns, and
they vibrated tremendously at best speed. By 1900, coal-fired water-
tube boilers began to displace the customary cylindric (Scotch) boiler
and thereby allowed a reduction in weight. Experiment with
turbines, which in a cruiser promised further to reduce weight by
about 120 tons, pioneered by the Parsons Marine Steam Turbine
Company at Wallsend-on-Tyne, had commenced on British destroyers in 1901 (*Velox*) and light cruisers in 1903 (*Amethyst*); the
latter managed to develop 14,000 hp and reach a best speed of
23.6 knots. The *Dreadnought*, launched in Febrary 1906, was the
first battleship outfitted with turbine engines.

Tirpitz had at the end of 1901 asked a special commission under
Rear-Admiral v. Eickstedt to look into turbine development, but the
various German prototypes (Schichau, Schulz-Germania, Riedler-
Stumpf [AEG], Zoelly, and Curtis) were not yet ready for service.
Moreover, in 1902 a special commission that visited Britain and
Scotland concluded that only the Parsons turbine was fit for sea
duty. The Navy Office included in the budget of 1903 sufficient
funds to install Parsons' turbines on an experimental basis in the
torpedo-boat *S 125* and the *Lübeck*. Brown, Boverie & Cie. on
behalf of the German Parsons-Marine AG offered the turbines for
Lübeck at 750,000 GM. The battleship *Kaiser*, built in 1911–12,
was to be the first German battleship to be outfitted with turbines.
The turbine was lighter, more compact and produced more power
for engine weight than the reciprocal engine; it also used less coal
at higher speeds and possessed a greater endurance at high speeds
as it had fewer moving parts. By 1908, all German cruisers received
turbine plants, while torpedo-boats ended the use of reciprocal
engines in the previous year with *V 161* (Table 8).

A second series of light cruisers, the *Nürnberg* class, was also laid
down during this period at a cost of 5.56 million GM each. Three
vessels of 3,500-ton displacement were built between 1905 and
1908 : *Nürnberg, Stettin* and *Stuttgart*. The three ships carried ten
10.5 cm guns as well as the standard two side underwater torpedo
tubes. As with the previous *Gazelle* class, these cruisers first served
with the battle fleet and then were dispatched to overseas stations.

Torpedo-boat building also continued during the 1900–7 period.
The *S 90* built by Schichau in 1900 was the first modern large "T"
boat designed for use with the fleet (see Chapter 2). A fairly representative series during this era *T 137–T 197*, consisted of 660-ton
boats with 10,000 to 16,000 hp propulsion plants permitting a best

speed of up to thirty-three knots. The *T 137* was built between 1904 and 1905 at a cost of 1.76 million GM, while the later *T 180–T 185* vessels increased in cost to 2.02 million GM each, having a range of 1,250 sm (North Sea service) at an average speed of seventeen knots. Diesel oil was introduced as fuel for "T" boats by 1908.

This hectic pace of naval construction permitted little time for organizational or administrative alterations. In February 1900 the Navy School and Navy Academy were officially separated; the former was relocated in Mürwik, near Flensburg, in November 1910. In March 1909, Wilhelm II opened the Catholic chapel in Kiel.

The flurry of German capital-ship building, seen in retrospect, came at a critical point in European affairs. The Second Navy Bill was passed in 1900 immediately on the heels of the outbreak of the Boer War and during the Boxer rebellion. The Reich's involvement with Great Britain and Italy in an international blockade of Venezuelan ports in 1902–3 further aggravated Anglo–German relations, prompted the Kaiser temporarily to seek naval increases in 1904, and raised serious doubts in the United States concerning Germany's intention of seizing territory in the western hemisphere. The period of construction under the first two Navy Bills ended in 1905 with the annihilation of the Russian East Asian and Baltic Sea fleets by Japan in Port Arthur and the Korea Straits, near the island of Tsushima. This, in turn, elevated Germany's fleet of sixteen battleships into third position in the world, behind Great Britain and France.

But Germany's unilateral challenge to Great Britain's dominant sea power, as expressed in the Second Navy Bill, caused concern in Germany, especially among senior Army officers. General v. Waldersee had noted as early as January 1896 that the Kaiser appeared to be "completely involved with naval expansion", and cautioned that German involvement with Great Britain in a naval race would be "presumptuous"; "we can only make asses of ourselves in this". And in the Far East in May 1901 as Wilhelm's *Weltmarschall,* Waldersee, who had done not a little to bring about Bismarck's dismissal in March 1890, was having second thoughts about the "New Course" of *Weltpolitik*: "Matters here would have quite a different appearance if he [Bismarck] were still alive; the world lacks a Bismarck."

The reaction in Great Britain was one of anger as well as determination to meet the German challenge head-on. To be sure, no one could deny the Reich a right to acquire sea power sufficient to protect her growing overseas trade and her scattered colonies. By March 1889, with the "Naval Defence Act", Britain had encouraged naval construction by defining the requisite strength of the Royal Navy as a fleet equal to those of the next two maritime powers (then France and Russia). This programme had called for no fewer than 70 ships, including 10 battleships and 42 cruisers; it was further refined by Lord Spencer in December 1893 to achieve series production of homogeneous types. The Netherlands in 1900 passed a ten-year building programme; Spain followed in January 1908 with a long-term plan. Nor were lesser naval powers immune to the virus of "navalism". Portugal in 1895 had launched a five-year programme, as had Mexico in 1901. But the cardinal difference was that Germany possessed the industrial capacity and technical knowledge as well as the will to realize her mammoth building plans: the Netherlands in 1914 were still planning their 6,530-ton battleship; Spain in 1914 possessed one 15,700-ton battleship; Portugal in 1914 claimed one 3,000-ton battleship, originally launched in 1876; and Mexico in 1914 still planned construction of two 2,400-ton cruisers. Germany, on the other hand, in 1914 had realized a force of fifteen battleships and six battle-cruisers in commission, with another six capital ships under construction. In short, it would be misleading to agree with Professor Jürgen Rohwer that German naval expansion can simply be integrated with Spanish, Mexican, Portuguese, or Dutch plans under the general umbrella of "navalism".

No one appreciated this more than Admiral Sir John Fisher, First Sea Lord between 1904 and 1909, and again from 1914 to 1915. When he became Second Sea Lord in 1902–3, Fisher found that British warships missed more than twice out of every three rounds during target practice. The Royal Navy had, in fact, last fired a shot in anger against a major naval power in 1856 off the Crimean coast. Fisher at once gave full rein to gunnery reforms initiated by Captain Percy Scott, "the pocket Hercules", who managed to hit the target 80 per cent – against the fleet average of 30 per cent. "I don't care if he drinks, gambles, and womanizes; *he hits the target!*" Moreover, Fisher also introduced sweeping recruiting reforms, to be discussed later, designed to increase the level of training and to remove age-old prejudices and methods.

Fisher's early personnel reforms as well as his gunnery improvements naturally frustrated Tirpitz's plans to be able to test Britain with a battleship ratio of 2:3 because of superior German personnel and gunnery. Still more crushing was Fisher's thorough fleet reorganization as First Sea Lord during 1904–5. "With one courageous stroke of the pen", as the Prime Minister, Balfour, put it, Fisher in 1905 scrapped no fewer than 154 warships, including 17 battleships. Fisher depicted his revamping policy as being "Napoleonic in its audacity and Cromwellian in its thoroughness". Not only did he trim the Royal Navy's motley collection of slow and inefficient ships; he also reshuffled Britain's existing naval commands. Independent squadrons in the Pacific, South Atlantic, North America, and the West Indies were consolidated into an Eastern Fleet based on Singapore. The Home Fleet, renamed Channel Fleet, was increased to twelve battleships and based on Dover. The late Channel Fleet, now Atlantic Fleet, was stationed on Gibraltar – within four days' steaming of home – with a force of eight battleships. The Mediterranean Fleet was now stationed on Malta, and each squadron in European waters was assigned a flotilla of six armoured cruisers. *Matériel* and tactics were also updated to bring them into line with recent technological advances. As in Germany, smokeless powder was introduced in the 1890s; armour-piercing shells were deployed, gun calibres increased, rapid-fire cannons built; and torpedo improvement centred round the new "heat" engines as well as the Obry gyroscope. The Nelsonian tactic of laying ships within one mile of the enemy and then smothering him with a hail of superior fire was still in vogue; battle ranges increased between 1900 and 1903 only from 2,000 to 3,000 m. Fisher, as will be shown, radically ended this by 1906.

But above all, developments on the international scene made possible such sweeping changes. The Anglo–Japanese treaty in January 1902 permitted a reduction in the Royal Navy's presence in East Asia. It also greatly infuriated Wilhelm II, who declared that Britain with this step had deserted Europe and the white race. The Entente with France in 1904 further allowed a reduction of Britain's Mediterranean forces, and conversely made a concentration in the North Sea – the crux of Tirpitz's master plan – a distinct possibility. And the great naval victory at Tsushima eliminated the Russian menace at sea to Great Britain. The Kaiser at the time sadly noted: "The situation begins to look increasingly like that before the Seven Years War."

The old British two-power standard could now be abandoned without risk, and attention could be turned instead to the new challenge from across the North Sea. Fisher in October 1906 bluntly stated : "Our only probable enemy is Germany. Germany keeps her *whole* Fleet always concentrated within a few hours of England. We must therefore keep a Fleet twice as powerful concentrated within a few hours of Germany." Two years later, Fisher informed the king that "we have eventually to fight Germany . . . just as sure as anything can be". Accordingly, by 1909, given the Anglo–French–Russian Entente of 1907, Fisher's reorganization schemes permitted Britain to make three-quarters of her battleships ready against the Reich. The First Sea Lord never tired of quoting Nelson's dictum : *"The battle ground should be the drill ground."* The redefinition of the two-power standard constituted a crippling blow to Tirpitz's master strategy.

Germany's intense Anglophobia contributed in no small way to Fisher's ability to carry out his bold reforms. The prevailing "invasion scares", in particular, played into his hands. As early as February 1896, Captain Baron v. Lüttwitz of the General Staff in Berlin had published an article – quickly translated – wherein he claimed that "the unassailableness of England is legend". Four years later General v.d. Goltz, and in 1901 Lieutenant Baron v. Edelsheim, published tracts raising the possibility of invading Great Britain. Admiral Livonius assured his countrymen that the Royal Navy no longer possessed either the character or the ability of the days of Trafalgar and Cape St Vincent, and that Germany could defeat her at sea. This invasion talk coincided with the expansion of the docks at Emden for the embarkation of 300,000 troops, and with Admiral Prince Heinrich's visit to Britain in May 1902 at the head of a squadron of eight battleships.

The Boer War, quite apart from the "Krüger telegram" of 1895 in which Wilhelm had pledged German support to the insurgent Boers, produced a tidal wave of anti-British sentiment in the Reich. The press denounced the British "buccaneering" adventure, insulted the British Army as a pack of "mercenaries", slandered Queen Victoria in gross caricatures, and hailed British reverses with gusto. Secretary of State for the Colonies Joseph Chamberlain, in turn, poured oil on the fire by alluding to the alleged cruelty of Prussian troops during the Franco–Prussian War. And while the Bülow government maintained a correct posture, it could not muzzle the press. In 1904 August Niemann's novel, *Der Weltkrieg: Deutsche*

3a. Wilhelm II and Admiral Scheer at Kiel, October 1918

3b. Admiral Scheer

3c. General v. Hindenburg and Admiral v. Schröder inspect German defences in the West

Träume, caused a sensation by calling for a Franco–German–Russian alliance against Great Britain in order to secure a new division of the world. In addition, the Kaiser's signature as "Admiral of the Atlantic" on a letter to the Tsar in October 1902 hardly soothed British fears and suspicions. When Edward VII visited Kiel in June 1904, Wilhelm II, against Tirpitz's better judgment, brought out every available German warship for a show of strength. British reaction came in the form of the first official war plans drawn up against Germany in the summer of 1904 under Admiral Prince Louis of Battenberg.

Still the "invasion scares" continued. During the winter of 1904–5, British warships were recalled from the Far East and all leaves cancelled. The press immediately suspected German machinations at the root of a new scare, and *Vanity Fair* in November 1904 argued : "If the German Fleet were destroyed the peace of Europe would last for two generations." Erskine Childers made his effort for peace with the novel *Riddle of the Sands,* and Spenser Wilkinson with *Britain at Bay.* The Socialist *Clarion* warned of a German "bolt from the blue" across the North Sea, and Alan H. Burgoyne, editor of the *Army and Navy Gazette,* published *The War Inevitable. Nineteenth Century* and the *National Review* joined the trend, as did William Le Queux with *The Invasion of 1910,* also serialized in the *Daily Mail* and, upon direct orders from the Kaiser, analysed by the German Admiralty and General Staffs. Le Queux and Major A. J. Read actually reported the presence of 6,500 German spies in Great Britain.

The crux of the matter was that Wilhelm II continued to furnish the fuel for these imaginary invasion novels. His unfortunate speech in March 1905 at Tangier, upholding Moroccan independence in the face of French incursions, was a maladroit effort to break up the Anglo–French Entente. As such it failed miserably. Although the move forced the resignation of the French Foreign Minister, Théophile Delcassé, the international conference convened at Algeciras in the following year revealed the bankruptcy of German diplomacy. The Reich's statesmen managed to alienate four great powers (Great Britain, France, the United States, and Italy), and were left with only Austria–Hungary. In a dramatic attempt to extricate himself from self-imposed diplomatic isolation, the Kaiser concluded a close offensive and defensive alliance with Tsar Nicholas II at Björkö – the very agreement that he had overthrown against Bismarck's express desires in 1890. But the pact proved to be still-born: the governments both in Berlin and in St Petersburg refused to ratify this *tour de force*. Wilhelm glumly spoke of "the dreadful Gallo–Russian vice".

Perhaps no single act could have stemmed – much less reversed – the rising tide of Anglo–German hostility and suspicion. Diplomacy had failed by 1906, and no one seemed anxious to try it again. The Germans were by now paranoid in their belief that "Fisher was coming". Early in 1907, this cry prompted parents in Kiel to keep their children from school for two days. Panic broke out in the Berlin Bourse as well. Moreover, there also continued what Jonathan Steinberg has called the "love–hate relationship between a half-English Emperor and an England which never entirely accepted him". On 28 October 1908 the *Daily Telegraph* published remarks which Wilhelm II had made to Colonel Stuart-Wortley at Highcliffe Castle the previous winter, in which the Kaiser had claimed that he had provided Queen Victoria with the successful operations plans against the Boers; that he, unlike the majority of his subjects, was pro-British; that he had rejected Franco–Russian overtures to mediate the Boer War, even sending these proposals on to the Queen; and that the German Navy was built not against Britain, but to secure the Reich's Far Eastern trade, that is, against Japan. Yet Britannia had not repaid these favours, and the Kaiser exploded: "You English are mad, mad as March hares." That same year Wilhelm perhaps best delineated his feelings with regard to the Anglo–German naval rivalry:

> I have no desire for good relationship with England at the price of the development of Germany's Navy. If England will hold out her hand in friendship only on condition that we limit our Navy, it is a boundless impertinence and a gross insult to the German people and their Emperor. . . . The [Navy] Bill will be carried out to the last detail; whether the British like it or not does not matter! If they want war, they can begin it, we do not fear it!

Professor Arthur Marder concluded that "the root cause of the English distrust of Germany in 1900–5 lay in the almost psychopathic suspicion of the methods and aims of German foreign policy".

It is against this background of international developments and Anglo–German fears and suspicions that subsequent naval developments must be seen; without such an understanding, what follows makes little sense. For with the laying down on 2 April 1906 of the world's first "all big gun one calibre battleship" by the Royal Navy at the Portsmouth Dockyard, Europe feverishly launched a fateful naval arms race.

IV

The Dreadnought Challenge

The Master Plan Goes Awry, 1905-1911

Admiral v. Tirpitz claimed after the war that the Dreadnought "leap" in 1905–6 had been a cardinal mistake on the part of Admiral Fisher because it allowed all major naval powers to commence new construction only slightly behind the British, who thereby surrendered their crushing superiority in pre-Dreadnought battleships and especially in cruising ships. These views, first expounded in Tirpitz's *Memoirs* (1919) and later expanded in his two-volume publication of *Politische Dokumente* (1924–6), were quickly accepted at face value not only by the grand admiral's erstwhile aides but also by numerous naval historians; moreover, all agreed that Tirpitz managed to accept, and eventually to offset, this nefarious British challenge. But recent archival work has proved them to be in error. Above all, Volker R. Berghahn's *Der Tirpitz-Plan* (1971) has revealed that the issue was far from being as simple as was once supposed. Various subtle strategic, financial and tactical factors were at work that ultimately undermined Tirpitz's master plan.

The argument that Fisher carelessly gambled away the British advantage in heavy units and cruisers with his decision to build the "all big gun one calibre battleship" is, of course, extremely superficial. The First Sea Lord had an option only in terms of time. The naval battle at Tsushima had clearly shown where the future lay: the encounter was won by Japan owing to superior speed, gunnery control, the new high-explosive shells, and, above all, the large 30.5 cm guns which decided the issue. And the Japanese decision, based on information gathered in the Russo-Japanese War, to commence building two 20,000-ton ships (*Satsuma* and *Aki*) naturally affected Fisher's decision to lay down the first "super" battleship.

Fisher was aware that other maritime powers were on the verge of creating "super" battleships. The Russians in 1904–5 contemplated such designs; the United States had in 1904 drawn up plans for a new, large battleship, and in 1905 Congress authorized two vessels (*Michigan* and *South Carolina*) that were already in this category. Not surprisingly, German naval scholars provide the most cogent attacks upon Fisher: the Reich, according to them, was "not in the least surprised" (Siegfried Breyer) by the "super" battleship, because it was fully ready for the new class. Spurred on by Wilhelm's pet project for a "fast capital ship" armed exclusively with heavy guns – which he had advocated since the 1890s, and discovered during a visit to Italy in the *Vittorio Emanuele* class – the design department of the Navy Office by March 1904 submitted plans for a battleship armed solely with heavy guns and with a displacement of about 14,000 tons. This initial design, entitled "Battleship Project No 10 A", yielded in October 1905 to "Project C", which envisaged a 17,000-ton vessel with eight heavy guns of uniform calibre. This was to be the forerunner of the German *Nassau* class of Dreadnoughts. If the Reich was this close to "super" battleship building, how could Fisher possibly have put off his plans?

Fisher was not the man to sit idly by and allow the initiative to go over to his most probable foe. He instructed Gard to draw up several designs for a project known as HMS *Untakeable,* and when appointed First Sea Lord in October 1904 he at once established a "Committee on Designs" that included Gard. By January 1905 it had come up with design "H", the forerunner of the *Dreadnought,* a 17,000-ton battleship with a best speed of twenty-four knots, and armed with twelve heavy guns of uniform calibre (30.5 cm). Fisher had undoubtedly been encouraged in this design by Vittorio Cuniberti's article in *Jane's Fighting Ships* (1903), wherein the chief designer of the Italian Navy had described precisely a type such as the "H" design as "an ideal battleship for the Royal Navy". Wilhelm's amateurish attempt in 1905 to influence Admiralty planning by sending retired Admiral Victor Montague details of elderly German battleships, in the hope that Montague would pass them on, must have given Fisher at least a moment of amusement.

Once in possession of design "H", Fisher moved with alacrity. The keel plates were laid on 2 October 1905, and the "super" battleship was launched by the king after only 130 days on 10 February 1906. Her sea trials were conducted on 3 October, one year and one day after she was laid down. She was commissioned on 3 December 1906, after a record building time of only fourteen months. She was named *Dreadnought*. The first of her six predecessors of that name had fought off the "invincible" Armada in 1588; the fifth had been with Nelson at Trafalgar. Fisher called his creations "Old Testament Ships". David Lloyd George was not so charitable. He termed the *Dreadnought* a "piece of wanton and profligate ostentation".

The *Dreadnought* displaced 17,900 tons and was the first major warship propelled by turbines. The greatest revolution, however, came with her armament. She received ten 30.5 cm and twenty-two 7.6 cm guns. Whereas ships before her fired two 30.5 cm cannons ahead and four on a broadside, *Dreadnought's* arrangement of five twin turrets (one fore, two aft, two side) gave her the firing-power equivalent of two pre-Dreadnoughts in broadside firing, and three in firing ahead. The Nelsonian "hail of fire" method was abandoned in favour of long-range duels with 30.5 cm guns, directed by a range finder in a tripod guiding an entire broadside (metal weight 3,085 kg).

Professor Marder, in his brilliant analysis *From the Dreadnought to Scapa Flow*, I (1961), has laid to rest the German claim that the *Dreadnought* was specifically designed as a deterrent to German naval ambitions. Germany was not mentioned in a single document even indirectly in any committee or design report. Nor had Fisher built this vessel with only Germany's need to widen and deepen the Kaiser-Wilhelm Canal and locks in mind, although later he pointed out that the "super" battleship construction would necessitate the expenditure of £12.5 million sterling to dredge the canal. What Fisher had, indeed, done was to give Britain a huge lead in this revolutionary type development by the secrecy as well as the speed of building the *Dreadnought*. He assured his countrymen in November 1907 that they could now "sleep quiet in their beds".

Fisher's "Committee on Designs" had yet a further surprise in store. Project HMS *Unapproachable* had reached fruition by 1906 with the "E" design of a special class of large armoured cruisers. The series was launched with the *Invincible*, built between April 1906 and March 1908 by W. G. Armstrong at Elswick under greater secrecy than even the *Dreadnought*. Designed to displace 17,000 tons, *Invincible* was driven by four Parsons turbines, and her eight 30.5 cm guns were arranged in twin turrets (one fore, one aft, and two side diagonally offset). The increase in firing power and speed was accompanied by a reduction in armour. The "all big gun cruiser" during the Great War vindicated her armament at Falkland; Jutland, on the other hand, revealed her shortcomings in protection. The problem, in a nutshell, was that these vessels had exaggerated demands made upon them. For overseas service, speed was paramount and armour of minor importance; for service with the fleet, however, they lacked even remotely adequate protection. The collective term "capital ships" for battleships and battle-cruisers was introduced during the naval scare of 1909, and generally adopted in the Royal Navy by 1912.

Fisher's *Dreadnought* and *Invincible* "leaps", coupled with the other reforms affecting personnel, training, gunnery, tactics, and fleet concentration, effectively blunted the German naval challenge of 1900. In terms of both quality and quantity, Fisher in 1906 torpedoed Tirpitz's calculated risk embodied in the 2:3 ratio. Superior German personnel and *matériel* were now a fiction. Moreover, Germany already spent about 60 per cent of her total income on the Army. Where was the money for the Dreadnoughts to come from? These ships entailed a cost increase of 15–20 million GM per unit over the last class of *Deutschlands* and, taken together with the requisite canal and harbour-channel dredging and widening (that between 1907 and 1918 cost 244 million GM), posed a horrendous dilemma. Failure to accept the British challenge meant, in effect, abandoning Tirpitz's master plan. Acceptance would inaugurate a monstrous naval race until financial attrition forced one of the participants out of the contest.

It is interesting to note that Tirpitz in 1906–7 did not once put forth the argument that Fisher's Dreadnought policy cancelled British naval superiority and hence accorded all other naval powers an equal chance to catch up. In fact, Tirpitz was deeply disturbed by the news of the "super" battleship and battle-cruiser building across the North Sea. Throughout the summer of 1906 he buried himself in his Black Forest retreat and did his best to avoid the Kaiser. For the latter had quickly recognized that the *Dreadnought* was, in reality, Cuniberti's design from *Jane's Fighting Ships* in 1903, and he once again harassed Tirpitz with his "fast capital ship" project.

Tirpitz was in a quandary. A decision to build Dreadnoughts would now remove all camouflage from German intentions and make it clear to British leaders that Berlin intended to compete with the Royal Navy. Such a mammoth fleet could not be hidden. But the cost factor was highly alarming. Tirpitz had carefully worked out his *Etappenplan* so that naval construction would be based upon the expansion of German industry and trade, that is, displacement of ships would be raised only slowly, about 2,000 tons per series, over an extended period, in order not to cause alarm in London and to keep cost increases within limits.

Tirpitz initially still hoped that he could get away with an increase in displacement to 16,000 tons. German canal, harbour and shipyard facilities would be taxed to the utmost even with this increase; the locks at Wilhelmshaven restricted beam to 23.2 metres, and any ships of greater displacement than the *Braunschweig* or the *Deutschland* threatened to run aground in the Kaiser-Wilhelm Canal. On 22 September 1905 the decisive meeting concerning Dreadnought building was held in Tirpitz's Berlin office; the opening of parliament was, by then, only a few weeks away. The state secretary from the start placed a unit cost ceiling of 36.5 million GM on Dreadnoughts. The cost limit for battle-cruisers was simultaneously set at 27.5 million GM. The displacement of the new battleships was to be kept below 19,000 tons. Tirpitz's staff came up with a figure of 940 million GM to be requested from the Reichstag – in addition to 60 million GM for dredging the Kaiser-Wilhelm Canal. Captain Eduard v. Capelle, Tirpitz's most trusted intimate, calculated that the naval expansion would necessitate an annual increase in taxation of 130 million GM. It was estimated that this budget would take the Reich as far as 1910–11, when a sixty-ship plan was to be laid before the deputies.

In other words, Tirpitz now decided to pick up the gauntlet that he felt Fisher had thrown him. For in order to stand a genuine chance against a British fleet in the North Sea, he could not allow his forces to be more than numerically one-third weaker than the enemy's. Nor could he permit British quality to be substantially higher than his own. If the master plan were to be salvaged, there was no choice other than to proceed with the naval race. Chancellor v. Bülow accepted the naval increases by 19 September 1905; Wilhelm II gave his approval on 4 October 1905.

But there remained the Reichstag. The international crisis over Morocco was now exploited to the full for this purpose. In addition, the Russian fleet's skirmish with British fishing trawlers off the Dogger Bank and Arthur Lee's indiscreet "Copenhagen" talk had whipped up public enthusiasm for naval increases. In May 1906, after a final altercation with the Kaiser over the "fast capital ship" project, during which Tirpitz tendered his resignation in pure Bismarckian fashion in order to force approval of his plans, the expansion was passed as a Supplementary Bill (*Novelle*). It called for the construction of six cruisers as well as the aforementioned outlay of 940 million GM for Dreadnought building and canal, harbour and dock improvements. The total constituted a 35 per cent increase over the Second Navy Bill of 1900. Three Dreadnoughts and one battle-cruiser were annually to be laid down.

The four ships of the *Nassau* series (*Nassau, Posen, Rheinland, Westfalen*) were laid down between June and August 1907 with the greatest secrecy ever attempted by German yards. In contrast to the *Dreadnought,* the chief designer, Hans Bürkner, placed greater stress on protection than on armaments, and accordingly established the general principle that the thickness of the belt armour was to be equivalent to the calibre of the heavy guns. The first German "super" battleships were launched in 1908 and completed in 1909–10 at an average cost of 37.4 million GM each, thereby surpassing Tirpitz's ceiling of 36.5 million GM.

Bürkner's insistence on optimum underwater protection resulted in a honeycomb type of hull subdivision; the *Nassau* had sixteen, and her successors nineteen, watertight compartments. This, in turn, required the wider beam which enhanced stability. But the main innovation centred round *Nassau's* armament. Reciprocating engines took up a great deal of space at midlength, and hence the mounting of the six turrets, all at the same level, was not very successful. Superfiring turrets were out of the question as no room could be found for their magazines and lifts. Bürkner therefore had to choose hexagonal mountings with two turrets at the sides. This, of course, meant that in firing broadsides, *Nassau* had to do without two turrets (four guns) at the sides. The Germans were in this way inferior in design to the British one-centre line, one-wing system. Only in firing forward and aft were the Germans able to bring a maximum number of guns to bear. In other words, trebling the number of guns resulted only in doubling the metal weight of broadside over the *Deutschland* class. Turbines were out of the question, partly because Tirpitz favoured them only for cruisers, and partly because the Navy Office's construction department had in 1905 still ruled that "use of turbines in heavy warships does not recommend itself". The *Nassau* class was outfitted with twelve 28 cm, twelve 15 cm and sixteen 8.8 cm guns, and eventually comprised the First Squadron of the High Sea Fleet.

German Dreadnoughts were known up to 1914 for their smaller calibre guns (28 cm as opposed to 30.5 cm at first), their thicker armour (300 mm compared with 279 mm), and their slower speed (20 kn versus 22 kn). They were recognized as having better underwater compartmentation and hence greater stability. (Table 9).

Germany also laid down her first battle-cruiser in March 1908. She was the *Von der Tann*, built at the Blohm & Voss yard in Hamburg which, up to 1918, constructed five German battle-cruisers. Her construction costs amounted to 35.5 million GM, about 9 million GM above the state secretary's budgetary ceiling. She was lightly armed with eight 28 cm guns, fitted in one twin turret fore and aft each, and two diagonally offset on the side decks. The novelty was that *Von der Tann* was the first major German warship with turbine propulsion. Two Parsons turbines gave her a best speed of twenty-seven knots; cruising range was contracted for 4,400 sm at an average speed of fourteen knots. She was commissioned in September 1910 and joined the fleet as a spearhead battle-cruiser. *Von der Tann* created a great impression at the Coronation Naval Review in 1911. (Table 10).

Light cruiser building continued with the *Dresden* and *Emden,* built between 1907 and 1909 at costs of 7.5 million GM and 5.96 million GM respectively. The *Emden*, destined to become the most famous German light cruiser during the Great War, was built with thirteen watertight hull compartments, and her twelve coal-fired water-tube boilers delivered 16,171 hp for a best speed of twenty-four knots; cruising range was 3,760 sm at an average speed of twelve knots. She was poorly protected with armoured deck plates of 10–15 mm and belt armour of 80–100 mm. Her armament consisted of ten 10.5 cm guns single mounted; these were rapid-fire weapons, sixteen shots per minute, and supplied each with 150 rounds of high-explosive shell. The ship held a midway place in German light cruiser construction, and she was an exception in so far as she did not initially join the fleet, but was sent directly to the Far East after commissioning in July 1909.

Hard on the heels of the *Dresden* and *Emden* came series production of the *Kolberg* class. *Augsburg, Cöln, Kolberg,* and

Mainz were built between 1907 and 1911 at a cost of about 8 million GM each. The ships displaced 4,400 tons and were armed with twelve 10.5 cm and four 5.2 cm guns. They were the first cruisers to be outfitted with mines, carrying about 100 each. The entire class received turbine engines, and in 1916 supplementary oil burners. German light cruisers were generally very seaworthy; the five ships of the *Hertha* class (1896–9), however, were relatively useless in high seas owing to their high decks. (Table 11).

This rash of naval building was felt painfully by the German Treasury. British construction costs over the first three generations of Dreadnoughts actually declined, from £1.783 million for the *Dreadnought*, to £1.765 million for the *Bellerophon*, and £1.754 million for the *St Vincent* class ships. The German picture, in contrast, showed the reverse trend: costs rose meteorically from 38.399 million GM for *Nassau* to 46.196 million GM for *Helgoland*, and 44.997 million GM for *Kaiser* class vessels – a rise in three years of 17.2 per cent, compared to a British reduction of 1.6 per cent. In other words, Germany was spending almost 20 per cent more for Dreadnoughts by 1909 than Great Britain. In terms of battle-cruisers, German units increased in cost from 36.523 million GM for *Von der Tann* (1908) to 56 million GM for *Derfflinger* (1912), a rise of 53.3 per cent in four years. British battle-cruisers, on the other hand, jumped from £1.67 million for *Invincible* (1906) to £2.08 million for *Lion* (1909–11), an increase of 24.6 per cent over five years. Here, also, Berlin suffered almost a 30 per cent increment over London's costs. Moreover, these figures do not include the Reich's outlay for canal, harbour and dock expansion. Tirpitz's original estimate of 60 million GM for the Kaiser-Wilhelm Canal proved to be unrealistic. Expansion of this connective link was started in 1909 and completed on 24 June 1914 at a cost of 114.8 million GM!

The expenditure for the Navy had, by now, become horrendous. In 1907 about 291 million GM were spent on the fleet, and between 1897 and 1914 naval building added no less than 1,040,700,000 GM to the national debt. It was estimated in Berlin that by 1908 expenditure would exceed income by 500 million GM. Albert Ballin, director of the Hamburg–America Line, came to realize in 1908 that 'we cannot let ourselves in for Dreadnought competition with the much richer English''. Parliamentary opposition was also mounting. The Conservatives, who had never enthusiastically endorsed the fleet, now viewed it with "cold hearts". The Agrarians

joined them and thereby destroyed the so-called "Bülow bloc" in
the Reichstag, depriving Tirpitz of the certain passage of new naval
funds. The state secretary also witnessed a cooling-off with regard
to naval support among the Catholic Centre Party, whom he
accused of carrying "a dagger in their garments" over this issue.
Chancellor v. Bülow was being boxed into a corner by the Reich's
dire financial straits. As early as 1907 he had brusquely asked
Tirpitz : "When will you finally be sufficiently advanced with your
fleet so that the . . . unbearable political situation will be relieved?"
Front-line officers with the fleet in 1908 also began to grumble over
the unending shortage of funds. With the new addition of Dreadnoughts, which required about 200 to 300 more men, personnel
was constantly overworked. And many were slowly realizing that
the British were not permitting Germany to close the battleship gap
which, in turn, produced an atmosphere of inferiority at the front.
Admiral Büchsel in 1908 bluntly stated that the German fleet was
"insufficient" to meet a "serious" challenge. Tirpitz, of course,
attributed such pessimism solely to the evil machinations of the
Admiralty Staff and the Foreign Office, and in January 1909
managed to obtain from Wilhelm II a ruling that the Navy Office
was "the only agency which can fully oversee" all naval matters.

The period since the 1906 *Novelle* had also brought a deteriora-
tion in Germany's international situation. The disaster at Agadir
had been compounded in 1907 by the Anglo-French-Russian
Entente, and Anglo-German relations had deteriorated in the wake
of the invasion scares, "Copenhagen" threats, *Daily Telegraph*
interview, and the unsuccessful missions of David Lloyd George
and Sir Charles Hardinge to Germany between 1906 and 1908 to
attempt some arrangement concerning the intense naval race. As
Professor Berghahn points out, German diplomatic isolation,
coupled with domestic stresses, produced in the Reich an atmosphere
of fear as well as a simplistic friend-foe mentality.

Yet the more his master plan came apart at the seams, the greater
became Tirpitz's resolve to cling to it at all costs. British increases
in battleship displacement from 17,900 tons (*Dreadnought*) to
20,000 tons (*Colossus*) forced Germany to shell out ever greater
sums in order not to be left behind. The result, of course, was that
the funds of the 1906 *Novelle,* designed originally to see the Navy
through to 1911, were rapidly drying up. Naval building therefore
required a booster in order to keep up with Britain.

Tirpitz found his chance after the elections of January 1907 –

the so-called "Hottentot" elections held by the government over the refusal of the Centre and Socialist parties to vote the necessary funds to suppress a native uprising in German South-West Africa – which brought a loss to the Social Democrats and a corresponding gain for the middle-class parties. In fact, Tirpitz was carried away with visions of grandiose naval expansion, urging his advisors to wring from parliament as much money as they "legally" could. With regard to Britain, he urged the greatest secrecy in order to camouflage his plans. Ceilings for battleships of 47 million GM and for battle-cruisers of 44 million GM were to be kept confidential; technical improvements, which could easily be detected in higher prices, were to be hidden by releasing only flat-rate figures for construction; launching and commissioning dates were to be regarded as state secrets; and the Imperial Treasury was asked not to release statistics concerning the increase in naval personnel. The latter had, in fact, risen from 40,800 in 1905 to 60,800 in 1911.

But the Treasury reserves were at full ebb. Naval outlay alone had increased from 207.8 million GM in 1901 (17.9 per cent of expenditure), to 347.4 million GM in 1908 (23.7 per cent). Hermann Freiherr v. Stengel, State Secretary of the Treasury, was not swayed by Tirpitz's argument that the victory of the Liberals in the British general election of 1906 would allow a reduction in the Navy budget and, being unable to see a way out of Germany's fiscal jungle, tendered his resignation early in 1908.

This notwithstanding, the Reichstag in March 1908 passed the *Novelle* with a sizeable majority. The Supplementary Bill reduced the life of all capital ships from twenty-five to twenty years, therefore encompassing an increase in the strength of the fleet because outdated battleships and cruisers would be replaced more rapidly with Dreadnoughts and battle-cruisers. In terms of quantity, this meant that Germany abandoned her pace of three battleships per year in favour of four units per year between 1908 and 1911. The Reich by 1914 would possess 16 battleships and 5 battle-cruisers, and by 1920 a fleet of 58 capital ships (38 battleships and 20 battle-cruisers) as well as 38 light cruisers and 144 torpedo-boats.

To be sure, the *Novelle* of 1908 temporarily forced Tirpitz to stray from his master plan in order to acquire the requisite funds to keep in step with British construction. Yet ironically, the Supplementary Bill had built into it already the *raison d'être* for future naval expansion : the four-ships-per-annum rate would expire in

1911 and be reduced to a two-per-annum rate in 1912, thereby creating a so-called "hole' in the programme. If at that time he could persuade parliament to agree to the new construction of just two capital ships, Tirpitz would attain his erstwhile goal of a fleet of sixty capital ships, to be replaced automatically every twenty years.

Yet, according to Berghahn, even this was only a minimum programme. German industry had by now become extremely dependent upon government ship-building contracts, and Tirpitz fully counted upon the major purveyors of naval *matériel* to launch "with large funds" a campaign for three ships per annum by 1911. If successful, this would allow Tirpitz to construct eighteen capital ships between 1912 and 1917, and thereby reach that magical – albeit elusive – ratio of 2 : 3 *vis-à-vis* Britain that he had pursued since the turn of the century.

The increases of 1908 heated the Anglo-German naval race to a fiery white. In April 1907, the Germans had established a special "Naval Artillery School" at Sonderberg, and experiment with the new 30.5 cm gun revealed its applicability to the second-generation Dreadnoughts. Range-finders at maximum height were now just over the horizon – Germany fitted all capital ships during the Great War with spotting tops on the masts – and centre-line turret mountings were introduced in most major navies by 1909. A "large calibre" mania also set in. Krupp by 1914 was testing 38 cm, 40.6 cm, 45.6 cm, and even 50.8 cm guns.

Between 1908 and 1912, Germany built the four ships of the *Helgoland* class (*Helgoland, Oldenburg, Ostfriesland,* and *Thüringen*) at an average cost of 46 million GM. The vessels displaced 22,800 tons, had a best speed of twenty-one knots, and were powered by coal-fired triple expansion engines (supplementary oil burners were installed in 1915, and 197 cbm oil stored in the ships' double bottoms). The major innovation, as previously mentioned, was the adoption of the 30.5 cm guns; the *Helgoland* received twelve 30.5 cm guns, mounted in six twin turrets, one fore, one aft and two on the sides (hexagonal design). The calibre of torpedoes was increased to 50 cm, which now became standard through the *König* series. By reverting, for only this class, to triple funnels, the designers inadvertently increased the ships' silhouettes. Finally, it should be pointed out that the gun mountings remained the same as in the *Nassau* class, rather than super-firing turrets in centre-line design.

The plans for the third generation of German Dreadnoughts, the *Kaiser* class, had been drawn up by 1907 before the *Helgoland* class vessels were completed. Built between 1909 and 1913 at an average cost of 45 million GM, they displaced 24,700 tons. The most important design alteration centred round the propulsion plant. Three turbines developed 55,000 hp and permitted a best speed of twenty-two knots. The *Prinzregent Luitpold,* however, had been structured to receive one large diesel engine for cruising, but when the Howaldt power plant failed to meet the required standards for sea service, she remained with only two Parsons turbines. These ships were also the first German battleships with supplementary oil burners. In addition to the normal four replacement ships, *Kaiser, Kaiserin, König Albert,* and *Prinzregent Luitpold,* an additional vessel, *Friedrich der Grosse,* was built as fleet flagship (1912–19). All *Kaiser* class units in 1914 formed the Third Squadron of the High Sea Fleet. (Table 12).

The changeover to turbine propulsion finally allowed the Imperial Navy to abandon the hexagonal gun mountings. The ships of the *Kaiser* class had their ten 30.5 cm guns arranged in five twin turrets: two wing turrets diagonally offset so that they could fire in both directions; one fore turret; and two aft turrets, with the centre one raised above the other. It was the first design of this type in Germany. With one turret (two guns) less than the *Helgoland* class, the *Kaiser* ships did not, however, lose any firing-power because they were able to discharge all five turrets in a broadside (weight of metal fired 3,900 kg), while the *Helgoland* could only train four of her six turrets to any one side (weight of metal fired 3,120 kg). The five *Kaiser* class vessels were roughly similar to the British *Neptune* (1909–11).

After 1909, commencing with the *Orion,* Britain built three series of four battleships and three battle-cruisers with all heavy-gun turrets along the centre line of the ship. The ten 13.5 in guns were arranged in five twin turrets, two each fore and aft (with the centre one raised above the other), and one turret in the centre amidships. This permitted the deployment of all ten heavy guns in either direction for a broadside and ushered in the era of "super" Dreadnoughts. The design had been taken from the United States' *South Carolina* class (1906–10) – only the centre turret was added – and was quickly adopted also by Russia, Japan and several South American states. German designers, on the other hand, continued to use the smaller 30.5 cm gun, laying much stock in their 15 cm secondary guns.

Nor did the Reich go over to the larger calibre for the second series of battle-cruisers, the *Moltke* class, built between 1908 and 1912 at a cost of 42.6 million GM for the *Moltke* and 41.6 million GM for the *Goeben*. These two ships were outfitted with two Parsons turbines and possessed a best speed of twenty-eight knots. The 28 cm cannon was retained and, as in *Von der Tann,* the ten barrels were arranged in twin turrets, one fore and two diagonally offset on the side decks. However, a super-firing fifth turret (and hence an additional two 28 cm guns) was inserted forward of the after one, and the forecastle was accordingly extended much further aft. These were the first battle-cruisers to receive the larger 50 cm torpedo tubes. *Moltke* in September 1911 joined the High Sea Fleet; *Goeben* in July 1912 was attached to the German Mediterranean Squadron, and on 16 August 1914 entered the Turkish Navy as *Jawus Sultan Selim.*

The single ship *Seydlitz* retained the basic concept of the *Moltke* class. The armament, in terms of both calibre and arrangement, remained unchanged. *Seydlitz* was the first German capital ship to reach 200 m in length, and she attained a best speed of twenty-nine knots from her two sets of Parsons turbines. The heavy guns had a range of 18,100 m, but this was increased in 1915 to 19,100 m by cutting away some of the armour protecting the gun openings in the turrets. As with almost all German capital ships, the 8.8 cm rapid-fire guns were discarded in 1916 and replaced with two or four 8.8 cm anti-aircraft guns. Moreover, as in a number of other vessels, the material in the boiler tubes had a tendency to pitting, which required back-breaking frequent retubing for the engineers and stokers. (Table 13).

The German type of uniform light cruiser continued uninterrupted. The *Magdeburg* class (4,600 t) was built between 1910 and 1912 at a unit cost ranging between 7 and 8 million GM. All four ships were outfitted with steam turbines, and were the first German light cruisers to receive supplementary oil burners. Armament consisted of twelve 10.5 cm guns, two side submerged 50 cm torpedo tubes – the first use of the larger calibre torpedoes on this ship type – and 120 mines.

A second series consisting of *Karlsruhe, Rostock* and *Graudenz* was built between 1911 and 1915. The displacement of these ships was increased by 500 tons, while their armament (gun, torpedo and mine) was not altered. The vessels were all turbine-driven and no appreciable changes were undertaken with regard to best speed, range, or horse-power output. (Table 14).

If, in an attempt to give an accurate overview of the *matériel* of the Imperial Navy, the impression has been given that naval building in Germany was carried out without major political repercussions, this would be misleading. Quite the contrary. The period between the *Novelle* of 1908 and the outbreak of war in August 1914 was perhaps the most hectic, chaotic and, for the Reich, fateful in modern European history. Battleships and battle-cruisers continued to be built on a regular rhythm of four keel-layings per annum. The ships increased in displacement by 2,000 tons per series. The calibre of the heavy guns continued to climb, as did that of the torpedoes. Draft increased. Beam expanded. Length went over 200 m for the first time in a German warship. Krupp armour plates steadily grew thicker. Turbines brought a revolution in propulsion as well as in gun mountings. Best speed for battleships reached twenty-two knots; almost thirty knots for battle-cruisers. And super-firing turrets arranged along the ships' centre line greatly enhanced the weight of metal fired in a broadside. The Dreadnought was already in the past; the "super" Dreadnought had arrived.

Nor was naval construction isolated from German policies, either domestic or foreign. On the local scene, armaments, steel, electric and machine manufacturers worked feverishly to fulfil ever-increasing naval contracts; by the same token, they became ever more dependent upon government orders. In the five years to 1909, Krupp's industrial empire in Essen more than doubled in size to 100,000 workers. The Blohm & Voss yard in Hamburg grew from 4,500 employees in 1906 to 10,000 in 1914, primarily as a result of battle-cruiser construction. And a host of workers, rammers, pile-drivers, dredges, tugs, barges, cranes, and the like, laboured from 1909 to ready the Kaiser-Wilhelm Canal and other inland waterways for the new Dreadnoughts. Locks had to be widened and slipways lengthened at great expenditure of men, money and time – especially in Wilhelmshaven, where the ground proved extremely difficult. In 1907 Admiral Fisher had predicted that Germany could not have the North Sea–Baltic Sea link operable for Dreadnoughts before the late spring of 1914. It proved to be a good guess. (Table 15).

And it all cost money – lots of money. Estimates in 1911 revealed that the next battle-cruiser (*Derfflinger*) would jump in cost by an additional 10 million GM in order to keep pace with the British *Lion* and *Tiger* ships. It was becoming clear to even the most diehard opponents of tax reform that indirect levies on consumer goods could no longer pay for this mammoth battle fleet. Moreover, there emerged a group of German political and military leaders with second thoughts about Tirpitz's grand strategy. First and foremost, the new chancellor, Theobald v. Bethmann Hollweg, who succeeded Bülow in July 1909, was most concerned about the financial as well as the diplomatic ramifications of the "Tirpitz" plan. Army leaders also tired of taking a back seat in German armaments programmes and clamoured for restitution to top priority in order to build up their forces for a possible two-front war against France and Russia. And when the joint armed forces in 1911 submitted a budget of 1,000 million GM, Germany was on the verge of an internal *débâcle*.

V

"We Have Them Up Against the Wall"

Dénouement, 1912-1914

The *Novelle* of 1908 triggered the great "naval scare" of 1909. Under its provisions, Germany would lay down 3 battleships and 1 battle-cruiser per annum, for a total of 16 capital ships between 1908 and 1911. Great Britain, on the other hand, planned to build only 2 new capital ships by 1908, 8 by 1909, and 5 each in 1910 and 1911 – a total of 20. This, of course, would create an unfavourable 5 : 4 ratio for Britain in Dreadnought construction. The Liberal government in London, hard pressed especially by David Lloyd George and Winston Churchill for much-needed social reform, argued lamely that by 1912 Britain would have 20 new capital ships in commission, against a maximum of 17 for Germany; Conservatives countered with a possible German advantage of 21 : 20. To compound the situation, Tirpitz ordered German yards to stockpile vital raw materials, especially nickel, and to step up ordnance capacities. And to muddy darkened waters even more, he awarded a contract for one battleship (*Oldenburg*) and one battle-cruiser (*Goeben*) before parliament had approved the funds. This illegal proposal was also adopted by Tirpitz's Austrian counterpart, Admiral Graf Montecuccoli, who in 1910 ordered two (later raised to four) capital ships of the *Viribus Unitis* class, thereby increasing Austria–Hungary's fleet to twenty-eight capital ships. When the British suggested that the respective naval attachés be allowed to monitor Dreadnought building, the Kaiser exploded : "They must be mad." The panic of 1909 had arrived.

If Tirpitz had hoped to catch the British napping with the

Supplementary Bill of 1908, he was to be sadly mistaken. Britannia rallied round the Royal Navy with the slogan "we want eight, and we won't wait". The Admiralty, in turn, responded by requesting six, rather than the normal four, capital ships in the 1909 Estimates. The left wing of the Liberal Party, as Tirpitz had hoped, opposed this 50 per cent increase in one year. After acrimonious debates, especially between Fisher, on one side, and Lloyd George and Churchill on the other, Parliament compromised and agreed to the construction of the normal four capital ships, adding a proviso that a further four would be laid down if German actions proved them necessary. In no event, however, would they jeopardize the expected customary four ships of the 1910 Estimates. And when news reached London that Vienna planned to lay down four capital ships, the issue was decided. Fisher got his three Dreadnoughts and one battle-cruiser in 1909 . . . and more. The Royal Navy again increased the calibre of its heavy naval guns; the *Orion* class received ten 34.3 cm (13.5 in) guns.

Berlin responded with the four ships of the *König* class. *König*, *Grosser Kurfürst*, *Markgraf*, and *Kronprinz* constituted the fourth generation of German Dreadnoughts; the ships were laid down between October 1911 and May 1912 at an average unit cost of 45 million GM. They were commissioned in August and September 1914, became part of the Third Squadron of the High Sea Fleet, and saw service at Jutland in May 1916.

The ships of the *König* class, the last complete series of the Imperial Navy, displaced 25,800 tons and their three triple-stage Brown–Boverie–Parsons steam turbines provided a best speed of twenty-one knots. The *König*'s main battery consisted of ten 30.5 cm guns in five twin turrets, all on the centre line (as opposed to the *Kaiser*'s wing turrets), and two super-firing fore and aft. The changeover to turbine propulsion had made possible this new arrangement by making available substantially more space inside the ship. Each turret had a working chamber below the gun house and a revolving ammunition hoist leading down to the magazine. The guns were hydraulically raised – either separately or together – and each turret was completely electrically operated. All furniture was made of steel to reduce the fire hazard. Torpedo nets were reintroduced and carried until Jutland, thereafter discarded because they reduced speed to eight knots – entirely inadequate for fleet operations – and because, rolled up, they could foul the screws if damaged (Table 16).

The four ships of the *König* class were unique in that they had originally been scheduled to receive each one MAN six-cylinder, two-stroke diesel engine producing 12,000 hp and allowing a cruising speed of twelve knots. However, as had been the case with the *Prinzregent Luitpold* of the *Kaiser* class, the diesel engines were not ready in time.

In the meantime, organizational changes of far-reaching strategic importance were undertaken. In the spring of 1910 the First Division of the High Sea Fleet, composed of the newest *Nassau* Dreadnoughts, was moved from Kiel to Wilhelmshaven in the North Sea – about 120 km closer to Britain. Work on port facilities at Brunsbüttel, where the Kaiser–Wilhelm Canal links up with the estuary of the Elbe river and the North Sea, proceeded under full steam. And at Wilhelmshaven, two docks capable of containing the largest warships were ready, with a third nearly complete. The Admiralty in London not surprisingly feared that the Reich would base its entire fleet on North Sea harbours.

In addition, Britain was feeling the financial pinch of the naval race in areas other than base facilities. The eight keels laid down in 1909 fully taxed her shipyard capacity. Building costs for battle-cruisers had increased 25 per cent from *Lion* (1909) to *Tiger* (1911); Dreadnoughts were to jump 21 per cent from *Iron Duke* (1911) to *Queen Elizabeth* (1912). Overall, the Navy Estimates were by 1914 to increase fully 74 per cent since 1899–1900, and the increment rise since the launching of the *Dreadnought* amounted to 39 per cent (from 681.1 million GM in 1905–6 to 945 million GM in 1914). Whereas in 1905 Britain had spent 54 per cent of her defence budget on the Navy and 46 per cent on the Army, by 1914 the Navy's share had risen to 64 per cent and the Army's fallen to 36 per cent.

The German picture was even bleaker. The Reich's defence budget rose from 928,609,000 GM in 1905 (compared with 1,257,269,000 GM for Britain) to 2,245,633,000 GM in 1914 (compared with 1,604,874,000 GM for Britain) – an increase of 142 per cent. The total German defence bill in 1914 was 641 million GM (40 per cent) *higher* than the British, as opposed to 1905, when it had been about 330 million GM (35 per cent) *lower* (Table 17).

In terms of naval outlays alone, the bill for Tirpitz's master plan had risen from 233.4 million GM in fiscal 1905–6 to 478.963 million GM in 1914 – a meteoric rise of 105 per cent in nine years; British Navy Estimates during that period increased only 28 per cent. Vice-Admiral Friedrich Ruge, well-known author of naval histories and a servant of both Wilhelm II and Adolf Hitler, claims in his English-language publications that German naval expenditure increased by only 100 per cent between 1903 and 1913. Walther Hubatsch, another naval officer turned historian, readily admits to a 300 per cent fiscal upturn!

Specifically, Germany's greatest budgetary overruns continued to rest with battle-cruisers. Navy Office estimates in 1910 revealed that the next design (*Derfflinger*) would require 56 million GM, a sharp rise of 25.3 per cent over *Seydlitz*'s cost of 44.685 million G.M. Worse yet, the 1913 estimates for the projected *Mackensen* series entailed yet a further rise to 66 million GM, or a 47.7 per cent increase over *Seydlitz*. Wilhelm II was not in the least disturbed by the financial strains imposed by the naval race, informing Admiral v. Müller in August 1911: "Money is sufficiently available. The Imperial Treasury does not know what to do with it all."

This view was not shared by the Treasury. The Kaiser's assurances to the contrary notwithstanding, most responsible German leaders recognised by 1910 that indirect taxes on consumer commodities could no longer pay for the fleet – regardless of how much beer and brandy were consumed. The problem was that any solution would automatically bring with it social and political changes. And these both Conservatives and Agrarians were not willing to accept at any price. Under Stengel they had agreed to an inheritance tax – the first direct levy by the Reichstag – but further they would not go. In addition, the special "donations" by the various states never reached even 25 million GM per annum, with the result that by 1904 the national debt had climbed to 3 billion GM while annual expenditure outdistanced income by 24 million GM.

The elections of 1907 had given Chancellor v. Bülow the opportunity to rally a "bloc" consisting of the old cartel parties of Bismarck's day, the Conservatives and National Liberals, and the democrats and left-wing liberals united in the Progressive People's Party. Under the direction of Reinhold v. Sydow, Stengel's successor, Bülow in 1909 introduced a tough budget designed to cover the annual deficit, now at a colossal 500 million GM. Specifically, Bülow sought to increase the inheritance duty and to raise old, or introduce new, consumer taxes on brandy, bottled wine, champagne, tobacco, beer, gas, electricity, and so on. It was not to be. Social Democrats and Progressives balked at the consumer tax rise while the Conservatives and Agrarians adamantly opposed the succession, or inheritance, levy. The resulting resignations of Bülow and Sydow did little to resolve the financial nightmare.

Theobald v. Bethmann Hollweg, Bülow's successor, tried to tack a new course. Through the good offices of Albert Ballin he initiated indirect talks with British leaders between August 1909 and June 1912. Bethmann Hollweg's proposal, in a nutshell, was to offer London a slowdown in German naval building in return for a neutrality agreement in case Germany were attacked by a third power. It was a high price to ask, and the chancellor deemed it wise to stretch the negotiations out and attain concessions "drop by drop".

But foreign events were once more to interrupt the course of diplomatic discussions. The State Secretary of the Foreign Office, Alfred v. Kiderlen-Wächter, was willing in the summer of 1911 to leave Morocco to the French, but demanded as *quid pro quo* German concessions in the Congo. In order to give the French a nudge in this direction, he authorized the dispatch of the gunboat *Panther* to Agadir – without the approval either of the Navy Office or of the Admiralty Staff. The "*Panther* leap", as it came to be known, of 1 July 1911 had the effect of drawing the French and British closer together; joint talks between their respective general staffs were at once authorized both in London and in Paris. Isolation had, indeed, ceased to be possible – much less, splendid.

British reaction to the *Panther* affair so exacerbated Tirpitz that he was determined to bring about yet another naval increase. The historical parallel was almost too perfect : as the First Moroccan Crisis in 1905 had been exploited in order to pass the *Novelle* of 1906, the Second Moroccan Crisis was to serve passage of the Supplementary Bill of 1912. Already on 8 July 1911, a spokesman for the Navy Office had bluntly noted "that the Agadir undertaking, however it comes out, will be very profitable for the Navy's propaganda" on behalf of a new *Novelle*. The increases of 1908 had dictated a slowdown in construction to two ships per year between 1912 and 1917, and this "hole" Tirpitz now had to fill if the entire naval programme were to be salvaged.

The Navy Office in the winter had optimistically prepared a Supplementary Bill calling for an additional six capital ships between 1912 and 1917; in other words, restoration of the three-per-annum rate. But Bethmann Hollweg flatly refused to consider such an increase in the size of the fleet at a time when he was attempting to reach an understanding with London on this matter. Moreover, elections were just round the corner in 1912 and the Conservatives stood adamant in their refusal to discuss the introduction of a more stringent succession duty to offset naval outlays.

The Kaiser became a problem once more. Having recovered from his humiliation in the wake of the *Daily Telegraph* affair, he was now ready to direct the German ship of state. During 1910–11 Wilhelm insisted upon personally telegraphing orders for ship building to the respective yards; this would crassly have underscored his oft-criticized "personal regime". Above all, the blustering tone of the pre-1908 days was here again. The "risk" fleet was explained to the British ambassador to Berlin, Sir Edward Goshen, with the words : "We do not want to be Copenhagened." Bethmann Hollweg was cautioned when he raised objections to the vast armaments increases planned for 1912, that in Wilhelm II he was addressing a descendant of the Great Elector and Frederick the Great. In fact, the ruler repeatedly informed the inner circle of trusted aides that Bethmann Hollweg was of no value, and that he could rely for help only on Tirpitz, General Helmuth v. Moltke, Chief of the General Staff, and General Josias v. Heeringen, the Prussian War Minister. "I must be my own Bismarck." The banker Arthur v. Gwinner, when he had the audacity to point out Germany's dire financial straits to Wilhelm, was informed : "That makes no difference to me." And diplomats who dared to allude to the Reich's international isolation were told that they were "in a blue funk".

Anglophobia continued to be given full rein. The German ambassador to the Court of St James' Paul Graf Wolff-Metternich zur Gracht, especially suffered as a result. His efforts towards arranging an understanding with Great Britain were denounced to Tirpitz in December 1911 : "Nonsense, coward, weakling, pure Metternich rubbish." The German naval attaché (Wilhelm Widenmann), who stood under Tirpitz's influence, was permitted to report directly to the Kaiser, with the result that the latter continuously received conflicting evaluations from the two envoys in London. When the omnipresent Ballin in March 1912 suggested that Wilhelm could greatly reduce Anglo–German tension by sending coal to strike-bound Britain, the emperor retorted : "Coal? I will send them a grenade, nothing else!" That same year Wilhelm II informed his naval officers that if he were ever in the position of his grandfather in 1871, his first condition of peace would be "the surrender of the French fleet", and he ended this tirade with the familiar Anglo-phobic rhetoric : "The English are all sheep. Mr Balfour is a sheep, Mr Chamberlain is one, Sir Edward Grey is the biggest."

Such remarkable volatility could have been excused on the part of naval officers; as the pronouncements of the key figure in the German constitutional system, they could not easily be dismissed. The Kaiser's autistic behaviour, accompanied and witnessed by these irrational outbursts as well as the numerous marginal comments set to state documents, stood in direct relationship with his simplistic and self-consuming friend–foe schema concerning Anglo–German relations.

In August 1911 Wilhelm in Hamburg called for naval increases "so that we can be sure that nobody will dispute our rightful place in the sun". The address was a historic repeat: in 1899 he had delivered his famous "dire-need" speech on behalf of naval building, a speech that had come on the heels of the Boer War; the latest one came in the wake of the Second Moroccan Crisis. But there were in 1911 other, powerful suitors for the German taxpayers' Goldmarks. The Prussian Army had long stood by and grudgingly watched the Navy estimates increase more than two-fold in a decade. Between 1904 and 1912, Army outlays had risen 47 per cent from 647 million GM to 948 million GM; Navy funds during that same span, by contrast, had climbed 137 per cent from 206.555 million GM to 461.983 million GM. In fact, as the following table clearly shows, the naval budget had steadily progressed since 1898 in relationship to the Army budget:

Navy Budget 1898 = less than 20.0% of the Army Budget
Navy Budget 1901 = 30.7% of the Army Budget
Navy Budget 1903 = 34.1% of the Army Budget
Navy Budget 1905 = 35.3% of the Army Budget
Navy Budget 1907 = 37.8% of the Army Budget
Navy Budget 1909 = 48.5% of the Army Budget
Navy Budget 1911 = 54.8% of the Army Budget

General v. Heeringen in 1911 attempted to restore the Army to primacy in armament expenditure, proposing an increase in strength of three Army Corps, about 19,000 officers and 117,000 men. Heeringen argued that the Reich in 1911 had only 0.99 per cent of the populace under arms – compared with 1.53 per cent for France.

Adolf Wermuth, Sydow's successor at the Treasury, and Bethmann Hollweg were mortified with the joint Army–Navy budget of 1,000 million GM for 1911. Elections were due in January 1912, and the prospect of going to the polls with such a budget did not appeal to the chancellor. Tirpitz, on the other hand, still refused to budge from a minimum of four new capital ships and accused Bethmann Hollweg and Wermuth of "surrounding the Imperial Treasury with barbed wire". His intimate aide, Capelle, in October 1911 bravely – if incorrectly – argued that "England must and will opt in the coming years for Germany and against France. . . . England must and will come to us." However, the elections of January 1912 – which brought out 84.5 per cent of the voters – were to soften this position : the Social Democrats, ardent opponents of any defence spending, scored a spectacular success with 4.25 million votes and 110 seats in parliament. This made them ("the rabble of humanity", according to the Kaiser) by far the largest faction in the Reichstag. It was at this critical juncture that Richard Burdon, Viscount Haldane of Cloan, the British War Minister since 1905, journeyed to Germany with Sir Ernest Cassel in order to discuss a possible reduction in the naval race.

Haldane, who had received the nickname "Schopenhauer" from Sir Henry Campbell-Bannerman partly because he had translated the philosopher's *Welt als Wille und Vorstellung* into English, arrived in Berlin in February 1912 in the guise of a private traveller. He was received by Wilhelm II as well as by Admirals v. Tirpitz and v. Müller. Haldane conducted the initial discussions alone with the emperor and was extremely optimistic : "The new atmosphere which has resulted is marvellous . . . the prospect for the moment is very good, and I seem to have been inspired by a new power."

Nothing could have been further from the truth. Absolutely nothing was to come from his mission – primarily because Tirpitz had decided that nothing should, or must, come from it. The state secretary knew full well that any agreement with Britain could only be obtained at the cost of dropping the proposed increases for 1912, a turn of events that would have shipwrecked his master plan of creating a fleet of sixty capital ships. He accordingly received Haldane with the words : "You see in me the bogeyman of old England." He denounced Haldane's companion Cassel as "a Jewish renegade in whose house the Anglo–French Entente was sealed". And he used that old Bismarckian standby, the threat of resignation, when all else failed – actually tendering such a note on 10 March 1912. It is hardly surprising, then, that Haldane a few days later described Tirpitz to Bethmann Hollweg as "a dangerous man".

The surprising thing about the Haldane mission is not what *was* discussed, but what London and Berlin later *alleged* had been discussed. Haldane claimed that he had only dangled before the Germans the possibility of some minor colonial concessions in return for British participation in the Baghdad–Berlin railway and a general naval agreement. Berlin, on the other hand, maintained that Haldane had made a firm offer of Zanzibar and Pemba, two islands off the coast of Tanganyika. Winston Churchill, who in 1911 had become First Lord of the Admiralty, did not make Haldane's task any easier. On 9 February 1912, at the very moment when Haldane was in Berlin, Churchill in Glasgow announced that "from some points of view the Germany Navy is to them more in the nature of a luxury". It proved to be a veritable bombshell. The German word *Luxus* has a pejorative air of sumptuousness about it, and its application to the High Sea Fleet was greatly resented.

Wilhelm II quickly saw himself as the victim of a British plot. "My patience as well as that of the German people is at an end." Admiral v. Tirpitz, on the other hand, was ready now to take advantage of the public furor over the Agadir crisis and Churchill's speech in order to bring the new naval increases safely into port. The Anglophobic rhetoric designed for public consumption was quickly cast aside. Moreover, the demand for six new capital ships as an addition to the fleet had purposely been set high for the benefit of the chancellor. Only two new vessels would realize the dream of the sixty-unit fleet. In April 1912 the new defence estimates were submitted to parliament, and passed four weeks later. Bethmann Hollweg's attempt in October 1911 to bring about a basic decision between Army and Navy priority had foundered in the meantime on General v. Heeringen's refusal to be involved in inter-service rivalry.

The total budget, even after Wermuth's trimming, amounted to 831 million GM. The Navy's share came to three new Dreadnoughts and two light cruisers as well as personnel increases of 15,000 officers and ratings. The three new ships were to form the nucleus of a new squadron of the fleet, along with the second fleet flagship and the four battleships of the material reserve. The High Sea Fleet was thus to be composed of one fleet flagship and five squadrons each of 8 battleships, 12 large and 30 light cruisers; the overseas forces of 8 large and 10 light cruisers. A sixth squadron, composed of replacements for the elderly "coastal-defence" squadron, would be added later, as would 8 battle-cruisers either built or building. Furthermore, Tirpitz planned now to convert the 8 large cruisers on overseas service into an additional squadron of battle-cruisers, to be permanently stationed on Wilhelmshaven. Thus by 1920, the Imperial Navy, with personnel of 100,500 men, would possess a fleet of 41 battleships, 20 large (battle) and 40 light cruisers. These figures do not, of course, include the plans for a sixth fleet squadron, or the 8 battle-cruisers to be gained from the overseas squadron. Perhaps most important of all, the fleet was to be maintained in full battle-readiness at all times and the material reserve was to be abolished.

Wilhelm II was beside himself with joy. Haldane had been sent packing. Bethmann Hollweg's cherished Anglo–German naval agreement had been scuttled – without the chancellor's resignation, which almost certainly would have precipitated a new state crisis. Tirpitz had managed with his exaggerated initial demands to give the "Socialist-dominated" Reichstag a feeling of satisfaction for having pruned his budget down to three new capital ships. The "hole" in the naval programme had been plugged for at least three years, through 1914–15. The Kaiser was on the crest of a wave of success, and he gloated: "We have them [the British] up against the wall."

Only the nagging problem of finances refused to disappear in the general euphoria of the spring of 1912. In March the Conservatives for a third time rejected a progressive inheritance tax, which prompted Wermuth, as Stengel and Sydow before him, to insist upon acceptance of his letter of resignation. A capital gains tax was finally passed in 1913, but the outbreak of the war, and the abandonment of the tax, preclude comment upon its possible effectiveness. Germany by 1913 spent 90.1 per cent of her income on defence; the national debt in 1914 had reached 5,000 million GM, up about 125 per cent from 1898.

The *Novelle* of 1912 had come extremely dear. It had to be introduced into the Reichstag jointly with the Army budget, a first for Tirpitz. The Army was now firmly re-established as the dominant force in German defence needs. Whereas in 1911 the Navy budget had amounted to 54.8 per cent of Army outlay – the high point of a steady thirteen-year advance – it declined precipitately thereafter: from 49.4 per cent in 1912 to 32.7 per cent in 1913. In addition, the Army's strategic concept concerning the inevitability of a continental war in the near future supplanted Tirpitz's *Weltpolitik* schema from 1898. When General v. Moltke in December 1912 announced, "I consider war to be unavoidable, and: the sooner, the better", Tirpitz could reply only that the Navy required at least an eighteen-month postponement of the conflict. Admiral Prince Heinrich felt in August 1912 that the Reich could no longer afford Dreadnoughts. The prince informed his imperial brother that he had "long ago" given up hope that Tirpitz's grand scheme could be realized.

The worst was yet to come from cross the North Sea. The First Lord of the Admiralty proved to be as resolute and aggressive on behalf of naval appropriations as he had once been opposed to them as Home Secretary. In March 1912, Churchill had informed the House of Commons that the Admiralty would lay down two capital ships for every one added by Tirpitz. In that same month the Admiralty transferred the battleships based on Malta to Gibraltar and shifted the Atlantic Fleet stationed at Gibraltar to the Home Fleet as the Third Battle Squadron. This shuffle constituted the realization of Fisher's belief that *"we cannot have everything or be strong everywhere. It is futile to be strong in the subsidiary theatre of war and not overwhelmingly supreme in the decisive theatre."*

Strategic alterations in the Mediterranean were also undertaken. The Germans in 1910 had sold Turkey the pre-Dreadnoughts *Kurfürst Friedrich Wilhelm* and *Weissenburg*, and in November 1912 created a special Mediterranean Squadron with the new battle-cruiser *Goeben* and several light cruisers. In addition, Austria–Hungary now burst upon the scene by announcing that she would build an additional fourth capital ship (*Ersatz Monarch* class), as she felt that her so-called ally, Italy, was no longer reliable. Churchill correctly drew the conclusion that "the naval control of the Mediterranean is swiftly passing from our hands whatever we do, while we remain single-handed". Talks with the French rapidly reached fruition : in September 1912, France moved her Atlantic Squadron from Brest to Toulon in the Mediterranean (the erstwhile "windpipe" of the British Empire), and by April 1913 plans were ready for joint defensive operations in the English Channel and the Mediterranean Sea.

Churchill also pushed forward Fisher's personnel reforms ("Selborne Scheme") by proposing in August 1912 to admit exceptionally talented petty and warrant officers to commissioned rank after a year's probationary period. Merit alone was to be the criterion for the Royal Navy. The First Lord accordingly passed over several senior admirals in order to make Rear-Admiral David Beatty his Naval Secretary, and in December 1911 he moved John Jellicoe, the second most junior among twenty-two vice-admirals, to Second-in-Command of the Home Fleet.

Churchill did not shy away from a public confrontation with Germany. On 18 March, 1912, he referred to the Reich in the House of Commons as Great Britain's only possible enemy at sea. Along with this he proposed that summer a so-called "naval holiday", whereby both Germany and Britain would agree to build no capital ships for one year. Wilhelm II was furious over what he termed an "arrogant" speech, as Churchill's proposal would, of course, have maintained Britain's battleship superiority. Tirpitz feared that Churchill's call for a "naval holiday" was merely the disguise for a British "Copenhagen". The Anglo–German naval arms race had by now enveloped Berlin with an air of suspicion, fright and hostility. Tirpitz spoke openly of a "vicious circle". Wilhelm II recalled Ambassador Wolff-Metternich from London.

The First Lord, who could find for the 1912 *Novelle* "no example in the previous practice of modern naval powers", had a final ace to play. Churchill revealed in 1912 that Britain would build five new "super" Dreadnoughts to act as a new wing of the main battle fleet. These *Queen Elizabeth* class ships had a best speed of twenty-five knots; their displacement ranged between 31,000 and 33,000 tons. They were the first British battleships with purely oil-fired engines, and were considered to be the world's first fast battleships. Admiral Fisher, who already a decade earlier had been dubbed the "oil maniac", had pioneered supplementary oil burners with the *Dreadnought*; in 1911, the United States Navy had fitted the *Oklahoma* and *Nevada* for oil only. Britain, unlike Germany, could be assured of a steady supply of oil from the Middle East. Just to be on the safe side, in August 1914 the London government for £2.2 million bought a controlling interest in the Anglo–Persian (later, Anglo–Iranian) Oil Company.

A second revolutionary development came in armament. The United States had in 1910–11 gone over to the 35.6 cm (14 in) heavy gun with the *Texas* class, as had the Japanese at the same time with the *Kongo* class. Fisher had raised British ordnance from the 50-calibre 12 in gun to the 45-calibre 13.5 in gun, and weight of shell from 850 lb to 1,400 lb, a projectile that was 40 per cent heavier than the largest fired by the German Navy. Churchill now introduced the 15 in (38 cm) gun, which hurled a 1,920 lb projectile thirty kilometres. As calculations proved that eight 38 cm guns were superior to ten 34.3 cm guns, it was decided to eliminate the single twin turret amidships and to mount four raised super-firing turrets of eight guns fore and aft.

The First Lord's energetic counter-measures during 1912, coinciding with the outbreak of the Balkan Wars of 1912–13, caused yet another near-panic across the North Sea. Many Germans, including "high-ranking officers", withdrew their savings and deposited them in Swiss banks. Wilhelm II, according to the Bavarian military attaché, "ordered the General Staff and the Admiralty Staff to work out an invasion of England in a grand style". Britain was again denounced as "a nation of shopkeepers", as opposed to the German nation of "hero-warriors". In his fit of rage, the Kaiser quite forgot that he had years ago accepted Tirpitz's battle-fleet programme, and now recommended "immediate submarine warfare against English troop transports in the Scheldt or by Dunkirk, mine warfare in the Thames. To Tirpitz: Speedy build-up of U-boats, etc." The state secretary was not, however, about to overturn his entire fleet concept in favour of *guerre de course*.

Germany was to follow British *matériel* developments one year later with the *Bayern* class, but during 1912–13 she concentrated instead on building the *Derfflinger* class battle-cruisers. Three ships were designed between the summer of 1911 and the autumn of 1912, and laid down in 1912–13 at a cost of between 56 and 59 million GM each. *Derfflinger* was commissioned in September 1914, *Lützow* in August 1915 and *Hindenburg* in May 1917. The Imperial Navy changed over to the 30.5 cm gun for battle-cruisers with this class, and hence only eight barrels in end arrangement were mounted in four super-firing turrets. The centre turret was thus eliminated. The *Bayern* class was to continue this design, which had been taken from the United States' *South Carolina* (1905). *Lützow* and *Hindenburg* were equipped with the newer, larger 60 cm torpedoes, while *Derfflinger* was the first German capital ship to receive 8.8 cm anti-aircraft guns. However, these ships possessed an Achilles heel as their bows were inadequately protected; the customary torpedo bulkhead had been omitted owing to lack of space, thereby rendering the broadside torpedo department forward of the fore turret vulnerable to shelling. Jutland revealed this flaw to be fatal. The *Derfflinger* vessels displaced about 27,000 tons and had a best speed of twenty-six to twenty-seven knots.

London's *tour de force* in building the *Queen Elizabeth* ships left Tirpitz no choice but to accept this latest British qualitative challenge. His answer in 1912 was the *Bayern* series. The first two units, the last Dreadnoughts completed by Imperial Germany, were laid down in September 1913 at a unit cost of between 49 and 50 million GM. The two battleships were completed in March and October 1915, not in time to see action at Jutland, but to be interned at Scapa Flow in November 1918. *Bayern* and *Baden* were turbine-driven ships with a best speed of twenty-two knots. They each displaced 28,600 tons and carried a complement of 1,171 officers and ratings (Table 18).

The British change-over to the 38 cm gun in the *Queen Elizabeth* class had naturally caused consternation at the Leipzigerplatz (Navy Office) in Berlin. The Admiralty's adoption of the 34.3 cm gun with the *Orion* series had not particularly troubled the Germans because they felt that their 30.5 cm gun was superior to the British 13.5 in cannon. But Churchill's decision to introduce the 38 cm gun left Germany no choice but once again to follow the British lead or be left behind. It was therefore decided in 1913 to outfit battleships with the 38 cm gun and battle-cruisers with a new 35 cm gun. Experiments with triple turrets, already used by Italy, Austria–Hungary and Russia, revealed that major technical difficulties would first have to be surmounted, and that in terms of weight, six twin turrets corresponded to four triple turrets. It was therefore agreed to increase the calibre of the heavy guns, but to retain twin turrets. *Bayern* and *Baden* as a result were outfitted with eight 38 cm guns, arranged in two super-firing raised twin turrets fore and aft, sixteen 15 cm and (in 1917) four 8.8 cm anti-aircraft guns.

Two additional units, *Sachsen* and *Württemberg*, were laid down in 1914 and 1915, but were never completed. Ordered in April and August 1914, work was stopped on them at the end of the war; *Sachsen* was by then nine months away from completion and *Württemberg* twelve months. They were broken up and scrapped in 1921. Siegfried Breyer claims that German Dreadnought building with the *Bayern* class had reached its "peak of perfection", and that the next twenty years were to bring no major design changes.

The *Bayern* class ended German Dreadnought building. Only the *Mackensen* class battle-cruisers were to be laid down after 1914. These will be discussed in a later chapter (p. 203). Germany by 1914 had copied most British design innovations: supplementary oil burners, 38 cm heavy guns, steam turbines, super-firing twin

5. Dreadnought *Prinzregent Luitpold*

6a. Battle-cruiser *Derffling*

6b. Sponging out a ship'
guns

turrets, and centre-firing as well as end mountings. Purely oil-fired ships alone were not adopted, partly because German planners insisted that side coal bunkers afforded added underwater protection in addition to the torpedo bulkheads, and partly because Tirpitz could not ensure Germany a steady supply of this fuel.

Germany in 1912–13 also placed contracts for the last two series of light cruisers during peacetime. *Regensburg, Pillau* and *Elbing* were built between 1912 and 1915 at a unit cost of about 8.8 million GM. These vessels had initially been started for the Imperial Russian Navy, but were seized on 5 August 1914. The *Wiesbaden* and *Frankfurt,* on the other hand, were larger, 5,200-ton ships. All five light cruisers joined the fleet in 1915 (Table 19).

Three special river gunboats designed solely for service in China were also built between 1902 and 1910. *Tsingtau, Vaterland* and *Otter* were the last gunboats completed in Germany prior to 1918, and all three – as their predecessors, the "predators" – were driven by triple expansion engines. *Iltis, Jaguar, Tiger,* and *Luchs* were destroyed in 1914 in Kiaochow; *Panther* was scrapped at home in 1913; *Eber* was scuttled after being interned in Bahia in 1917, and *Tsingtau* in 1917 when China declared war against Germany; *Vaterland* and *Otter* were confiscated by the Chinese in 1917.

In terms of torpedo-boat building, the period since the *T 180– T 185* series (1909–10) brought little change. Germania in Kiel by the end of 1911 had completed the *T 192 –T 193, T 195–T 197* boats. These 660-ton craft, costing 1.8 million GM each, were armed identically to the *T 180–T 185* boats, and possessed almost the same speed and cruising range. Vulcan in Kiel by 1914 had built the 800-ton *V 25–V 30* units, armed with three 8.8 cm guns and six 50 cm torpedo tubes. Also turbine-driven, these boats attained a best speed of thirty-four knots and had a cruising range of 1,080 sm at twenty knots. All were designed for duty in the North Sea with the High Sea Fleet (Table 20).

Germany had also made a modest beginning in naval air reconnaissance. Observation balloon trials had been conducted as early as 1891 off Helgoland, but the then State Secretary of the Navy Office, Admiral v. Hollmann, reported that owing to haze and rough weather, no military value could be derived from them. Tirpitz concurred, and suspended all further trials. Both Army and Navy in 1895 also attached little value to Ferdinand Graf v. Zeppelin's dirigible. Eleven years later, the Navy again rejected Zeppelin's invention, arguing that emergency landings at sea were too hazardous and that the dirigible's best speed of twelve miles per hour was insufficient against strong North Sea gales. And in 1909 the state secretary refused an offer from "Flugmaschine Wright" to demonstrate that aircraft could be launched from warships – despite the fact that Wilhelm II encouraged the Navy to look into aerial development. In the following year, Tirpitz finally permitted one naval officer to go to Lake Constance to observe Zeppelin's test flights, but he again remained opposed to any discussion of aircraft development. Only in 1911 did he permit the formation of an experimental air station at Putzig, near Danzig.

The Navy's Zeppelin programme officially got under way in 1912, when Tirpitz agreed to make available 2 million GM for a "Navy Airship Detachment" after trials in 1911 had convinced him that airships could be used for reconnaissance in the North Sea, deployed against enemy submarines and mines, and used to drop bombs on enemy docks, locks and munition plants. Consequently, the Navy bought its first dirigible, commissioned in October 1912 as *L 1,* at a cost of 850,000 GM. It had a range of about 1,440 km (an endurance of thirty hours in the air), insufficient for use off the British coast. *L 1* was armed with two machine-guns for anti-aircraft protection and had places for experimental 80 kg bombs.

During 1913, Tirpitz followed up with the purchase of ten dirigibles with a life expectancy each of four years, a step which the Kaiser endorsed. In May of that year the state secretary created a "Navy Airship Division" at Johannisthal, near Berlin. But that autumn disaster struck twice. During fleet manoeuvres in September, *L 1* was destroyed in heavy storms with the loss of fourteen of her crew of twenty; the following month *L 2* was lost with all hands when her oxy-hydrogen gas mixture accidentally exploded. The *L 3* came to the Navy in July 1914, but the two previous disasters had cooled Tirpitz's interest in airship development, and he cancelled the order for the ten dirigibles, to be delivered between 1914 and 1918. Even two Zeppelin orders from the past were never filled, and by August 1914 the Imperial Navy possessed only the *L 3.* A surprising lack of large hangars (pre-1914 ones were too small for the 32,000 cubic metre Zeppelins) meant that *L 3* as well as her successors had to be manoeuvred out of existing small hangars, a risky undertaking especially during a crosswind, and hence were not at all times available for fleet reconnaissance. Only Admiral Jellicoe was awed by the possibility of Zeppelin naval reconnaissance, constantly lamenting that the Imperial Navy possessed excellent "eyes" for the fleet with these airships.

Aircraft development was even slower. Only in October 1910 did Tirpitz agree to look into this matter, and meagre funds came forth the following year (100,000 GM). The Imperial Yard in Danzig was charged with naval aircraft development, which received a tremendous boost in November 1910 when Grand Admiral Prince Heinrich, Inspector-General of the Navy, had at the age of forty-eight become the first naval officer to receive his pilot's licence.

In the meantime, Lieutenant Ely in 1910 and 1911 managed to take off from the deck of the cruiser *Birmingham* and to land on the deck of the armoured cruiser *Pennsylvania*. However, there was to be no further deck landing anywhere until 1917, and the German Navy Office continued to spurn all attempts to land aircraft on ships. In Britain, Churchill from the start favoured the pioneering of seaplanes, and in May 1913 the elderly cruiser *Hermes* was converted into a seaplane-carrier. She was to be replaced by the converted merchant ship *Ark Royal* in 1914; by the outbreak of the war, Britain possessed 7 airships, 31 seaplanes, and 40 aeroplanes. But apart from Fisher, Jellicoe, Scott, and Captain Sueter, most Royal Navy officers viewed seaplanes as the "First Lord's playthings".

In Germany, seaplane experimentation had in 1911 centred round single-pontoon models developed by the Albatros Company. In the following year, twin-pontoon craft were favoured, and in 1912 Tirpitz allotted 200,000 GM for seaplane competitive trials. The regular budget allowed 150,000 GM for an airfield, and twice that much for naval air development. A "National Air Donation" spurred this competition, won by the United States Curtiss seaplane after German prototypes developed by Albatros and Rumpler were delivered too late. The Admiralty Staff now advocated the use of seaplanes as scouts against submarines and mines in the North Sea, but Tirpitz argued that this was premature. In a compromise move, he laid out a long-range plan whereby Germany would by 1918 create six naval air stations (two in the Baltic), each with eight naval aircraft. By March 1913, four craft were on hand, including the United States Curtiss and a British Sopwith, because "German industry had brought nothing of use". Tests in September 1913 with hoisting seaplanes aboard the cruiser *Friedrich Carl* to and from the water, convinced Tirpitz that this was of little military use as the planes could carry only 5 kg bombs and possessed neither bomb bays nor accurate target finders.

During the High Sea Fleet's manoeuvres in 1914, four aircraft were tried out as scouts. Of these, *D 14* crashed off Helgoland, *D 7* could not lift off the water, and only *D 12* (the British model) could pass tests. In addition, of the two land planes that were sent to Kiaochow, the first crashed on its maiden flight on 31 July 1914. By August 1914, twelve seaplanes and one aeroplane were available to the Navy. The budget for airships and seaplanes in 1914 amounted to 8.45 million GM. Overall, by 1914 Germany had paid out 18.4 million GM for naval air development – compared with 56 million GM for a single battle-cruiser (*Derfflinger*).

By 1914 the submarine had also been added to the arsenal of *guerre de course*. In January 1898, France launched the *Gustave Zédé* which, in mimic warfare, sank the battleship *Magenta*. Interest in this new weapon ran extremely high in Paris, where it was widely hailed as an ideal against British surface strength. The problem, however, was the submersible's application to warfare. American revolutionaries had failed with the one-man hand-driven submersible *Turtle* to drill and place a charge of gunpowder against the copper-sheathed hull of HMS *Eagle*. It was only in 1864 in Charleston harbour that an underwater craft, the Confederate *Hunley*, sank the Federal corvette *Housatonic* by suspending a torpedo ahead of her bow and ramming the warship. Above all, problems of surface as well as submerged propulsion continued to render the submersible's wartime value negligible. Early British prototypes had proved to be unreliable and primitive; in particular the engine's exhaust fumes were highly toxic and explosive. Vice-Admiral Sir A. K. Wilson, Commander of the Channel Squadron and destined to succeed Fisher as First Sea Lord in 1909, expressed the view of many in 1902 when he described submarines as "underhand, unfair, and damned unEnglish", and wanted their crews captured and hanged as pirates.

Ironically, Germany, whose submarines (*Unterseeboote*) were twice in the twentieth century to become the scourge of the world, was a late arrival in submarine development. Tirpitz's passion for battleships left little leeway for pioneering in other areas of naval weaponry, and the state secretary refused to create what he termed "a museum of experiments". Nevertheless, under pressure from close aides, on 4 April 1904 he finally agreed to place the first order for a submarine. As late as December 1899, German shipyards, heavily engaged in more profitable capital-ship building, congratulated the Imperial Navy "for not having allowed itself to be dragged into expensive and tedious experiments with U-boats". In the fiscal year 1905, Tirpitz allotted 1.5 million GM for submarine experiments, with the result that on 14 December 1906 Krupp's Germania yard in Kiel delivered the first U-boat (*U 1*) to the Navy's Inspection of Torpedo Development which, until 1913, was in charge of all submarines. *U 1* caused little excitement in German naval circles at the time. *Nauticus* and *Marine-Rundschau* did not report the commissioning of *U 1* until October 1907, and both stated that the Navy had built the craft "only with extreme reluctance".

U 1 was built at a cost of 1.9 million GM and displaced 238 tons on the surface and 283 tons submerged. Her Körting six-cylinder two-cycle petrol or heavy oil (paraffin) engine permitted a surface speed of 10.8 knots and a range of 1,500 sm at 10 knots; the electric cells gave a submerged speed of 8.7 knots and a range of 50 sm at 5 knots. Armament consisted of one bow 45 cm torpedo tube (three torpedoes) but no guns; she could dive to eight metres water above the tower in 100 seconds.

The basic German model remained this double-hull boat, which had been perfected by the Frenchman Laubeuf by 1897, with the diving tanks outside the main compartment over the last three-quarters of the boat. The introduction of the diesel engine for submarines in Germany – unlike France, where this conversion had been made by 1904 – also came rather late. The first eighteen German boats, with the exception of *U 2*, all used heavy oil as fuel. The petrol engines, especially in *U 5–U 18*, often betrayed the boat's position through the emission of heavy white smoke and the loud explosions of the fuel which, at night, could be detected by their glare at great distances. Therefore, after 1905, trials were undertaken with diesel propulsion plants. The changeover to diesels in August 1910 elevated the submarine for the first time in German plans from a weapon of *Kleinkrieg* to a decisive strategic unit designed to decimate the enemy's battleship strength. The erstwhile plan to deploy submersibles as floating batteries along the North Sea line Jade estuary – Helgoland – Lister Tief was now abandoned. There existed as yet no plans to use the U-boats against merchant shipping.

Krupp once again had the right design at the right time. Apart from the Imperial Yard in Danzig, only his Germania yard produced U-boats prior to the Great War. The Navy Office in 1907 decided to order three additional submarines, and from 1910 to 1914 twenty-six diesel-powered boats (*U 19–U 41, U44 –U 45*) were under construction. The Navy's budget for submersibles increased from 1.5 million GM in 1905 to 15 million GM in 1910, and 20 million GM by 1913.

German submarine building made rapid progress after the *U 1* in 1906. The *U 19*, for example, built in 1910–13, had more than doubled in size to 650 tons displacement, and to a cost of 2.9 million GM. Its range had quintupled to 7,600 sm at eight knots – a fact not generally appreciated in London. Diving time to eight metres water above the tower had been shaved to ninety seconds. Armament had been stepped up to two bow and two stern tubes with six 50 cm torpedoes stored; one 8.8 cm gun was later fitted. Building time was thirty-one months.

The *U 19* was the first German submarine fitted with two MAN 850 hp diesel engines, providing a best speed of fifteen knots on the surface and nine knots submerged. These twin-screw vessels were equal to the British "D" class. The *U 19* series had been designed for diving depths of 50 m (164 ft), but on occasion were known to reach slightly more than 80 m (275 ft). The Navy Office in 1913 also planned to build minelaying submarines ("UC" craft), but did not realize this plan until November 1914.

The budget for the fiscal year 1912 had foreseen an ultimate submarine fleet of 72 U-boats, but when war broke out, Germany possessed only 28 – compared with 77 submarines for France, 55 for Britain and 38 for the United States. Adoption of the gyro-compass in place of the magnetic compass in 1908 had greatly enhanced the submersible's use in war; and the improvement of the torpedo through "heater" propulsion and gyrocompass in itself made U-boats a force to be reckoned with.

Submersibles had first been allowed to participate in the High Sea Fleet's manoeuvres – albeit at a distance and only on an experimental basis – in 1909, but Tirpitz remained extremely cool towards them and repeatedly voted against their participation in the autumn manoeuvres. In 1912, however, Admiral v. Capelle took advantage of Tirpitz's absence from Berlin to include them in the annual exercises. In September a "U-boat Flotilla" and a special "U-boat School" in Kiel had also been established. Yet Admiral v. Tirpitz continued his unbending faith in Mahan's battleship concept. Neither the German "lighter-than-air" craze nor the U-boat spurt before 1914 – both "dangerous" *guerre de course* departures – found favour at the Leipzigerplatz.

Germany's sea power in 1914 was expanding at the most rapid pace possible. The "risk" period, during which the Reich was vulnerable to a British "Copenhagen", had been safely traversed. Of the High Sea Fleet of one fleet flagship and five squadrons each of 8 battleships as well as 12 large (battle) cruisers laid down in the *Novelle* of 1912, Tirpitz could count by the end of 1914 on the following: 17 Dreadnoughts (1 fleet flagship, *Friedrich der Grosse*; the First Squadron composed of 4 ships each of the *Nassau* and *Helgoland* classes; the Third Squadron comprised of 4 ships each of the *Kaiser* and *König* classes); 8 pre-Dreadnoughts (4 ships each of the *Braunschweig* and *Deutschland* classes); 4 battle-cruisers (*Von der Tann, Moltke, Seydlitz,* and *Derfflinger*); and 4 armoured cruisers (*Blücher, Prinz Adalbert, Roon,* and *Yorck*). In the future lay the 4 *Bayern* Dreadnoughts and 2 *Derfflinger* class battle-cruisers – as well as 3 projected replacements in 1916 for the elderly *Hertha* class large cruisers.

It was a creditable performance for the nascent German Navy but, coupled with the most recent need to develop auxiliary weapons such as dirigibles, aircraft and submarines, one that left it constantly in dire financial straits. When Widenmann reported – quite incorrectly – from London in October 1913 that the British were considering lowering the calibre of their heavy guns, the Kaiser at once let out a sigh of relief: "That would be a blessing." In the following month Wilhelm informed Tirpitz that the fleet of the *Novelle* of 1912 had "exceeded the limits of available personnel, to say nothing of the purse". The monarch spoke openly of the "ghastly" nature of "this screw without end". He informed Widenmann in London that "the bow is overstrung here as in England".

There was by now a discernible change in Wilhelm's character and actions. Whereas in the 1890s as self-appointed *roi des gueux* – another model borrowed from Frederick the Great – he had met with Reichstag deputies and even workers' delegations, after 1900 he saw no more of the latter and in the wake of the *Daily Telegraph* affair (1908) no more of the former. Moreover, up to 1906 he had been a frequent visitor to Great Britain and Russia; now he gathered his information from diplomatic and, more frequently, military/naval reports selected by his staff to buttress his preconceived ideas and prejudices. Wilhelm gravitated into isolation, seeing only generals, admirals, ministers, courtiers, and the like, and developed a dangerous and simplistic "friend–foe" mentality. Accordingly, when Churchill in 1914 repeated his call for an Anglo–German naval "holiday", Wilhelm's frenzied reaction was: "The British surprise attack is here."

The fleet, for its part, continued to bombard Tirpitz with incessant complaints concerning the lack of funds. When it suggested in 1913 the creation of a special "Commander of Torpedo-Boat Forces", Tirpitz vetoed this owing to financial considerations. In a similar manner, he developed a plan not to use specific elderly ships to train recruits, but to place them permanently aboard the newest battleships, in the hope thereby of easing the personnel shortage. Rear-Admiral Reinhard Scheer, Director of the General Department of the Navy Office, argued in 1912 that in terms of engineers alone the fleet would have to wait until two years after completion of the sixty capital ships, that is, 1921–22, before it possessed a full complement. In November 1912, Admiral Oldekop rendered a dismal evaluation of naval personnel after a visit to Kiel and Wilhelmshaven. The fleet, he argued, was "totally exhausted" by the rigours imposed upon it by the frenzied building under the *Novelle* of 1912, with "every available man" used to staff existing vessels:

> There is almost no more personnel on land. Garrison watch duty can no longer be conducted according to regulations. The machinists and apprentice-machinists with the Divisional School, for example, must be utilized for nightly guard duty. From the station chief [in Wilhelmshaven] to the youngest officer, I received complaints without end about these conditions. The Navy units [in Kiel] are equally exhausted as in Wilhelmshaven. Complaints concerning lack of personnel on land are the same.

Admiral v. Tirpitz was fully cognizant of this sad situation, but his concern was first and foremost with *matériel*. Once the ships were available, he reasoned, personnel could be found. Therefore in the winter of 1912–13 the Navy Office worked out a Supplementary Bill designed to place Germany on a permanent three-per-annum capital-ship building rate. Only in such a manner could a 10:16 ratio *vis-à-vis* the Royal Navy be attained. But it is indicative of the changed situation in Germany by 1912–14 that the chancellor and the Army immediately quashed this proposal. The Army, by contrast, received in 1913 about 136,000 new personnel, and Tirpitz, who had significantly contributed to the fall of Treasury chiefs Stengel, Sydow and Wermuth, had in 1913 to allow the new head of the Treasury, Hermann Kühn, to inform him that in no circumstances might 1914 Navy estimates pass the legally determined amount. And when Tirpitz in April 1914 let up a trial balloon by informing the Kaiser in the most fawning manner imaginable that the Navy over the next six to eight years would require an additional 150 to 200 million GM in new tax revenues in order to be at full strength, it proved to be a non-starter. Bethmann Hollweg in particular, backed by solid Army support led by General v. Moltke, quickly deflated this proposal. Kurt Riezler, the chancellor's intimus, in 1914 expressed the conviction that with regard to Dreadnoughts "the English can, and always will be able to build twice what we can".

The programme that Tirpitz had worked out for Wilhelm II by 1897 had been a comprehensive design to shore up internal dissension and to allow "great overseas" expansion. The state secretary had argued that the building of a mammoth fleet would unite German political parties against the Social Democrats, rally German workers round the Empire with steady work and higher wages, unite the various particularist states through one great *German* armed force, raise the image of the Crown at home and abroad, remove the "disturbing influence" of the Reichstag upon the Kaiser's policies, make Germany more attractive as an ally to minor naval powers, and wring colonial concessions from London by threatening Britain's European security with a massive battle fleet concentrated off her eastern shores. In addition, superior *matériel*, personnel and tactics would allow the High Sea Fleet a "genuine chance" of victory against the Royal Navy with only a 2 : 3 numerical ratio.

Instead, by 1914 the master plan had gone awry. The Social Democrats had by 1912 become the largest party; the bourgeois parties that had once been included in the "Bülow bloc" were at odds with one another over the ruinous finances; the Navy was no longer the unifying force, the "darling of the nation", that it had once been touted by Tirpitz; the Crown's glitter had been badly tarnished by the Boer War, the Moroccan crises, the *Daily Telegraph* affair, the Björkö agreement, and the Anglo–French–Russian Entente; the Reichstag held the purse strings more firmly than ever; not a single European naval power had sought an alliance with Germany; no colonies were volunteered by Britain; and after Algeciras (1906) the Reich stood isolated in Europe, with the fateful exception of Austria–Hungary. In addition, Tirpitz's tactical calculations had also proved to be in error. Britain had reacted to the unilateral German naval challenge with Fisher's reforms, relocation of forces at home and Dreadnought quality production in 1906, all programmes that Churchill six years later was to continue and to advance in face of German increases in 1908 and 1912. The Admiralty had not been left behind in terms of quality. Personnel were highly trained. Their selection and education methods were progressive. The German 2 : 3 ratio had not been accepted. Battleship strength had not been squandered among numerous overseas posts. The North Sea had not been surrendered to Germany. And Britain had not been brought to the brink of financial ruin. Rather, the Imperial Navy in 1914 found its building programme eight battleships and thirteen cruisers in arrears.

The most crushing blow to Tirpitz, however, was that in 1912 the Prussian Army had been restored to first priority in armaments considerations. General v. Waldersee as early as 1898 had commented bitterly :

> The Navy more and more cultivates the notion that future wars will be decided at sea. But what will the Navy do if the Army should be defeated, be it in the East or in the West? Those good gentlemen do not like to think that far ahead.

The Balkan Wars of 1912–13 in particular once more brought home the realization that battleships could not protect Germany against huge Russian and French armies. Moreover, a victorious land war might bring Germany the hegemony in Europe that the naval arms race had promised – but failed – to provide. Annexations and indemnities would serve to restore internal harmony as well as the lustre of the Crown in its ensuing battle against democratization, especially in Prussia. This gamble apparently was all that remained to Wilhelm II after the demise of Tirpitz's master plan. General Friedrich v. Bernhardi's *Germany and the Next War*, published in 1912, was merely an outward symptom of this development. That neither the German Armies nor the Navy was fully ready for the *Flucht nach vorn* of July 1914 was not the least of Admiral v. Tirpitz's contributions to the history of Wilhelmian Germany. However, before turning to the events of July 1914, a few words are in order on naval policies other than ship construction.

Part Two

VI

A Place in the Sun

*The German Colonial Empire
and the Navy, 1884-1918*

When Admiral Prince Adalbert in 1870 suggested that Prussia seize French global bastions such as Saigon, Martinique, St Pierre and Miquelon, Chancellor Otto v. Bismarck rudely interjected: "But I do not want colonies. They are only suitable as supply bases . . . this colonial business for us would be similar to the silken pelts of Polish noble families who do not possess even shirts." The British historian, A. J. P. Taylor, hardly a Germanophile, concluded his study of *Germany's First Bid for Colonies* as follows: "The German colonies were the accidental by-product of an abortive Franco-German entente."

Taylor's claim notwithstanding, German naval officers and historians like to point out that the Reich possessed "one of the oldest and richest colonial traditions". Certainly, allusions are not hard to come by. Apart from the Viking and Hansa legacies, there were early colonial ventures by the Welser and Fugger patrician houses in Venezuela, Paraguay and Uruguay. Jacob of Courland in the seventeenth century briefly held land in Tobago and Gambia. The Great Elector of Brandenburg/Prussia after 1650 purchased Tranquebar in India, and built Fort Great Fredericksburg on the Gold Coast of Africa. Yet little came of these undertakings. King Friedrich Wilhelm I disposed of the Prussian African holdings to the Dutch for the ridiculous sum of 7,200 ducats and twelve slaves. Only the dream of a fleet remained.

The revolutions of 1848 briefly rekindled the quest for colonies. Admiral Livonius called for a Prussian overseas empire. Admiral Prince Adalbert foreshadowed later arguments: "For a growing people there is no prosperity without expansion, no expansion with-

out an overseas policy, and no overseas policy without a Navy."
This stance was to become a perfect *circulus vitiosus*: colonies
required a fleet to protect them, while a fleet required colonies in
order not to be tied down to one's shores. Until the early 1880s,
Bismarck stood squarely in the path of such aspirations. In 1871
he refused a French offer of colonies in Cochin China; three years
later he turned away offers of a protectorate from the Sultan of
Zanzibar as well as land in Borneo; in 1876 he rejected a proposal
from German merchants to establish a colony in South Africa; in
1880 he likewise turned down a scheme to settle in New Guinea;
and two years later he refused any part in a projected German
colonial society. Moreover, his negative comments concerning
colonies are legion. In 1881 he stated: "As long as I am chancellor
we will carry on no colonial policies." And in 1889 he made perhaps
his most widely-publicized announcement on the issue: "From the
start I have not been a colonial person."

That a German overseas empire was established during the years
1884–6 is the result primarily of European developments. To be
sure, German colonial enthusiasts had systematically organized their
efforts in the 1880s. A "Kolonialverein" had been established in
1882 for "the necessity of applying national energy to the field of
colonization"; its membership grew from 3,260 in 1883 to 10,275
two years later, and a newspaper (*Kolonialzeitung*) propagated its
policies throughout the German states. French expansion in Tonkin
and Tunis, Italian influence in the Red Sea area, and British con-
quests in India and Egypt prompted the Kolonialverein to merge
in 1887 with Karl Peters' "Gesellschaft für deutsche Kolonisation"
to form the "Deutche Kolonialgesellschaft". However, while Article
IV of the Constitutions of 1867 and 1871 made provisions for
extending German laws "over the Colonies and the settlements in
the lands oversea", no such colonies as yet existed.

The German colonial empire was acquired during the so-called
"Great African Hunt" in 1884. For over a year Bismarck pursued
the elusive dream of a Franco-German *rapprochement*. As he
remarked at this time to the French Ambassador to Berlin, Baron
Alphonse de Courcel: "England must slowly get used to the idea
that an alliance between Germany and France does not lie beyond
the realm of the possible." And conditions seemed ripe for German
expansion. Bismarck had ended his struggle with the Catholic
Centre Party (*Kulturkampf*). The Triple Alliance and Three
Emperors' League (1881–4) left Germany secure in Europe. Jules

Ferry put an end temporarily to the most militant French *revanche* notions. Britain had rejected Bismarck's alliance offers in 1875 and again in 1879. And France seemed to be on the verge of forgetting the "gap in the Vosges" for Tunisia. Under this favourable alignment, the German empire was forged almost overnight.

In 1884, Bismarck extended protectorates over Togoland and the Cameroons, German South-West Africa, German East Africa, and the former "New Britain Archipelago" (extended now to include the Marshall Islands, a quarter of New Guinea, and a group of the Solomon Islands). The British historian, Lewis C. B. Seaman, later summed it up well: "To the Germans, circumstances were a mere anvil and policy a series of irresistible hammer blows shaping the inevitable."

Yet the dream was quickly dissipated. In May 1885 Ferry fell from power; Boulangism was in full swing in France; and Bismarck's enemy William Gladstone departed in favour of the more congenial Benjamin Disraeli. The French connection was now dropped. While Kaiser Wilhelm I proudly commented upon the acquisition of German South-West Africa, "Now I can look the Great Elector in the face when I cross the long bridge in Berlin", Bismarck spoke openly of Germany's future role as a "sea power of secondary rank". The African policy, which had always been an extension of his continental policy, now lay dormant. In December 1888, the Iron Chancellor explained brusquely to the African explorer Eugen Wolf the cardinal points of his colonial policy: "Your map of Africa is very nice, indeed, but my map of Africa lies in Europe. Here lies Russia, and here lies France, and we are in the middle; that is my map of Africa."

For Bismarck the colonies were protectorates, and he sought out chartered companies to administer them in order to avoid government expenditure. He had taken them partly to still the clamour of minority lobbyists, but his plans never reached fruition. Heavy industry at first regarded the African holdings as "colonial empires that lie on the moon"; Emil Kirdorf declined to support them with "one ton of coal". And when no chartered companies could be found for Togoland and the Cameroons, Berlin reluctantly entered the field of colonial administration. (Table 21).

As these territories were taken peacefully, the Navy's role was limited to transport. The warships *Elisabeth, Leipzig* and *Wolf* in 1884 helped raise the Imperial banner in German South-West Africa, while *Elisabeth* and *Hyäne* performed similar tasks in New

Guinea. Only the Sultan of Zanzibar opposed the German claims in East Africa, but a naval demonstration by four armoured frigates quickly convinced him of the lack of wisdom of this act. *Bismarck* and *Olga* in 1884 landed troops in the Cameroons, and *Habicht* three years later brought a punitive expedition against the Duala tribe.

The accession of Wilhelm II to the throne in 1888 seemed to promise a vigorous overseas policy. In October of that year, *Eber* raised the German flag on the phosphate island of Nauru in the South Sea; a "New Course" also in colonial expansion seemed at hand. But when two years later Wilhelm recognized British protection over the Witu and Somali coasts, Uganda and Zanzibar in return for the rocky North Sea isle of Helgoland, German colonial enthusiasts were bitterly disappointed. Karl Peters caustically announced that "two kingdoms" had been "sacrificed for a bathtub in the North Sea".

Indeed, the first decade of Wilhelm's rule saw German naval expeditions primarily against rebellious natives. Rear-Admiral Karl Deinhard between 1888 and 1890 fought a pitched encounter with African slavers who incited a native rebellion against German rule in East Africa. Order was restored by six German warships only after Deinhard had blockaded the entire coast and a German naval battalion had stormed Dar Es Salaam as well as other lesser coastal ports. Native uprisings in the Cameroons in 1891 and again in 1894 forced the Navy into action, while yet another East African revolt in 1894 required the intervention of the cruising ships *Möve* and *Seeadler*.

The Navy, for its part, entered the colonial sphere with a flourish in 1897–8. For years there had been speculation and rumours concerning a possible concession in China. Rear-Admiral Alfred Tirpitz in the spring of 1896 as Commander of the German East Asian Squadron scoured the coast of China for a possible German settlement. Like Admiral Eduard v. Knorr before him, Tirpitz initially favoured the mouth of the Yangtze river, later changing his choice to a more northerly spot, Kiaochow in Shantung province. A problem arose in so far as the so-called Cassini Convention had accorded Russia a fifteen-year lease of the bay; the Wilhelmstrasse feared complications with Tsarist Russia on this matter. But a stroke of good fortune arose in November 1897, when two German missionaries in the area were murdered. Wilhelm II saw his chance at once. Without asking either the Foreign Office or the Navy

Office, he ordered Vice-Admiral Otto v. Diederichs to seize the Kiaochow region. On 10 November 1897, Diederichs put into the bay with the cruisers *Kaiser, Cormoran,* and *Prinzess Wilhelm* as well as the *Irene* and *Arcona;* a landing force of 717 men quickly dispelled the 2,000 Chinese soldiers. Possible Russian intervention was bought off by guaranteeing Russian ownership of Port Arthur; the British, for their part, were more than willing to have a German "buffer" between their Yangtze holdings and the Russians in Manchuria. Rear-Admiral Prince Heinrich was hastily dispatched from home with the *Gefion, Deutschland* and *Kaiserin Augusta* as well as 1,155 marines and 303 naval artillerymen under Captain Oskar Truppel. On 6 March 1898, Germany obtained a formal 99-year lease on the Shantung peninsula.

Wilhelm II was in a state of euphoria. He at once spoke of the creation of "the new German Hansa". Nicholas II was informed that "Russia and Germany at the entrance of the Yellow Sea may be taken as represented by St George and St Michael shielding the Holy Cross in the Far East and guarding the gates of the Continent Asia". Prince Heinrich, upon departing for China, had been informed "that the German Michael had set his shield, decorated with the Imperial eagle, firmly in the ground". All opposition, the prince learned from his brother, must be routed: "Drive in with the mailed fist." Bülow later claimed that Germany's foothold in China "had been internally most directly connected with the Navy Bill" of 1898, and the "first practical step on the way to *Weltpolitik*". A more sober analysis was to come from General v. Schlieffen in 1905 during the Russo-Japanese War: "This Kiaochow can give one sleepless nights." But more on the Navy's model colony below (p. 103). (Table 22).

The year 1898 seemed to offer still greater prospects for German expansion in the Far East. Already in January 1897, Tirpitz had anxiously wired to Berlin that the Spanish Empire appeared to be on the verge of collapse. Wilhelm II again was ready. "I am determined, when the opportunity arises, to purchase or simply to take the Philippines from Spain – when her 'liquidation' approaches." Tirpitz, now in Berlin, was no longer quite so enthusiastic, lamenting that "*the Spanish-American conflict came politically too early*" for him, that is, before German sea power could play "a decisive role". Nevertheless, he counselled that German warships should be stationed off Manila, and that the

Spanish-American conflagration offered the *"last opportunity* for us to purchase Curaçao and St Thomas".

The Navy's commanding admiral, Knorr, concurred. On 20 April 1898, he informed the Kaiser that the time was ripe to seize a base in the West Indies. In fact, lamenting that the globe was almost totally "divided among the major powers", Knorr urged the monarch to "seize" suitable bases (*Stützpunkte*). As such he defined especially the Dutch and Danish islands that would guard the future eastern terminus of the Panama Canal.

The German Admiralty at the same time urged action upon Wilhelm. "We lack a secure base almost everywhere in the world." The Admiralty sought "systematic planning" to ascertain the most suitable *Stützpunkte,* identifying as possible objectives the entire Samoan group, the Carolines, part of the Philippines (Mindanao), and Fernando Po on the west coast of Africa. More specifically, the head of the Foreign Office, Bülow, informed Lord Salisbury that Germany "expects not to go empty-handed at any new division of the globe".

On 18 May 1898, the Kaiser ordered Vice-Admiral v. Diederichs from Kiaochow to Manila; between 12 and 20 June, Diederichs concentrated there a naval armada larger than Commodore George Dewey's blockading force: the cruisers *Cormoran, Irene, Kaiser, Kaiserin Augusta,* and *Prinzess Wilhelm.* This display of force, in turn, prompted Admiral v. Knorr on 1 July 1898 to present Wilhelm II with a new shopping list of possible acquisitions. The admiral recommended primarily Mindanao in the Philippines, along with the Sulu Archipelago and Palawan to supplement Berlin's holdings in New Guinea and Oceania. Bülow again shared this policy: "His Majesty the Kaiser considers it the primary task of the German government not to leave unexplored any possible opportunity resulting from the Spanish-American conflict to acquire naval bases in East Asia."

But the German presence at Manila constituted a classic example of "overkill". It greatly annoyed Dewey. Several minor incidents concerning the American inspection rights on 10 July brought about a confrontation between Dewey and Diederichs' flag lieutenant, Paul v. Hintze. According to the latter, Dewey lost his temper at the meeting: "Why, I shall stop each vessel whatever may be her colours! And if she does not stop, I shall fire at her! And that means war, do you know Sir! And I tell you, if Germany wants war, all right, we are ready." Given such bitter feelings, it is not surprising that the Spanish-American War was resolved without any major gains being made by Berlin. President William McKinley decided instead to annex Guam, Hawaii, Wake Island and Puerto Rico, and to accept the Philippines "as a gift from the Gods" in order to "uplift and civilize and Christianize" the islands.

The United States action effectively crossed Diederichs' plans to seize one of the Philippine Islands, the Carolines, the Marianas, and Palau island. The admiral in his cables to Berlin railed against the "Anglo-Saxon world", warning that America's "violation of Spanish possessions" and Britain's "rape of the Transvaal" only pointed to the creation of an Anglo-American "trade monopoly brotherhood". Wilhelm II informed Bülow on 29 October 1898 that Germany's misery stemmed from her lack of sea power. "After twenty years," when the battle fleet would be ready, "I will adopt a different tone."

Admiral Tirpitz, on the other hand, now State Secretary of the Navy Office, provided some insight into his *Stützpunktpolitik*. In April 1898 he informed Wilhelm II that he regarded as his primary function "especially the further expansion of [our] colonial possessions, but above all the creation of a chain of maritime *Stützpunkte* [bases] overseas". In January 1899, Tirpitz revealed to Bülow that he supported a scheme recommended by a Captain v. Christmas-Dirkinek-Holmfeld to have German entrepreneurs purchase for the government the island of St John in the West Indies. Moreover, Tirpitz acknowledged that Albert Ballin of the Hamburg-America Line favoured the plan, which would afford the Reich a naval base on the vital strategic eastern terminus of the Panama Canal – when completed. Unfortunately, the Kaiser did not at this juncture relish such a deceptive and potentially explosive scheme.

In the Far East, Tirpitz desired a coaling station on the route to Kiaochow. As such he coveted the island of Langkawi in the Straits of Malacca. "The island would most favourably fit as a link into the chain of station bases that we must in the distant future complete." The state secretary also envisaged Langkawi as a vital base in the world-wide submarine cable network that Berlin had, of necessity, to create within the next decade. Finally, the island would be absolutely essential for "our future further expansion in East Asia". Though these were mainly expansionist aspirations and hopes, they nevertheless point to the future direction of

German ambitions – if international relations allowed such development.

More concretely, the Reich in 1898–9 finally managed to bring about partition of the Samoan group among Great Britain, the United States and herself. Initially, the Wilhelmstrasse did not especially desire acquisition of these lava heaps. Bülow confided that "the entire Samoan question" had "absolutely no material but only ideal and patriotic interest for us". His Undersecretary, Baron Oswald v. Richthofen, sarcastically commented that Samoa was "not worth the money spent upon telegrams to and from Apia". But Tirpitz was adamant on their strategic value. On 11 October 1899 he informed Bülow that Samoa was "already today of the greatest strategic value for the German Navy as an important station on the route from Kiaochow to South America". In addition, the islands would provide some control over the new sea routes opened by the Panama Canal; they were also indispensable for the projected "German world cable" that would be laid from South America to Samoa, from there via New Guinea to East Africa, and across that continent to the German colonies in West Africa. Rear-Admiral Felix Bendemann, Chief of the Admiralty, that same day seconded Tirpitz's dictum that "the military point of view" necessitated German control of the Samoan group. Bendemann specifically desired Samoa as a further link between the Reich's holdings in the South Sea and South America. In fact, the peace accord in the autumn of 1899 gave Germany most of the Samoan Islands (Upolu and Savaii), while the United States received Tutuila and Britain the Tonga group, Savage Island, Lord Howe Island, and most of the German Solomon Islands. Colonial enthusiasts in Berlin were jubilant, referring to what Sir Thomas Sanderson termed 'that miserable Archipelago" as "the pearl of the South Sea".

In a final rush of overseas expansion, Germany in 1899 for 4.2 million dollars purchased from Spain the Caroline, Palau and Mariana islands (save Guam). This host of coral islets and lagoon islands was designed for the eventual "German world cable", and furthered Bülow's belief that the Reich was "well along" the "road to *Weltpolitik*". As it turned out, these holdings – along with the "appetizer" (Bülow) Samoa – completed Berlin's colonial ventures under Wilhelm II. The total increase under the "New Course" amounted to a paltry 2,000 square miles, or a net gain of 0.18 per cent. This notwithstanding, the Kaiser by the turn of the century proudly announced that the "German Empire" had now been transformed into a "world empire". As Wilhelm put it at another time : "Where in the world he could find a nail to hang his shield, there he would hang it." On the lighter side, Admiral v. Diederichs, as Chief of the Admiralty Staff, between 1898 and 1900 acquired one of the Farasan Islands in the Red Sea as a vital coaling station on the route to East Asia. Apparently, no one in Berlin bothered to point out not only that cheaper coal could be had at Aden, but that the Farasan Islands were totally dominated by the British through the Suez Canal and the Gulf of Aden.

Among these holdings, the brightest future was planned for Kiaochow. It was at once transformed into a free port to rival Hong Kong and, unlike the Reich's other colonies, was placed directly under the Navy. Its governor was always the highest-ranking naval officer, who in practice, if not in theory, was responsible for his actions to Tirpitz. Even matters such as health, education and public works came under naval supervision. In the early years, about 1,500 troops guarded the German toehold in China : 22 officers and 1,132 men of the newly-created Third Marine Battalion, 7 officers and 272 men of the Naval Artillery, and about 100 Chinese troops. In 1902, a company of cavalry and an additional artillery command arrived in Kiaochow, raising the total force to 1,850 men.

The artillery was permanently established on two emplacements overlooking the city from Bismarck and Iltis Mountains. Yet there were few troubles in the leasehold. Not even during the so-called Boxer Rebellion in the wake of the murder of Minister Klemens v. Ketteler in Peking did a single foreigner die in Shantung. Fifty-one marines from Kiaochow took part in the relief of the capital, while Field-Marshal v. Waldersee's expeditionary force, which arrived after the siege of Peking had been lifted on 14 August, busied itself suppressing local uprisings near Kiaochow, specifically at Chihli. It should be noted that Tirpitz opposed this gaudy and utterly unnecessary show of force, which cost German taxpayers over 100 million GM.

The Navy had chosen to rule the colony in order to turn it into a model leasehold, and thereby to ensure future parliamentary support for itself as well as for its place in colonial administration. During the first two years alone, Germany poured about 23 million GM into the colony. Each year a lavish progress report was meticulously prepared for parliament in order to accentuate the

Navy's model administration in economics, health, education, and
the like. Indeed, much had to be done. Health conditions were
abominable in 1898 : dysentery, malaria, colitis, venereal disease
and typhus were uncontrolled. But by 1907, Kiaochow enjoyed a
wide reputation as the healthiest port in the Far East. The disease
rate among the German troops that year approached the level at
home, and foreign diplomats sought out the "Brighton of the Far
East" for their holidays.

Governor v. Truppel, whose maxim was that "in Shantung the
German governor is lord", ruled the leasehold almost as an
eighteenth-century enlightened despot. The Chinese section of the
town was razed and German "urban renewal" set in. Deep-water
wells were dug and special reservoirs built. Trees were planted to
hold the water on hillsides and prevent flooding. The good coal
deposits (bituminous and anthracite) were slowly exploited. By 1904,
the 247 miles of railroad from Kiaochow to Tsinan were ready for
service. And in less than a decade, the number of Europeans in the
colony had increased from 200 to 1,650. On the eve of the Great
War, there were 53,000 Chinese and 2,700 Europeans (1,855
Germans) in the leasehold. Kiaochow had become the sixth most
important port in China, and the Japanese in particular eagerly
sought its local dark and light "Germania" beer. The Navy not
only operated the town's slaughterhouse and electricity plant, but
also bought about 8 per cent of the locally mined coal (613,000
tons in 1913).

The Navy further hoped to convert Kiaochow into a first-rate
naval and merchant shipping centre. During the first year of
occupation alone, 14 million GM were set aside to dredge the
harbour to a depth of 10 m. Eventually, a great semicircular
mole three miles long protected the main harbour area of 725
acres; a railway ran the length of the dam, at the end of which
were raised both a private and a government wharf. The harbour
soon housed three piers : two were for cargo ships and carried a
rail spur to the ship's side; the third was for petroleum with a
pipeline from ship to shore. The Navy's shipyard on the tip of
the dam in the Large Harbour was one of the most modern enter-
prises ever attempted in the Far East by a European power. By
1907, there existed about 1,100 yards of docks, including a 16,000-
ton floating dock; the latter was the largest of its kind, equipped
with an electric crane that could hoist up to 150 tons. Over the
next seven years, Kiaochow built twenty-two ships, 70 per cent of

which were for the Imperial Navy. The leasehold in 1914 was the Reich's first (and only) first-rate naval base overseas.

But the undertaking cost money. Lots of money. John Schrecker estimates that by 1913 Germany had lavished almost 200 million GM upon its model colony. Of this amount, only 36 million GM had been raised locally, prompting the Centre Party delegate Matthias Erzberger sarcastically to note that with such subsidies one could "make the finest garden in the world even out of the Mark of Brandenburg". As late as 1913, the colony managed to raise only 7.2 million GM of its total budget of 16.8 million GM; the gigantic naval yard alone accounted for 50 per cent of the locally raised revenues. The government's statistical records support Schrecker's claims. The Reich spent well over 10 million GM p.a. in the period 1898–1909 in running the model colony. (Table 23).

Moreover, around 1905 it became clear to the Germans that Kiaochow did not represent the cherished entry into China, but rather the final phase of her Far East policy. Chinese nationalist reforms prevented the governors of Kiaochow from extending their influence beyond the leasehold into Shantung province, and the Anglo-Japanese alliance of 1902 – although directed primarily against Russia – further isolated the Germans in Shantung. Subsequently the Russo-Japanese War effectively eliminated the Russians as Britain's rival in the Far East, while at home the Reichstag Centre, Social Democratic and Progressive parties united against the soaring costs of *Weltpolitik*. By 1905, smuggling accounted for almost one-half of all goods brought into Kiaochow. Germany now reluctantly abandoned the free-port status of her leasehold and, in return for 20 per cent of revenues collected, placed Kiaochow within the Chinese Imperial Maritime Customs. In fact, Kiaochow imported only about 8 per cent of its needs from Germany, a figure roughly equal to that of other Chinese ports. The Japanese in time totally dominated the Kiaochow trade with roughly 55 per cent, forcing the Hamburg-America Line to reduce its sailings there to one per month. The Japanese also began to replace Germans as military instructors in China. And as a final and perhaps most telling blow, the Imperial government proved utterly unable to sell its installations in Kiaochow – especially the dock and electricity facilities – to private German businesses according to the master plan for the leasehold. Krupp repeatedly declined any interest in the floating dry-dock. As late as 1914, the Reich's exports to Kiaochow amounted to 2.2 million GM, while her imports from the colony stood at a modest 425,000 GM.

If the picture of the Navy's model colony in the Far East appears bleak with regard to financial solvency and German interest, the other possessions fared even worse. German South-West Africa turned out to be the greatest drain on imperial funds. Over 7 million GM had been spent building docks at Swakopmund harbour; in 1904, the annual subsidy for this colony still amounted to 32 million GM. The Herero uprising between 1904 and 1907, which has been described as the first war of Wilhelmian Germany, necessitated the further outlay of over 323 million GM.

The Navy also felt the financial pinch owing to these revolts. The China expedition, as previously mentioned, had cost more than 100 million GM, and involved the battleships *Brandenburg, Kurfürst Friedrich Wilhelm, Weissenburg,* and *Wörth* as well as 6 cruisers, 10 freighters, 3 torpedo-boats, and 6 regiments of marines. Nor had the Kaiser's over-reaction eased the German role in the Far East. Wilhelm had at once ordered naval infantry to China, announced that Peking "must be levelled to the ground", and grandiosely proclaimed the start of "the struggle between Asia and all of Europe". His "world marshal" v. Waldersee glumly noted in July 1900 : "We are supposed to conduct *Weltpolitik*. If only I knew what that is supposed to be."

Even the cost of showing the flag had begun to mount meteorically. Cruisers such as *Bussard, Falke, Gazelle, Geier,* and *Vineta* periodically appeared off Haiti, Venezuela, the West Indies, Mexico, Brazil, Chile, Peru, California, and British Columbia. In 1902–3, the *Vineta* and the gunboat *Panther* shelled the ancient Venezuelan forts at Puerto Cabello and Maracaibo. Two years later, the light cruiser *Habicht* put German marines ashore in Swakopmund during the Herero revolt, while in 1905–6 *Bussard, Seeadler* and *Thetis* were engrossed in the Maji-Maji rebellion in German East Africa. Even the small island of Ponape experienced native troubles that in 1911 required the presence of the warships *Emden, Nürnberg* and *Condor.* The cost of maintaining naval flotillas in time of peace in Germany's overseas colonies in a typical year (1909) amounted to no less than 1.4 million GM.

The returns from these outlays were most modest. The Reich's colonial trade between 1903 and 1914 rose from 71 to 263 million GM, but less than one-half (110 million GM in 1914) was with the homeland, and in 1914 represented only 0.5 per cent of

Germany's total trade. The aggregate gross value of Berlin's commerce with its colonies between 1894 and 1913 remained less than what was spent on them; subsidies, in fact, climbed from about 8 million GM in 1897 to over 32 million GM in 1909, with the result that in 1912 the colonial debt stood at 171.48 million GM. Only Samoa and Togoland paid their way. Finally, it should be noted that indirect support in the form of postal and shipping subsidies, naval defence, and special low-interest loans is not included in these figures.

The colonies also failed to become the suppliers of raw materials for German industry. They provided as late as 1910 only 0.25 per cent of her cotton, 2.12 per cent of her oils and fats, and 13.6 per cent (the highest figure attained for any import) of her rubber. Nor were the overseas holdings to emerge as the classic areas of capital investment for German bankers and businessmen : by 1913, only 505 million GM, about the same amount that the Reich in the 1890s invested in the South African Rand gold mines, had been channelled into the colonies. In fact, the latter by the outbreak of the Great War had absorbed only 3.8 per cent of Berlin's total overseas investment of about 25 billion GM. Generally speaking, Germany had placed only 10 per cent – compared with Britain's 27 per cent – of her national wealth overseas; the return on this investment, on the other hand, comprised a mere 2 per cent of her national income. Clearly, the colonies never laid the proverbial golden egg.

Nor did the overseas possessions absorb Germany's much-touted excess population. The Reich's emigration between 1871 and 1901 amounted to about 2.75 million people, and as late as 1893 over 90 per cent of these still preferred to go to the United States. The German colonial empire in 1904 encompassed an area of 2.5 million square kilometres, about five times the size of the mother country. Yet there were only 5,495 German residents – about the average size of a German village – in the colonies. Of these, most settlers had gone to South-West Africa. And by 1900, only one of every thousand Germans leaving the homeland chose to emigrate to her overseas territories. This notwithstanding, the old argument for colonies and sea power to protect them never subsided. As late as 1905, when the colonial venture had clearly been revealed as a failure, the German Colonial Congress passed a trenchant resolution that "a fleet is necessary as they [colonies] cannot exist without a background of guns". The simple truth of the matter is that colonies were regarded mainly as a token of German power and prestige rather than as an integral part of her economic or financial life. General Lothar v. Trotha, governor of South-West Africa, at the turn of the century ably commented on the Reich's colonial policy: "It was neither political because we lacked the enthusiasm, nor economic because initially we lacked the capital. . . . It was simply pure speculation."

And what of the highly touted role of the colonies as vital cogs in the future "German world cable"? Paul Kennedy argues that this, too, proved to be a dream. The Reich lacked even the *matériel* to build a submarine cable network: while Britain possessed twenty-eight cableships, Germany had one. In addition, most German cable stations employed numerous British subjects, who could hardly be relied upon in case of war. The major German cables – the joint German/Dutch line to Yap, the Emden–Vigio–Azores–New York link and the Monrovia, Liberia to Pernambuco, Brazil tie – were at all times exposed to British cutting. Finally, Kiaochow relied on Russian lines, Togoland on French, and German South-West Africa, East Africa, and the Cameroons on British. The Colonial Defence Committee in London estimated that by severing merely the Emden–Yap cable, "it would be possible to isolate Germany from practically the whole world, outside Europe". Only the neutral Scandinavia–United States tie was considered inviolate, and it was through it that Germany in January 1917 sent the fateful Zimmermann telegram to Mexico.

Great Britain's system of quadruplex cables, on the other hand, was by 1914 so complementary that when Germany did manage to cut several lines (at Cocos and Fanning Islands), it did little harm. In contrast, on the morning of 5 August 1914, when the British ultimatum to Germany had expired, the Admiralty severed both ends of the German Atlantic cable and secured it in Halifax and Falmouth. Under the provision of the Versailles Treaty, Japan and the United States took possession of the German cable in the Far East (Yap), France that in South America (Pernambuco), and Britain and France the Atlantic lines.

Wireless transmission, developed by the Marchese Guglielmo Marconi at the turn of the century, seemed to offer an alternative to British-controlled submarine cables. A chain of powerful stations was planned for Togoland, Kiaochow, New Guinea, Narau Island, Samoa, and, after purchase, Dutch Sumatra. However, in August

1914 only the Togoland link with the homeland was fully operational.

There remains the place of the colonies in Tirpitz's alleged *Stützpunktpolitik*. The period immediately prior to the turn of the century had, as we have seen, brought on frenzied hunts for suitable naval bases, especially by Admirals Tirpitz, Knorr and Diederichs, aided and abetted by Wilhelm II and Bülow. German attention had centred mainly round the Philippines, Samoa and the West Indies; that is, round possessions of colonial powers believed in Berlin to be "dying". No island had been too small, no coral reef too insignificant for German planners, who had accepted fully the British premise that "even the most unpromising detached ocean rock will, if kept long enough, develop some useful purpose". Yet Tirpitz's announced policy of creating for Germany a chain of naval bases girdling the globe to act as supply depots and submarine cable stations never reached fruition.

The answer to this apparent paradox lies both in the state secretary's naval strategy and in the Reich's international relations after 1900. Tirpitz had banked his entire plan upon an all-out naval Armageddon with the Royal Navy in the central or southeastern North Sea. The High Sea Fleet has been depicted by one historian as "a sharp knife, held gleaming and ready only a few inches away from the jugular vein of Germany's most likely enemy", Great Britain. Conflicts on the periphery of the North Sea, in East Asia, South America, or Africa, were not allowed to jeopardize the admiral's master scheme of concentrating sixty capital ships in home waters. Thus, colonial conflicts were often resolved to Berlin's detriment during a period that Tirpitz described as "dancing on eggs". Only when this "risk" period of naval building had been safely traversed would "a different tone", as Wilhelm II once put it, be heard from Berlin. With a fleet that stood a genuine chance of victory against Britain, the Reich would relentlessly press London for colonial concessions around the globe. Destruction in the North Sea or acceptance of the Reich as an equal colonial power would be London's alternative. This is the meaning behind Tirpitz's candid comment at the turn of the century, that the "bear skin" could only be divided once the "bear" had been slain.

On the international front, the years 1903 to 1907 witnessed the Kaiser's frenzied efforts to forge a sort of Continental League against Great Britain. In this he failed. Instead, between 1904 and 1907 France, Russia and Britain laid aside overseas rivalries for the sake of a common front against the Reich. The latter, for its part, countered with charges of "encirclement". In time, the monarch was forced to return to Bismarck's erstwhile policy of subordinating German expansion overseas to her safety in the European concert. Armaments priority was again accorded to the Army. Colonial gains remained negligible: in 1911, Berlin received 107,000 undesirable square miles of the French Congo, and two years later she was offered by Britain parts of Portuguese Mozambique and Angola. By 1914, she had created an overseas empire of about a million square miles and perhaps 15 million subjects. But the price had been high. Great Britain, Japan, Russia, and France had all at various times been antagonized by Germany's heavy-handed colonial policy.

Finally, it remains to be considered how well these far-flung holdings could be defended in a major war.

VII

"Men Fight, Not Ships"

*The Personnel of the
Imperial German Navy*

The Imperial German Navy was a relatively small entity when
Rear-Admiral Tirpitz became State Secretary of the Navy Office
in 1897. There were more than 1,000 officers: 827 executive, 128
engineer, 142 medical, 104 paymasters, 40 naval infantry, 57
ordnance, 41 torpedo, and several torpedo engineer and artificer
officers. In addition, there were 1,058 deck officers, 4,740 petty
officers, and 19,378 ratings, for a total contingent of about 26,000
men. By the outbreak of the Great War, the Navy consisted of
about 80,000 officers and men: 3,612 officers, including 2,388
executive and 585 engineer officers, 3,183 deck officers, 15,966
petty officers, and 54,369 ratings. There were in 1914 also 30
pastors in the Navy as well as 1,383 marines and 6,343 artillery
personnel.

The Organizational Regulations of 26 June 1899 divided the
Navy's personnel into "A. Officers, B. Men: petty officers, ratings".
The first category included all officers attached to the Navy Office,
Navy Cabinet, Admiralty Staff, and North Sea as well as Baltic
Sea naval stations, thus ending the system whereby seniority was
determined within each command post rather than the Navy as a
whole. The term "officer" was at the same time restricted to
Seeoffiziere (executive), *Marineinfanterie* (infantry), *Marineinge-
nieurkorps* (engineer), *Torpedo-Ingenieurkorps* (torpedo engineer),
Feuerwerks-, Zeug, and *Torpederoffiziere* (ordnance artificer,
ordnance, torpedo), and *Sanitätsoffizierkorps* (medical).

A. OFFICERS

The Imperial decree of 26 June 1899 established equivalent ranks

for Navy and Army officers. It also tied advancement strictly to
seniority of *Anciennität;* only the Kaiser could decide promotions.
Sea duty was no longer required for promotion. The Navy Cabinet
was entrusted with all matters pertaining to executive and engineer
officers and the Navy Office with those of torpedo engineer, torpedo
and artificer officers. Engineer and medical officers were designated
"military superiors of all naval ratings", but placed behind executive
officers in all cases. Finally, the order regulated the important
matter of marriage consent by the Kaiser (*Allerhöchste Konsens*).
Only executive, naval infantry and medical officers were granted
this social distinction; engineer officers needed the consent of their
naval station commander, while all other officers required that of
the state secretary.

The officers attached to the Naval Infantry formed a special
group. They had been recruited since 1866 exclusively from the
Prussian Army, and first appeared as "naval infantry", or marines,
only in the budget of 1889–90. The corps in 1905 consisted of 50
officers as well as 1,229 petty officers and ratings; added to this
should be the 69 naval artillery officers and 2,784 petty officers
and ratings. Throughout the period under discussion, marine officers
continued to be on loan from the Army, to which they returned
after two years' service with the Navy.

The First and Second Naval Battalions, consisting of four companies each, were commanded by a colonel or general who, after
12 March 1889, headed the Inspection of Naval Infantry. In
August 1901, a naval cavalry and a machine-gun company were
added to this corps. By 1895 the Naval Infantry no longer served
aboard ships, and instead received training for duty in the colonies.
It was ruled in April 1891 that all colonial troops were to come
under the jurisdiction of the chancellor, through the Navy Office;
in 1896 they were placed in the colonial department of the Foreign
Office, and after 1907 with the Imperial Colonial Office. The
Naval Artillery was in charge of fortifications at Helgoland,
Wilhelmshaven, Bremerhaven, Cuxhaven, and Kiel. However, the
coastal defence works in the Baltic Sea – other than those at Kiel –
remained with the Army.

In 1905 there were also 208 officers in the medical corps. The
latter was commanded by a *Marine-Generalstabsarzt* in the Navy
Office with the rank of rear-admiral. Immediately under him were
Generalärzte (captains) attached one each to Kiel, Wilhelmshaven,
Kiaochow, and the Navy's Education Department. *General-*

oberärzte, in the grade of *Fregattenkapitän,* customarily headed garrison hospitals and acted as squadron surgeons, while the *Oberstabsarzt* (commander) and the *Stabsarzt* (lieutenant-commander) served on board the heavy ships. These officers were commanded on board for one or two years; each year they had to take three- or four-week refresher courses, while the *Stabsarzt* was frequently sent to a university for one or two years to keep pace with the latest developments in his field. Medical student volunteers (one year) had to serve six months with the Naval Infantry and, after passing their state boards in medicine, six months with the Sailors' Division.

Torpedo officers and torpedo engineer officers (founded 1881) were yet another special corps. The Navy in 1905 maintained a complement of 61 torpedo officers who, in turn, commanded 4,513 petty officers and ratings in the Torpedo Inspection. Although this branch enjoyed the special patronage of Tirpitz, it nevertheless was regarded as too "technical" by many. Ernst v. Weizsäcker in 1906 was wary lest he become "too much of a locksmith . . . in the torpedo workshop. This must not happen under any circumstances. For me the executive officer comes before the technician."

Paymasters began as *Zahlmeister* with the grade of ensign, and advanced through *Oberzahlmeister* to *Stabszahlmeister* (full lieutenant); a lieutenant, usually with one aïde, served on each of the capital ships. Promotion to the rank of paymaster was only through the emperor, who assigned these men "special civil servant status with military rank".

There were also a number of "civil servants in uniform" in the Navy, most notably the construction engineers. Highest ranking among these, by order of 10 April 1899, was the *Geheimer Baurat,* with the grade of rear-admiral, followed by *Schiffbaudirektor* (captain), *Marine Oberbaurat* (commander), *Marine Baurat* (lieutenant-commander), and *Schiff-,* and *Maschinenbauingenieur* (lieutenant). Not proper officers in the true meaning of the word, these men with their Technical College education (*Diplom-Ingenieur*) naturally looked down on naval engineer officers and instead sought the company of executive officers in order to gain in military status. They constituted a specialized branch of the service as technical, rather than military, experts.

However, as previously stated, the premier officer corps in the Imperial Navy was that of the *Seeoffiziere.* The executive officers alone constituted a "commissioned" officer corps, received the

Supreme Commander's marriage consent, represented His Majesty
overseas, and were entitled to command a ship. They aspired to
attain social and military status equivalent to that of the more
prestigious *Garde* or cavalry officers of the Army, relying upon
Wilhelm's well-advertised love for naval matters to reach this lofty
goal. In short, they laid claim to being "the first estate" in the
realm.

The executive officer corps was divided into several grades: flag
officers (rear-admiral to grand admiral), staff officers (commander
to captain), and subaltern officers (ensign to lieutenant) (see Table
24). Each of these officers was *hoffähig,* that is, he had the right
to appear at Court. An ensign could usually hope to become a
lieutenant after five years, lieutenant-commander after twelve, and
commander after eighteen years, around the age of thirty-six.
Executive officers were first assigned to the Navy's main bases at
Kiel, Wilhelmshaven and Danzig. The first two were simultaneously the seats of the Baltic Sea and the North Sea naval stations,
each with an admiral as commander and governor of the port. The
main training areas were the Elbe and Jade river estuaries in the
North Sea and the Kiel Bight in the Baltic Sea. Helgoland did not
possess a first-class harbour, and only later were torpedo-boats based
there.

All ships carried in the Fleet List were anchored in Kiel,
Wilhelmshaven or Danzig and ready to sail at all times. Each
September, after conclusion of the Kaiser Manoeuvres, the ships
were dispatched either to Kiel or to Wilhelmshaven for overhaul
and refit. This usually lasted about four weeks, and constituted the
low point of the year. At this time, all reservists went from board
and the great changes in command took place. Early in October,
new recruits were assigned to their new vessels. It was a time of
unpreparedness, for the officers and men found their newly assigned
ships mostly still in drydock. The material reserve of the Navy lay
in port in three stages of readiness. Class one had coals as well as
munitions on board and could be sent out on sea duty at once;
class two had only coals on board; and class three constituted
strictly a material reserve.

The most cherished position was naturally that of skipper. Battleships and battle-cruisers were usually commanded by a captain,
light cruisers by a commander or lieutenant-commander, gunboats
by a lieutenant-commander, and torpedo-boats by a lieutenant.
Whatever the rank, the skipper was responsible directly to the

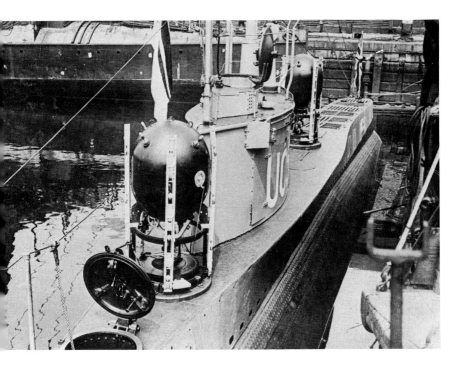

7a. Mine-laying *UC 5* with two mines on deck

7b. *U 35* in the Mediterranean. Commander Arnauld de la Perière is on the right

Kaiser for the combat-readiness, discipline and safety of his ship; he also had to see that proper homage was paid to the flag by crew and foreigner alike.

The captain occupied a lonely, almost Olympian position on the large ships. He had a private suite in the stern of the ship where he dined alone. The Kaiser's birthday (27 January) was one of the few dates on which the captain would eat with fellow executive officers in the mess.

The actual running of a capital ship lay primarily in the hands of her First Officer. Second in command, he usually had the rank of lieutenant-commander and was given one subaltern officer to assist him. The First Officer was the military commander of all on board save those directly under the captain : navigation officer, adjutant, medical officer, chief engineer, paymaster, and pastor. Above all, he was responsible for the discipline of the entire crew, whether officers, non-commissioned officers or ratings. All matters concerning maintenance, inventory, and training also came under his jurisdiction. The First Officer carried the *Rondelisten* (muster rolls), and he issued the daily orders to leading deck officers. He was also the head of the officers' mess (*Kasino*) on board. Not surprisingly, he usually was the officer most criticized, if not despised, by the men.

Third in command on the big ships was the navigation officer, often a lieutenant or lieutenant-commander. He supervised the course and speed of the vessel and monitored weather reports. The big ships also had an artillery officer, usually a lieutenant-commander, who was in charge of training the gunnery crew, directing the vessel's fire in case of war, and maintaining all guns and munitions. Working closely with him was the torpedo officer, who was entrusted with the ship's customary six torpedo tubes. The large units also had three or four officers of the watch, usually lieutenants, who were each responsible for training one division of sailors. An ensign was aboard the large ships to act as adjutant to the captain. Lastly, the Dreadnoughts carried sixteen sea cadets, and the large cruisers twelve. The Dreadnought *Prinzregent Luitpold* (24,700 tons), launched in 1912, carried a complement of 22 executive officers, 6 engineer officers, 2 paymasters, 27 deck officers, and 1,020 petty officers and ratings.

The executive officer corps received special uniform insignia from the Kaiser on 25 March 1890, and again on 19 December 1892; the latter order specified that adjutants wear a "W" on their

shoulder pieces and a royal (!) crown as well as Wilhelm's mono-
gram in their epaulettes. A basic change came on 1 January 1899,
when the epaulettes were altered to carry an anchor and eagle, and
the imperial crown was appended near the collar button.

Wilhelm II also introduced a number of uniform alterations for
staff officers and subaltern officers. In 1897 the *Korvettenkapitän*
was given the Army grade of lieutenant-colonel; on 23 November
1898 the new rank of *Fregattenkapitän* was introduced. On 29
June 1888, the corps received a gala uniform, and on 25 March
1890, the six-sided sleeve star was replaced by the imperial crown
(hitherto worn only by Admiralty Staff officers). In all, by the turn
of the century the *Seeoffizierkorps* possessed a gala uniform, a
regular naval uniform, a duty uniform, a special "day" uniform,
a mess jacket, a tropical uniform, and a cloak. Civilian clothes were
permitted only for sport. Already in 1873 the executive officers had
exchanged their side rifles for swords, and on 13 September 1901,
on the occasion of Tsar Nicholas II's visit to the fleet, Wilhelm
finally allowed them to lay down the unwieldy sword in favour
of a 34 cm dagger with ivory grips. (Table 25).

The Navy's uniform demands, which included no less than
thirty-six shirts, were not without motive. In settling a dispute in
1907 between the Education Department and the Navy Cabinet
concerning the admission of the son of a Danzig prison inspector,
the Kaiser noted: "A danger that too many naval cadets will enter
the service from such circles is already precluded by the fact that
only rarely will it be possible for the fathers to obtain the necessary
funds." Here, in precise terms, was an indication of how the Navy
used indirect monetary barriers to keep out undesirable elements.

The executive officer career was an expensive one. Estimates of
the cost vary; one source gives 7,900 GM for 1874, and 9,755 GM
for 1909 as the cost for the $3\frac{1}{2}$ years of training. The Navy Cabinet
in 1910 set the parental aid for the first year of training at 1,505
GM; the second year cost 1,090 GM; the third year, 1,000 GM;
but the final six months were expensive: 1,240 GM, including the
officer's uniform at 1,000 GM. Moreover, 600 GM per year were
required for the next four years, at which time the young man
would be promoted to lieutenant, in order to maintain his status
as officer and the accompanying social duties. Accordingly, the final
figure was set by the Navy Cabinet at 7,235 GM. If one adds to
this other expenses such as riding, fencing, dancing, and the like,
the training costs easily surpassed 8,000 GM.

This figure is not at all exorbitant by comparative standards. It was estimated in Great Britain that at the turn of the century naval cadet training costs had reached £1,000, or about 20,000 GM. As Fisher put it, "Surely we are drawing our Nelsons from too narrow a class." The figure of 8,000 GM was also not out of line with the 30–50,000 GM subsidy required for a judgeship, or the 7,500 GM for a court assessor (five years of training). However, the roughly 2,000 GM per annum demanded of parents of sea cadets was out of reach for the lower strata of society: the average yearly income of a skilled worker in 1913 was 1,300 GM, and that of deck officers about 2,500 GM.

Among those who could afford it, most came to the Navy either out of a sense of adventure, or because they saw quicker promotion and greater prestige in the new service than in the various German armies. Romantic sea stories, a longing for travel, and a hankering for "practical" rather than "academic" occupations also brought many young men to the Navy. The latter, in fact, never experienced a shortage of applicants; each year there was an excess of about 200 men above those admitted.

The *Inspektion des Bildungswesens der Marine* (Education Department) was created by imperial decree on 26 November 1895, and placed in charge of the Sea Cadet Entrance Commission, with its inspector as permanent head of this commission. The latter was responsible for all matters pertaining to officer recruitment, with final authority resting in the hands of the Kaiser. The commission deliberated from 1 October to 1 April of the following year, basing its arbitrary decisions upon information received from heads of administration districts (*Landräte*), police agencies, municipal magistrates, and military commanders. It held its deliberations in private, kept no minutes of its sessions, and was not required to reveal the reasons for its decisions – unless they involved a highly prominent member of society, in which case the person involved could appeal directly to the Kaiser. Undesirable applicants were often merely informed that the year's quota had been reached; if they applied a second time, they were failed in the entrance examination.

In addition to the parental support and good social standing of the candidate's family, the Navy also required passage of the aforementioned entrance examination as well as school graduation with *Primareife,* that is, high-school attendance, but without the final examinations and thus without certification as *Abiturient.*

Various attempts by Admiral v. Müller to introduce the *Abitur* as
entrance requirement were successfully blocked by senior naval
leaders, who preferred a conservative, Christian upbringing in a
middle- or upper-class home (*häusliche Erziehung*) to formal
education. Nevertheless, the percentage of candidates coming to the
Navy with the *Abitur,* usually at age eighteen or nineteen, increased
from 35 in 1900 to 90 by 1914. The Prussian Army also refused to
accept higher education as admission requirement; the Bavarian
Army, on the other hand, had required the *Abitur* since 1872. In
fact, young men could enter the Navy as officer candidates by
obtaining an imperial waiver for *Primareife* as well as for the
entrance examination; Graf Luckner was a prime example.

Who, then, qualified for admission to the executive officer
career? Gert Sandhofer has left a prescient analysis of the Crew
of 1907, which he deems highly "representative". Of the 197
applicants, only 22 (11 per cent) came from noble families, mostly
from the relatively impoverished lower Prussian Protestant nobility.
Overall, the number of noble cadets usually fluctuated between 10
and 15 per cent; only 14 per cent of all noble cadets between
1895 and 1914 were Catholic. Among the remaining 197 cadets,
90 had fathers who were academicians, 52 fathers were officers,
34 were merchants or manufacturers, 10 were landowners, and 10
were professional men. Each year the Navy also took about seven
candidates from the petty bourgeoisie as well as a few from downright "low" social circles, presumably in order to include a few of
them for the benefit of the Reichstag.

The analysis of the Crew of 1907 also revises some lingering
myths. The majority of the cadets came not from South Germany
but from the North. Of 197 members, only 25 came from south
of the Mainz–Coburg line; 130 came from Prussia, 13 from
Saxony, 8 from Bavaria, 7 each from Hamburg and Baden, and
the remainder from various other federal states and cities. No fewer
than 69 per cent came from northern coastal areas, while the
Hanseatic cities (Bremen, Hamburg, Lübeck) did not provide a
substantial percentage of the cadets. The Navy Office in that same
year defined "desirable" recruits as sons of officers with the rank
of Army colonel and higher, and civil servants from *"Rat II.
Klasse"* (colonel) upwards. Applicants of the Jewish faith were not
accepted, and were customarily rejected because of the "dietary
difficulties" that they would cause for the mess; a few baptized
Jews, such as Kurt Dehn in the Crew of 1910, which included

Martin Niemöller and Karl Dönitz were admitted, but they were generally members of what was popularly termed the "millionaires' club". Their presence spoke more for their parents' wealth than for the Navy's tolerance. No sons from Social Democratic and trade unionist homes were allowed to enter the executive officer corps, thus ensuring the social homogeneity, as well as isolation, of this corps.

The Navy attempted to increase the percentage of noble officers by elevating deserving senior *Seeoffiziere* into the Prussian nobility. The list of such cases is interesting : Knorr (1896); Koester, Müller, Tirpitz, Grumme, Hollmann (1900); Pustau (1901); Bendemann (1905); Hintze, Fischel (1908); Ingenohl (1909); Fischer (1910); Truppel (1911); Schröder, Capelle (1912); Coerper, Pohl, Lans, Karpf, Thomsen (1913); Henkel (1914); and, through the King of Bavaria, Hipper (1916). Moreover, Admiral v. Müller in 1913 sought to systematize this process in order to create "a new nobility of the sword for the partially dying out old nobility"; sons of the former would therefore in the future enter the Navy already as noble cadets. This self-perpetuating process would save the Navy from having to draw its recruits from the middle or lower-middle class. And the relatively high cost of admission to the nobility (4,000 GM) would automatically keep out "those without means". But the Great War precluded realization of this scheme.

The cadets entering the Navy after 1855 were attached to the *Seekadetteninstitut*. After admission at Mürwik in April, the sea cadets received 1.5 months' infantry drill, followed by 10.5 months of navigation, engine-tending and stoking aboard the Navy's school ships. Following promotion to midshipman (*Fähnrich zur See*), the cadets became members of the non-commissioned officer corps with sword-knot (*Portepee*); the Navy in 1890 had discarded the cumbersome side rifle for cadets in favour of a 60 cm dagger.

The approximately 200 *Fähnriche* next attended the Navy School for twelve months. Here they were given instruction in navigation (eight hours per week), seamanship (five hours), mechanics (three hours), as well as artillery, hydraulics, mathematics, shipbuilding, and dancing. One hour per week was devoted to the study of ship types, the use of mines, English, French, gymnastics, debating, and horse-riding. A major gap in the education of the cadets, according to the naval historian Admiral Otto Groos, was the lack of instruction in political affairs, in accordance with the general principle of keeping politics out of the armed forces. And with Admiral v. Tirpitz's decision to concentrate the fleet entirely in the North Sea, cruises in foreign waters were permanently suspended, and the cadets thereby deprived of their only opportunity to come into contact with different peoples, other forms of government, and other modes of life. Looking back in 1929, Germany's official naval historian, Admiral Eberhard v. Mantey, complained that the executive officer corps had become "a Prussian Army-Corps transplanted on to iron barracks".

The year at the Navy School ended with the main examinations for executive officer. Thereafter came special training courses in gunnery, torpedo warfare and infantry practice in the field, lasting six weeks. Finally, the *Fähnriche* were again placed on board ship for the last twelve months of training. Upon successful completion of this stint, they were promoted to and commissioned as ensigns (*Leutnant zur See*) and given the officers' uniform and sword. They ended their training and began their new career by swearing an oath of loyalty to the Kaiser :

> I, . . ., swear a personal oath to God the Almighty and All-knowing that I will faithfully and honourably serve His Majesty the German Kaiser, Wilhelm II, my Supreme War Lord, in all and any cases, on land and at sea, in peacetime and in wartime, regardless where this may be . . . and will act in a manner proper and suitable for a righteous, intrepid, honour- and duty-loving soldier.

The final step was election to the officer corps, a practice adopted by the Prussian Army on 6 August 1808. The election was carried out by the officer corps of each ship, from the light cruiser to the battleship, and by the flotilla or half-flotilla for torpedo-boats and submarines. Here was a final opportunity by secret ballot without appeal to reject any undesirable candidates who threatened the homogeneity or the exclusiveness of the corps.

Once members of the officer corps, the young men were much concerned about that mysterious entity called "honour". To maintain its notions concerning the latter, the Navy had copied the military courts of honour (*Ehrengerichte*) introduced by the Prussian Army on 3 August 1808. The courts were usually convened to cover behaviour not explicitly included in the Articles of War, such as offences against the unwritten laws of class morality (*Standessitten*). Only executive and infantry officers could sit on the courts;

neither medical nor engineer officers were permitted judgment over executive officers. The most severe sentence possible was "plain dismissal", with forfeiture of all officer rights and privileges.

"Honour" also revolved round the proposed marriage of *Seeoffiziere*. All active and, after 26 October 1907, all inactive officers were required to obtain imperial consent for their proposed marriages. In order to forestall *mésalliances,* executive officers had to submit not only a complete survey of the social backgrounds of the prospective bride and her parents, but also proof of financial support. On 19 January 1886, this amount, apart from the regular salary, was set at 3,000 GM per annum for an ensign, 2,000 GM for a second lieutenant, and 1,200 GM for a full lieutenant.

Neither gambling nor indebtedness was tolerated in the Navy, for fear that the officers involved would have to borrow from shady, often Jewish, money-lenders and thereby lower the prestige of the entire corps. The Kaiser on occasion even bailed out prominent officers who had partaken of champagne too often. In fact, drunkenness was frowned upon, especially by Admiral v. Müller, who conducted feared "milk" sessions in order to woo the officers from "the goblet". Wilhelm II, in his customary manner, carried the matter to comical extremes. During a speech to sea cadets at Mürwik in 1910, he described drinking as an "ancient heritage of the Germanic peoples", but warned that the "nation which consumes the smallest amount of alcohol" would win the next war. And despite the founding of the Navy Temperance League in 1903 in Kiel, many officers shared Admiral Ludwig v. Schröder's opinion: "A national drunkard is dearer to me than an international teetotaller."

There was also the matter of the duel. According to Articles 201 to 210 of the *Reichsstrafgesetzbuch,* all encounters with "deadly weapons" were to result in from two months' to two years' imprisonment for the offenders. Imperial decrees of 25 July 1895 and 1 January 1897, however, could not stem this practice. Duels were even fought on school ships, and it was not unusual for cadets to be asked to render "satisfaction" before being promoted to officer rank – a practice condemned by the Kaiser as well as the Navy Cabinet, without success. Executive officers both in Kiel and Wilhelmshaven in 1908 founded fencing clubs as "knightly" institutions. Although the Navy's first, and last, fencing match with Army officers in Dresden proved to be an utter fiasco, the Kaiser supported the clubs with money and trophies. In fact, Wilhelm at times chastised officers who did not accept a challenge to duel, stressing that executive officers should be infused with concepts of honour "in flesh and blood". In short, there existed a double standard on the issue of the duel. On the surface one realized that it was an anachronism in the modern industrial age; privately one still viewed it as a question of honour and a sign of social status.

Especially talented officers, usually lieutenants or lieutenant-commanders, were appointed to the Navy Academy in Kiel for detailed instruction designed to prepare them for staff work and for senior posts with the Navy. The Academy offered two semesters per year, one lasting six and the other nine months. However, such highly specialized training, and especially the accompanying elitist tendencies, were viewed with scepticism by Tirpitz. The latter was particularly worried that the Academy might become the training ground exclusively for officers of the Admiralty Staff, which he viewed uneasily as a rival.

Remuneration for executive officers was good. The basic monthly salaries for ensign (75 GM), lieutenant (125 GM), and lieutenant-commander (225–325 GM) at the turn of the century do not appear to be very high, but they were augmented by a host of bonuses and subsidies. *Servis* to supplement housing and heating costs on land, *Servis* to upgrade conditions on board ship, special adjutant's pay, re-enlistment bonuses, extra pay for sea duty, a special subsidy for married officers residing on shore – all these enticements to remain with the Navy could add up to, but not exceed, 1,800 GM per annum and make life in the Navy lucrative even in the lower officer ranks. Officer salaries were liable to state income tax when on station in home waters; overseas duty freed officers from this burden. Non-commissioned officers and ratings received wages, and these were not taxable.

After years of loyal service, the executive officers either retired (*a.D.,* or *ausser Dienst*) or were inactivated (*z.D.,* or *zur Disposition*) with sizeable pensions. There was an unwritten law in the Navy that executive officers retire at age sixty, and some were fortunate enough to get positions with naval purveyors such as munitions and powder factories, shipyards, or machine shops. Vice-Admiral Hans Sack, Admiral August Thomsen and Vice-Admiral Hunold v. Ahlefeld were most successful at this practice.

The Navy managed to maintain its rigid class structure (*Kastengeist*) even during the Great War. The Prussian Army experienced horrendous losses – 11,357 active and 35,493 reserve officers – and was forced to promote 82 non-commissioned officers (91 in the Bavarian Army) to active officer status. Even members of the Social Democratic Party, such as Julius Leber, Paul Göhre and Albert Südekum, were appointed reserve officers. The Navy, which lost only 647 executive officers (including 590 ensigns, lieutenants and lieutenant-commanders, mainly on the submarines), did not need to abandon its peacetime practices. Not a single non-commissioned officer between 1914 and 1918 was promoted to officer rank.

The executive officers had achieved their aim of attaining, socially and militarily, equality of status with the prestigious guards or cavalry regiments. By adopting the privileges and rights of the latter, while at the same time barring advancement of other officer corps, the *Seeoffiziere* developed a *Kastengeist* after the "ancient Prussian example". But the price was high. A number of specialized officer corps had been refused admission into the ranks of executive officers, and thereby were permanently relegated to a position half-way between executive and non-commissioned officers. As a result, the engineer officers especially were disgruntled and worked to improve their overall status on the basis of Napoleon Bonaparte's phrase, "La carrière ouverte aux talents."

The engineer officer corps of most modern navies underwent long and bitter struggles before they attained social and military status commensurate to that enjoyed by executive officers. In 1899, the United States Navy ended the division between "line" and engineer officers; even before then, the term "engineer officer" had been in use. Admiral v. Tirpitz only agreed to adopt the latter grade designation for "machinists" that very year, but denounced the American reforms as an attempt to create "one hodge-podge" of officers.

Admiral Fisher in Great Britain, on the other hand, basically approved the American reform, and, realizing at the turn of the century that the Royal Navy had only 961 engineers on duty out of the requisite 1,497, moved to close the gap between executive and engineer officers. The resulting "Selborne Scheme", named after the First Lord of the Admiralty, William, Second Earl of Selborne, between 1903 and 1905 introduced common entry and training for all cadets in the new naval academies at Osborne and Dartmouth. Moreover, while the highest grade for an engineer officer in the Imperial Navy after 1899 was *Fregattenkapitän,* technical officers with the rank of vice-admiral were to be found in the navies of Great Britain, France, Japan, and Italy, of rear-admiral in the United States Navy, and of captain in the Russian Navy. Most radical of all, France on 1 January 1907 decreed that 20 per cent of all executive and engineer officers were to be promoted from the ranks of qualified deck officers. Obviously, the times were changing.

But not in Germany. The 243 members of the *Marineingenieur-offizierkorps* in 1905 were not allowed to wear the officers' sash, the imperial crown on their sleeves, sleeve stripes, or a gala uniform. In addition, the Navy's Education Department ordered separate messes on board for executive and engineer recruits as well as an Engineer Officer School separate from the Navy School. Engineer officers did not have their own military courts of honour, but came under the jurisdiction of the executive officer *Ehrengerichte;* after 5 September 1909, in matters involving their corps, one engineer officer could replace the most junior *Seeoffizier* on the court. In Wilhelmshaven, there were separate officer messes for executive and engineer officers. In both Kiel and Wilhelmshaven executive, infantry and medical officers were designated "regular" members and engineer officers "irregular" members of the *Kasino;* the engineers were without a vote in the mess. This was especially degrading because parliament voted funds for these special clubs on the basis of *total* officer corps membership. The exclusiveness of the executive officers in 1891 militated against the engineers becoming regular members of the prestigious Imperial Yacht Club at Kiel.

Even at sea, the distinction between executive and engineer officer was clearly marked. The First Officer alone had disciplinary powers on the big ships. At the officers' mess, the most senior engineer had to wait for even a junior executive officer to give the signal to sit down and to start the meal. It is also revealing that in the Imperial Navy, where a strength relationship of 4 : 1 between executive and engineer officers was deemed desirable, there were sixty executive and only eight engineer officers in the Navy Office.

Until 1908, Tirpitz consistently opposed granting the engineer officers the promised (1899) rank of captain, but on 19 September 1912 this grade was finally awarded to the two senior engineers in the fleet, both men with almost forty years of service behind them. Wilhelm II as early as July 1906 had been willing to give engineer "applicants" the more appropriate title of "engineer cadets" as well as to grant engineer officers the desired imperial marriage consent, but both measures were blocked by the opposition of senior admirals, who feared that such actions would create "a state within a state" from among the barely 200 engineers. Indeed, the same officers expressly informed the Kaiser that were the two reforms granted, they "could no longer guarantee the combat-readiness of the fleet".

On 1 July 1908, the engineer officers were finally awarded the right to wear the officers' sash, again against Tirpitz's wishes. The state secretary managed to prevent publication of this imperial decree outside the Navy, and when it was printed in the official *MVOblatt,* it came under the innocuous heading of "uniform orders", hidden among items such as new lace boots for executive officers.

The main argument in favour of granting engineers higher social and military status was their growing importance in running the intricate machinery of the big ships as well as the acute shortage of this type of officer. Already in 1890–1, the Navy was only up to 68 per cent of the requisite technical personnel, and it was estimated that this figure would fall to 52 per cent over the next two years. Rear-Admiral Reinhard Scheer, then in the Navy Office, calculated in 1912 that the Navy would not be up to strength in engineer officers until 1921–2, or almost two years after completion of the building programme laid down in the Supplementary Bills of 1908 and 1912. By mid-1917, a crisis point would be reached, with 190–250 engineer posts in the fleet remaining vacant.

Piecemeal measures failed to alleviate this situation. On 1 October 1907, the practical experience asked of engineer candidates before they entered the Navy was reduced from thirty to twenty-four months; five years later, the overall training period was lowered from nine to eight years. Training facilities were also improved. On 1 October 1909, a new Engineer School was opened as a subsection of the Deck Officer School in Kiel, following an earlier parallel development in Wilhelmshaven. In 1916 a special Engineer and Deck Officer School was opened in Kiel in der Wik, again copying earlier examples from Wilhelmshaven.

But the engineer shortage continued unabated. In August 1914, there were 419 engineer officers on active duty as well as 114 retired – against a budget strength of 577, or 27.45 per cent below requirements. And the budget of 1918 called for 768 engineers,

whereas there were only 529 available and 32 imprisoned by the
enemy, a shortage of 31 per cent. During the Great War, 302
non-commissioned officers were promoted to engineer-officer grade.
A last-minute reform on 1 April 1918 failed to streamline engineer
training, which still lasted about 8 years and cost 3,735 GM for
the first 5½ years.

Indeed, the engineer officer career was neither undemanding nor
inexpensive. Parents had to pledge monthly support during the
period of training in addition to all uniform costs. In 1906, parental
support alone for the first four years of training amounted to
roughly 1,440 GM, not including uniform costs. Werner Bräckow
in his recent study of the engineer officer corps claims that it was
not unusual for a parent to subsidize his son in the amount of
7,000 GM. By November 1910, the Navy Cabinet estimated that
it cost about 6,450 GM for the engineer training, including 2,000
GM for uniform.

The young men who entered the service as engineer officer
candidates after 1903 were required to offer proof of thirty months'
experience in machine-work or shipbuilding as well as school graduation with *mittlere Reife,* that is, successful completion of
Untersekunda and status as *Einjährige* (one-year volunteers) with
Obersekundareife. Twenty-one years was the age limit. The
applicants were further asked to pass entrance examinations in
engineering, physics, mathematics, mechanics, engineering drawing,
and one foreign language, usually English or French. Upon successful completion of these hurdles, the young men were officially
enrolled as apprentice naval engineers (*Marineingenieuranwärter*).

The *Anwärter* received the basic three-month military training,
followed by nine months' technical sea duty in home waters as
seaman first class to gain experience in the stokeholds and engine-
rooms. Upon passing a practical examination, the young man was
promoted to *Applikant* and given petty officer status and sent to
sea for two more years, followed by one year at the Engineer School.
After yet another examination came advancement to *Aspirant,* and
deck officer grade.

The *Aspirant* was assigned sea duty for four years, followed by
an additional year at the Engineer School, where he concentrated
his studies on the theory of naval engineering. Then came the stiff
engineer examination, election to officer status by the executive and
engineer officer corps, and promotion to *Marineingenieur,* usually
at age twenty-nine. Thereafter, the engineer had to be at sea for

at least a full year before promotion, a requirement not set for executive officers.

On board ship, the engineer officer did the greasy work down in the bowels while the executive officer commanded from the conning bridge. The modern Dreadnought *Prinzregent Luitpold* was staffed with six engineer officers. The Chief Engineer (*Oberstabsingenieur*) was assisted by a Staff Engineer (*Stabsingenieur*) and a Leading Engineer (*Oberingenieur*) as well as by three engineers of the watch, one for each of the vessel's engines. In addition, the Chief Engineer on board had approximately 400 machinists and stokers immediately under his command. This, in theory if not in reality, made him the single most important officer on board. But as a member of a "technical" corps, he was not fully recognized as a *bona fide* officer. This was in keeping with the general bias against technical professions in Wilhelmian Germany, where the technical colleges were only at the turn of the century given parity with universities and the right to award the doctorate (*Promotionsrecht*).

To be sure, the engineer officer corps had risen from incredibly humble beginnings. The image of the engineer in the late nineteenth century was still one of "greaser" or "chauffeur admiral"; he was, according to Admiral Fisher, a "lesser breed" in the eyes of the "sacred priesthood of Executive Naval Officers". In the Reich, the first breakthrough for this corps came on 10 April 1899, when its name was changed from "Machine Engineer Corps" to "Naval Engineer Corps". And on 1 October 1903, the first fifty "Naval Engineer Candidates" entered the Imperial Navy.

A change in the social background of the engineer officer candidates can also be discerned during this period. Among the engineer aspirants accepted in October 1905, the majority (18) came from families of the lower or middle civil service, 16 from families of factory owners or directors and merchants, 7 of academicians, and 5 of engineers. Only 3 came from officer, or upper civil service, families, while 4 had fathers in the manual trades. A survey of the same year shows that the engineer officers generally married into the same, though slightly more affluent, social circles. But the efforts of leading engineers to raise the social level of the corps were slowly taking root. Among the candidates admitted in 1911, the most striking increase came with sixteen applicants from upper civil service background. Here the corps was recruiting from among the same social circles that provided the majority of executive officer cadets.

While the Chief of the Navy Cabinet, Admiral Gustav Baron v. Senden-Bibran, as well as his successor, Vice-Admiral v. Müller, generally supported the engineer officers in this matter, Tirpitz refused any and all attempts to raise their status to that of executive officers. For Tirpitz, the engineer officer was a "technical adviser", who could only aspire to take charge of machinery; the executive officer commanded men, was a "combatant", represented the Kaiser overseas, and could "possibly take the fate of the nation" into his hands. Was the state secretary thinking of himself? In any case, here in 1906 Tirpitz provided a clear definition of the two officer corps which remained in force for the Imperial Navy until the end of the war in 1918.

The years immediately preceding the Great War brought continued petty rancour and bitterness between executive and engineer officers. The Navy's records are filled with instances of petty class warfare, such as engineer officers refusing flowers sent by executive officers for their "women" because they were not allowed social intercourse with executive officers and their "ladies". The two corps wrangled over the right to exchange visiting cards, what courses each could attend at school, and the like. While junior executive officers, who had to work with the engineers on board ship, were generally sympathetic to the cause of the engineers, senior naval commanders stood firm with Tirpitz. Admiral Prince Heinrich, Admiral August v. Heeringen, Admiral Kurt v. Prittwitz, and Captain Friedrich v. Kühlwetter, head of the Deck Officer School, led the charge. Captain Karl Wilbrandt, Director of the Engineer School and head of the Engineer Candidates Admission Commission, was outraged that a particular engineer officer had audaciously paid a social call with his wife to the family of an executive officer. One commander of a warship had even invited his senior engineer officer into his home. "The only proper way of putting the engineers in their proper modest place is to accept only people from the lower middle class."

The discontent of the engineers, compounded by their mounting importance as well as shortage in the fleet, and by a bitter debate over their status in the Reichstag, led naval leaders on 6 June 1912 to introduce new regulations concerning the executive and engineer officer corps. Whereas up to now engineer officers had, in all cases, been listed as subordinates of *Seeoffiziere,* the relationship between the two types of officer was now to be based on their "professional relationship". This meant that the Chief Engineer on a ship was subordinate only to that vessel's captain and her First Officer, the Squadron Leader, and the Fleet Chief; the engineers under him only to the Chief Engineer and to the First Officer in disciplinary matters, while in theory to no other admiral or executive officer. The engineer officer became the military commander of all deck and petty officers as well as ratings, but the order also stated: "Nowhere do they appear as superiors to other officers of the Navy." In short, the order was absurd. According to Admiral v. Müller, Tirpitz promulgated it to assuage the Reichstag on this matter. Whatever the case, Bräckow attributes to Tirpitz "only a minimal insight into the dawning technical era" with regard to the engineer officer corps, and claims that even the state secretary's son, also a naval officer, spoke of his father's "antipathy towards the engineer officer corps".

Intra-service strife was temporarily laid to rest by the First World War. But as the struggle dragged on and the critical shortage of engineer officers that Scheer had predicted in 1912 materialized, the engineer officers became restive. The exigencies of the U-boat war further aggravated the shortage of engineer officers and conversely raised their military value. Their social status, on the other hand, remained unchanged.

To placate the military aspirations of the engineer officers, Wilhelm II on 1 May 1916 created the new grade of *Marineoberchefingenieur* for chief engineers, with the rank of captain. But other old grievances remained. Engineer officer candidates and executive officer cadets were still served in separate messes on board. They were not permitted to visit officers on land. The engineer officers had not yet been granted imperial marriage consent. The old adage that only executive officers could command ships was strictly adhered to. Numerous commanders, such as Captain Wilhelm Heine of the *Hannover,* still treated their engineer officers as "supply officers".

In July 1917, for reasons unknown, Admiral Scheer set new guidelines regarding the relations of the two corps. In a memorandum to all commanding officers on 3 July, he reminded executive officers that whereas they were trained to develop a *Führerblick,* engineer officers were limited by their education to the development of their "practical, technical capabilities". Hence, two completely different types of officer were required, "on the one side the commanding admiral on the conning bridge, on the other the military head of naval machinery". This was the criterion that regulated all aspects of the issue, necessitating "differences which permeate down to the selection of recruits". These "differences" could not be erased. *"The power to command is the concern of the executive officer"*; any change in this dictum would result in "the complete merger of the two corps". Here was the crux of the matter.

The memorandum marked the complete return to the hard-line position taken by Tirpitz in 1906. While allowing for occasional minor concessions to the social and military aspirations of the *Marineingenieure,* Scheer in fact relegated them to subordinate, technical status between executive and deck officers. Social mobility was thus denied to engineer officers. It is interesting to note Scheer's jab at the educational level of engineers at a time when almost twice as many engineers as *Seeoffiziere* possessed university degrees.

Scheer's treatise was somehow leaked to engineers, who naturally took umbrage. More than that, they boycotted the Kaiser's birthday celebration to accentuate their inferior social status in the *Kasino,* and during the winter of 1917–18 reacted with what amounted to passive resistance. Captain Andreas Michelsen, Commander of U-boats, complained to Scheer in November that engineer officers who had been placed under ensigns or lieutenants reported sick or "emotionally hurt". The Commander of Torpedo-Boats, Captain Paul Heinrich, informed Scheer in May 1918 that his engineer officers feigned sickness whenever they were placed under the command of a lower-ranking executive officer. And while Michelsen, Heinrich and Scheer agreed that only "firm and uncompromising" measures could stamp out this rash of "sickness", little was, or could be, done. As a result, military discipline on the big ships began to suffer. Many cases of military insubordination, especially on the part of the stokers, were not reported by engineers who did not want to call in the executive officers to assist them in the engine-rooms. Although no data are available on the frequency of such occurrences, there is little doubt that such situations existed and that they ultimately contributed to the mutinies of 1917 and 1918. On 8 August 1918, Admiral v. Müller made a fitting comment on the entire dilemma when he stated that the "uproar" over the engineer officer issue would end "either with the total equalization" of the two officer corps, "or with a political crisis".

B. PETTY OFFICERS AND RATINGS

The Organizational Regulations of 26 June 1899 divided the "Men" into petty officers with the sword-knot, petty officers without the sword-knot, and ratings. Recruits, according to the Constitution of 1871, were all men between the ages of seventeen and forty-five. It was customary to enter the service at age twenty, unless one opted to volunteer, in which case it was at the age of seventeen. Service in the Navy was for three years, followed by four years in the naval reserve as well as a further five years in the *Seewehr,* a last category of reserves. Volunteer re-enlistment was initially for four years, later raised to five and finally to six years.

The most difficult grade to define was that of deck officer. The very term is, of course, misleading; this corps was specifically designated as "Men" rather than as "Officers". However, *Deck-offiziere* received salaries rather than wages and, like executive officers, maintained their own batmen. In addition, they were allocated table-money as well as mess subsidies and other incentives given only to officers. And their uniforms were closer to those of executive officers than to those of petty officers.

The deck officer had no analogy either in the Prussian Army or in the British Royal Navy. Established by the Naval Regulations of 7 July 1854 as an independent officer corps, the deck officers supervised the various detachments of specialists on board: helmsmen and machinists in charge of mines and torpedoes, boatswains serving as carpenters, artificers, signalmen, and so on. They were, in short, the vital link between executive officers and ratings.

But times were changing. The sail was replaced by steam, wood gave way to steel for ship construction, and gun turrets appeared in place of mobile cannon on the side-decks. These changes, as well as the increasing electrification of the ship, created the need for a host of highly trained and specialized technicians who could be assigned neither to the ratings nor to the petty officer corps, and thus were placed among deck officers, whose ranks swelled rapidly as a result. The demanding technical functions performed by them increased their importance to a modern navy, but at the same time diminished their *military* role. Increasing numbers of executive officers now assumed the latter. In addition, engineers entered the service. As they tended to have a better formal education and often came from a superior background to that of the deck officers, the engineers threatened both the military and the social status of deck officers, as well as replacing them on board ship as technical specialists *par excellence*. The struggle of the deck officers in the "Tirpitz" Navy centred round their attempts to preserve inviolate their traditional status between executive and petty officers.

The *Deckoffiziere* came primarily from the ranks of the ratings; after three years' compulsory service, seamen could advance to petty officer (*Unteroffiziere*) grade. On the average, fifty months' sea duty were required before such a promotion was granted. Exceptional service as petty officer opened the door to the highest grade open to ratings, Chief Deck Officer. Advancement from petty to deck officer grade depended most frequently upon one's special technical skills. Gunnery experts were in great demand and hence promotion was rapid. On the other hand, the popularity of departments such as the torpedo service militated against quick advancement. In any event, promotion was accompanied by substantial financial benefits. Basic salary for Chief Deck Officers in 1908 was 2,580 GM annually, for Deck Officers 2,100 GM. In addition, they received 50 GM per month table money when on board ship and, like all officers, about 20 GM per month housing when residing in Kiel, Danzig or Wilhelmshaven. And, again like executive officers, after twelve years of service in the Navy deck officers were entitled to minor civil service posts set aside for them.

On the other hand, the social status of deck officers around 1900 remained low. They ranked militarily ahead of Army sergeants, yet socially were on the same level. In fact, they shared equal repute with machinists, carpenters, paymaster candidates, and sergeants of the watch. Nor did the deck officers receive support from the Kaiser for an improvement in their social position. When informed that deck officers in the Royal Navy would be allowed to mess with executive officers, Wilhelm II found this shocking.

Only in terms of quantity did deck officers enjoy a special place in the naval hierarchy. They were the largest single group of "officers". In 1905 there were 1,309 executive, 223 engineer and 1,652 deck officers in the Navy; nine years later, the figures were 2,249 executive, 537 engineer and 2,977 deck officers. The *Prinzregent Luitpold* carried a complement of 27 deck officers.

By 1910 the deck officers, in an attempt to enhance the social and financial position of the corps, formed a "Committee of Seven" (*Siebener Ausschuss*) composed of retired deck officers living in Kiel. Through pamphlets and public meetings the committee advocated economic concessions for active deck officers. Two years

later the "Committee of Seven" was joined in its endeavours by
the "Union of Retired Deck Officers" (*Bund der Deckoffiziere a.D.*).
It was politics by pressure groups in the best tradition of Wilhelmian
Germany.

Admiral v. Tirpitz initially was not particularly perturbed by
these developments. On 4 January 1911, he suggested to the
Prussian War Ministry that deck officers be recognized as an
independent officer corps, but the Army vetoed the plan. The War
Ministry had recently been confronted with similar pressure group
politics by a national *Bund deutscher Militäranwärter,* whose 35,000
members openly lobbied for improved conditions of employment
after retirement for non-commissioned officers. One final recourse
was open to Tirpitz: on 18 August 1911, he presented the case of
the deck officers to the Kaiser. To no avail. Wilhelm was in no
mood to force a confrontation with the Army, and Tirpitz could
only remind the deck officers that they, like petty officers, belonged
to the category "Men".

At this juncture, the struggle of the deck officers cropped up in
the Reichstag. On 15 May 1912, Dr Wilhelm Struve of the Progressive People's Party formally petitioned the Budget Commission to
ask the chancellor to "raise the social and economic status of deck
officers". Such public airing of naval personnel matters was
anathema to Tirpitz, and the admiral used all his wily parliamentary
skills to kill the measure in committee. But the issue would not die.
In July 1912 over 3,000 retired as well as active deck officers held
a rally in Kiel to publicize their grievances. This, in turn, led the
naval command to re-examine the entire deck officer controversy.

The naval stations in both Kiel and Wilhelmshaven as well as
the Navy Office in Berlin agreed that "all attempts" by the deck
officers "to obliterate the division between deck officer and officer"
were to be "emphatically opposed". This ruling was necessary for
the maintenance of proper discipline and had "its intrinsic justifica-
tion" in the low social origin of the deck officers and their lack of
higher formal education. On the other hand, the chiefs of the first
three squadrons of the High Sea Fleet seem to have sympathized
with the deck officers, showing that German naval leaders were
again sharply divided on personnel reforms.

The Chief of the High Sea Fleet, Vice-Admiral Friedrich v.
Ingenohl, in August 1913 made known his opposition to all attempts
that would *"raise the deck officers* as a category by themselves *out
of that of the ratings"*. In that same month, both the Baltic naval

station, commanded by Admiral Carl v. Coerper, and the North
Sea naval station, headed by Admiral v. Heeringen, supported
Ingenohl.

Thus the Navy, on the eve of the First World War, confirmed its
basic policy not to tolerate within the naval hierarchy any
subordinate officers who could claim to intervene between "officers"
and "men". To be sure, most senior naval commanders continued
to regard the deck officers as ratings. In November 1913 the North
Sea naval station ordered that all references to "deck *officers*" be
dropped from its daily orders. The First Shipyard Division in Kiel
that same month enjoined its officers to teach the deck officers "that
they fall into the category of . . . petty officers". In addition, Tirpitz
now concluded "that enough has been done for the deck officers.
. . . Even justified issues must no longer be taken up." The master
builder of the Navy obviously lacked in personnel matters the fine
touch he had shown in dealing with Reichstag deputies.

The deck officer issue contained all the components of very petty
class warfare. *Deckoffiziere* struggled, on the one hand, to advance
up the social and military ladder by acquiring various privileges
reserved for executive officers. On the other hand, they guarded
most jealously their own superior status with regard to petty officers
and ratings. This dual policy of aspiring to the social status of
higher military grades while at the same time resisting similar
challenges from below, would, the deck officers hoped, cement their
claim to be a separate, independent corps between officers and
ratings. The Navy repeatedly crushed this hope.

Germany entered the war in August 1914 with a corps of 2,977
deck officers. With the further development of mines, torpedoes,
submarines, and dirigibles, the technical industries outfitted the
rapidly increasing fleet with extremely intricate machinery, and
the technicians in charge of it were the deck officers. They were,
as Tirpitz once stated, the backbone of the Navy.

Once war had been declared, the deck officers dropped all
demands for reform. In the spirit of the *Burgfrieden* proclaimed by
Wilhelm II, Chancellor v. Bethmann Hollweg promised all retired
deck officers who volunteered for war duty that they would be
given commissions as engineer officers. But when they volunteered
almost to a man, only one *Deckoffizier* was promoted to officer.
Instead, even the most inexperienced officer recruits were appointed
"auxiliary officers" (*Hilfsoffizier*) and ranked above deck officers.
Worse yet, when the Navy followed the Army's example and created

"deputy officers" (*Offiziersstellvertreter*), it promoted only sergeants from the Naval Infantry to this grade; deck officers were outranked by and required to salute the "deputy officers".

The resulting uproar among deck officers caused Tirpitz in June 1915 to rule that deck officers would only be subordinate to "deputy officers" where this was militarily justified. In addition, on the Kaiser's birthday, 27 January 1916, an imperial decree established the special rank of "deck officer lieutenant" and "deck officer engineer" for retired deck officers who had completed twenty years of active service and had filled officer positions without being commissioned in wartime. It was a step in the right direction but, like so much else, it came too late and offered too little.

The deck officer issue never died during the war. Dr Struve in 1917 and his colleague Friedrich Hubrich in 1918 pestered the Navy on this matter, finally calling upon it to bestow officer status on all deck officers after a certain number of years in the service. Hubrich in May 1918 informed the Reichstag that 150 deck officers were at present serving as commanders of light naval craft, 300 as navigation specialists or as officers of the watch, 30 as leading engineers, 120 as regular engineers, and 360 as chief machinists on other light craft. Most of these posts were normally manned by executive or engineer officers.

But the naval command would not budge. Vice-Admiral Georg Hebbinghaus again stressed that deck officers were members of the petty officer corps. "They are not deputy officers. Their origins and their education relegate them to petty officer rank." This emphasis on education was most interesting : only 2 per cent of all executive officers (as opposed to 5 per cent in the Army) had attended the War Academy, and their tenure there had, according to Tirpitz, not been brilliant. This notwithstanding, the Navy Office "fully agreed" with Hebbinghaus.

Only in July 1918, when the corner had been turned in the war, did the Navy Office finally agree to make major concessions to the deck officer corps. In that month Admiral v. Capelle, who was already on his way out as state secretary, informed the Reichstag of his intention in December "to raise the deck officers from the ratings' ranks, and to form a special deck officer corps". This solution was nothing more than a redefinition of the Naval Regulations of July 1854; it would have made the Navy a force composed of three major grades – officers, deck officers and ratings. And yet, in all probability, this solution would have met the moderate demands which the deck officers had submitted ever since 1912.

It was not to be. The triumvirate of Scheer, Trotha and Levetzow (see p. 245) was not in a conciliatory mood in the autumn of 1918. Trotha in June had turned down several demands of the deck officers, such as officer status. Scheer, as we have seen, had in July blocked all progress for engineer officers. And in August the Navy Office advised against adopting Capelle's reforms, stating that the admiral had made a mistake when he committed himself on the deck officer question. The war ended without any change of status for the deck officer corps.

The petty officer corps, by contrast, enjoyed a relatively tranquil existence. *Unteroffiziere* were recruited especially from the ranks of ship boys as well as gifted seamen and one-year volunteers. Apart from the special category of deck officers, the grades of non-commissioned officers with sword-knot were distributed among seven naval divisions. The grade *Unteroffizier* included all sea cadets (*Fähnriche*), staff musicians and sergeants of the Naval Infantry, and supply sergeants and mechanics in the Naval Artillery. In addition, there were torpedo boatswains, artificers, machinists and sergeants in the Torpedo Division; engineer candidates, machinists, paymaster candidates, sergeants, and masters in the Shipyard Division; artificers, boatswains, chief quartermasters, gunners, and sergeants in the Sailors' Division; and artificers, sergeants, and staff musicians in the artillery branch.

The ranks of the non-commissioned officers without sword-knot included all petty officers and ratings. These men were the work force on the big ships, the stokers especially the beasts of burden. All petty officers and ratings were carried on special *Rollen,* or duty rosters.

The social status of non-commissioned officers was not very high. In case one of them married, there was no screening of the bride's social or financial background; it was not even necessary to state the intended's religious persuasion. No *Konsens* or annual independent income was required. Petty officers simply had to deposit 300 GM to show that they were not utterly destitute. All ranks from sergeant downwards received uniforms from the Navy, which withheld 9 GM per month for this expense. All were to maintain two blue, two white and two work uniforms; these remained their personal property upon retirement. And whereas civilian police could arrest *Seeoffiziere* only in "special cases", all petty officers and ratings from sergeant downwards could be arrested by civilian authorities without official permission from the Navy.

Pay at the turn of the century was not overly lucrative. A sergeant or an officer of the watch could expect 69 GM per month, a mate 45 GM, a seaman 19.50 GM, and a ship boy 12 GM. Sea cadets, on the other hand, already at this time received 40.50 GM per month, not counting table money or other bonuses. Wages were given out every ten days; ships on overseas stations were paid once a month. It was possible to make ends meet only by qualifying for special incentives and bonuses for housing, sea duty, re-enlistment, and the like.

All petty officers and ratings were, by order of 1 August 1890, to carry the letters "SMS" (His Majesty's Ship) before the ship's name on their caps. The navy-blue uniforms were given yellow sixty-degree chevrons to denote rank for the Naval Artillery, and red for the Sailors' Division. Metallic branch insignia were worn on the sleeve. As a general rule, technical personnel had silver insignia and nautical personnel gold. The members of the petty officer corps as well as ratings had to carry the cumbersome naval rifle as side weapon.

Rather than present a host of highly complicated and relatively trivial regulations for petty officers and ratings, it may be profitable to consider a sample case. Signal mate Richard Hubatsch, father of the naval historian Walther Hubatsch, has left his memoirs of life as a recruit in the Imperial Navy.

Richard Hubatsch reported to Wilhelmshaven in January 1901. The recruits were confined to barracks, where the day began at 6 am and ended at 9 pm. In between, the men were issued everything from sewing kits to sea boots, all properly tagged with their names. Clothing in the Navy was changed from head to foot twice a week, on Thursday and Saturday. The recruits received three months' infantry training, which was conducted by drill corporals on leave from the Army. It is interesting to note that the recruits were not taught Morse code; even signalling with lights was introduced into the training programme only in 1902.

Hubatsch recalls that his first ship assignment to the light cruiser *Gazelle* stood in stark contrast to land service. Duty was divided into a day and a night shift. While in port, the former began at 5 am with washing, laundry and ship cleaning. Breakfast was at 6.45 am. Additional duty and instruction continued until 11.30 am, at which time "clear deck" was piped. At noon lunch was

served, followed by a general rest period until 2 pm. Afternoon
duty and training ran from 2 to 6 pm, followed by supper, and at
8 pm all but those on watch were issued hammocks. Shore leave
was granted daily between 7 and 11 pm, while on Sundays the
men were given free time from noon to 5 pm.

Life on the *Gazelle* was crowded, with 250 people spread over
the 100-metre length of the ship. The captain and executive officers
were housed on the top deck in the stern; deck officers were on the
deck below, with nautical personnel a deck lower and all technical
personnel in the very bowels of the ship. The ratings slept in
hammocks strung up in the mess, whose mealtime tables and
benches were at this time suspended from the ceiling. Linoleum
covered most floors.

A special routine was observed on board. The flag was raised at
8 am while in port, and lowered at sunset. The least-liked chore
was coaling. In times of manoeuvres, this odious task was undertaken every fortnight and became a contest to see which ship could
take on the greatest tonnage in the least time. The work was
especially hard on stokers, who had to stand in coal-dust-filled
bunkers and receive the black material from above, often in a
temperature of 100-degrees. The Imperial Navy had tried coaling
with Chinese wicker baskets, passing these down the line from
hand to hand, but this system proved too slow in home waters,
where crews were trained to recoal even on the high sea.

Food in the fleet reminded the recruits more of the days of sail :
standard rations included hard bread, canned potatoes, and dried
salted meat. In home waters the daily meal usually consisted of
some form of *Eintopf,* or vegetables, meat and potatoes all boiled
together; this was supplemented twice a week by meat or fish main
dishes. When at sea, potatoes as well as bread spoiled easily and
thereby lowered the quality of the meals even further. Each recruit
received a loaf of bread weighing 6 lb every four days; coffee was
served in the morning, tea at night. But especially at sea the food
was monotonous and vitamin-poor. Recruits could purchase extra
bread rations, but at exorbitant prices. Neither sugar nor fruit
products were worked into the menu. The food allowance for the big
ships is interesting : 1.6 tons to be divided equally between the mess
for the admiral and the captain on the fleet or squadron flagship,
10.9 tons for officers, 1.1 tons for sea cadets, 9.2 tons for deck
and petty officers, and 16.1 tons for ratings.

Unbelievably, there was absolutely no intellectual or educational stimulation provided on board. There was no ship's library. No fleet magazines were printed. Daily newspapers were not allowed; they had to be purchased on land, and even there those of left-wing persuasion were banned. History was taught only as the glorious saga of the House of Hohenzollern. On Sundays the ship's captain held a brief religious service; occasionally the squadron pastor, Protestant or Catholic, arrived to give a longer sermon.

A sailor, even a mate, was rarely addressed by executive officers. The latter, according to Richard Hubatsch, formed "at all times a caste unto itself", while medical officers and paymasters were considered second-rate officers. The captain especially lived a monastic life. Rarely seen, he dined alone and appeared in the officers' mess only on special occasions. Hubatsch's skipper on the *Gazelle* was Lieutenant-Commander Reinhard Scheer, destined to head the High Sea Fleet in the Great War, a man known for strict discipline and popularly called "the man with the iron mask". Reserve officers came on board only for the autumn manoeuvres and were usually captains and officers from the major steamship lines. With this observation, signal mate Hubatsch closed his diary.

A final category of ratings were the ship boys. Every April about 1,000 of these young people, usually between the ages of sixteen and eighteen, were taken into the Ship Boys' Division at Friedrichsort, where they received eighteen months of instruction in seafaring. This was followed by sea duty aboard the old frigates *Stosch, Stein, Moltke,* and *Charlotte* for a minimum period of two years. After about seven years in the service, they were advanced to petty officer grade, and hence they formed the nucleus of the future noncommissioned officer corps.

The foregoing analysis of the personnel of the Imperial German Navy, however brief, may suffice to show that Admiral v. Tirpitz was rather less skilled in personnel matters than he was in handling parliament and in ship building. Perhaps the latter allowed him not enough time to devote to matters of personnel. Yet he might have remembered General v. Stosch's axiom that "men fight, not ships". For it was with these "officers" and "men", that the Imperial Navy in August 1914 entered the First World War.

Part Three

VIII

August 1914

The War that Came Too Soon

On the evening of 3 August 1914, Sir Edward Grey stood at the window at Downing St and sadly commented: "The lamps are going out all over Europe. We shall not see them lit again in our lifetime." But the "lamps" went out especially for Admiral v. Tirpitz. The Kiel Canal was ceremonially opened on 24 June, four days before the assassination of Archduke Franz Ferdinand in Sarajevo. Subsequent events confronted Tirpitz with the stark reality that war in late 1914 would constitute the "hour of truth" for his fleet before it stood a chance against the Royal Navy. Accordingly, the state secretary in July and early August feverishly sought to delay any German belligerency. A general European war now would be fought by the German armies not for a "place in the sun", but for defence of the borders of 1871. Tirpitz's fears that Bethmann Hollweg might seek an "understanding" with "perfidious Albion" in naval affairs were compounded by Captain Albert Hopman's reports that the Kaiser saw only France and Russia as possible opponents. He was also alarmed by news that the State Secretary of the Foreign Office, Gottlieb v. Jagow, believed that even a German occupation of the Netherlands would not bring Great Britain into the war. Both Hopman and Capelle still hoped that while "many swords will be rattled and much poisonous ink spilled, Europe will not tear itself to pieces over Serbia".

Tirpitz, on the other hand, knew full well that London would not stand by and allow a repeat of 1870–1. Only once, when erroneous news reached Berlin that Britain would remain neutral in a war against France, did he sip champagne with Wilhelm II and indiscreetly utter: "The risk theory works." For the most, Tirpitz was sullen, pessimistic, hoping against all hope to persuade Wilhelm

to keep the proverbial sword in its scabbard. On 31 July, when
both King George V and Wilhelm II informed the chancellor of
their love of peace, Tirpitz breathed a sigh of relief : "What, then,
is the point of war?" But Moltke was set on war and would not
hear differently. War came with Britain on 4 August against the
advice of Tirpitz. Admiral v. Müller believed that the conflict with
London had long been "unavoidable", and that the Berlin government had handled the situation well in making Germany appear as
the attacked. "The mood is brilliant." Wilhelm returned his insignia
of Field-Marshal and Admiral of the Fleet to George V. "This was
the thanks for Waterloo." With a heavy heart, Tirpitz on 26 July
had recalled the fleet from its manoeuvres off Norway – a step
designed to avoid a possible British "Copenhagen", but one which
he knew would greatly increase the likelihood of war and restrict
the government's diplomatic freedom. His last-minute pleas for
peace with Russia, if war with Britain were inevitable ("set the
whale against the bear"), were also ignored.

Across the North Sea, fleet exercises had been topped on 17–18
July by a spectacular review at Spithead. It was incomparably "the
greatest assemblage of naval power ever witnessed in the history of
the world", according to Churchill. When word reached the
Admiralty on 26 July that Serbia's conciliatory reply to the Austro–
Hungarian ultimatum had been rejected, Prince Louis of Batten-
berg, the First Sea Lord, moved at once. Demobilisation was halted,
the Royal Navy was placed on "preparatory and precautionary"
footing, and its newest vessels were ordered through the Channel to
the northern anchorages at Scapa Flow, Cromarty and Rosyth.
Admiral Sir John Jellicoe, ten years younger than Admiral Sir
George Callaghan, was placed in command of the newly constituted
Grand Fleet. At 11 pm on 4 August (midnight in Berlin), the
Admiralty gave the signal to commence hostilities. Churchill
accepted the outbreak of war in a packed House of Commons on
5 August with tears streaming down his cheeks. The years of tension
and stress were over.

What were the relative strengths and weaknesses of the two fleets
in 1914? On the surface, the picture was most bleak for Germany.
The Grand Fleet, dubbed the "Crown jewels" by the First Lord,
possessed 21 Dreadnoughts and 4 battle-cruisers in its northern
lairs; the High Sea Fleet 13 Dreadnoughts and 3 battle-cruisers
(without *Blücher*). Britain was eventually to add 11, and Germany 2
Dreadnoughts to their respective battle fleets. Moreover, 3 Dread-

noughts being built for foreign nations were immediately seized by the Admiralty: *Canada* (Chile) and *Agincourt* and *Erin* (Turkey) raised the British force to 24 Dreadnoughts. In terms of light cruisers, Britain had 18, with 8 being built, to Germany's 8 in commission, with 8 under construction. The destroyer forces were also in Britain's favour 225 : 152.

But the picture was not this lop-sided in terms of bases. In fact, the British situation was shocking. The first-class naval stations were at Chatham, Portsmouth and Devonport; their location had been dictated two or three centuries earlier when Britain's enemies had been Spain, France and Holland. Financial expenditure on floating *matériel* had since 1903 delayed improvement of North Sea facilities at Scapa Flow, Cromarty and Rosyth. Scapa in 1914 still had no anti-submarine nets or booms; the other two bases had only light coastal artillery guns and were highly susceptible to submarine and mine attacks; Harwich was too far south, and was used primarily by light cruisers and destroyers. The dockyard at Rosyth had just been begun in 1914, and Scapa possessed absolutely no provisions for fleet maintenance or repair.

Germany, on the other hand, was far better off. Principal bases at Kiel, Wilhelmshaven and Cuxhaven formed a right angle defended by the heavily fortified island bastion, Helgoland. The area "between Helgoland and the Thames", where Tirpitz planned to engage the Royal Navy, was linked to Wilhelmshaven through the Jade river, to Hamburg through the Elbe river, to Bremen through the Weser river, and to Kiel through the Kaiser-Wilhelm Canal. Borkum Island, fifty miles west of the Jade, protected the Ems estuary. Shoals and sandbanks off the Elbe restricted approach by capital ships to easily defensible narrow channels. Kiel was protected by mine barriers in the Great and Little Belt, which had been illegally laid in Danish waters. On the negative side, anti-submarine protection was completed only in 1915, and two high waters were needed to pass the entire fleet over the Elbe and Weser bars into the North Sea. This was to prove fatal early in the war when Admiral Beatty appeared off Helgoland.

And what about the fighting capabilities of the respective capital ships? In terms of armour protection, Britain had increased citadel belts by two inches from *Dreadnought* to *Queen Elizabeth*, and Germany the same from *Nassau* to *Kaiser*; German battle-cruisers had about two more inches of protection than British counterparts. German ships on the average had about 10 ft more on the beam than the British, which meant enhanced stability and permitted thicker armour, especially underwater against mines and torpedoes. German ships were also less sinkable than British with more intricate hull watertight subdivision. In torpedo and mine development, the Germans were far ahead of the British, who continued to look upon these as subsidiary weapons.

The First World War, like the Russo–Japanese War before it, was to prove the dominance of the heavy guns; not a single capital ship managed to fire a good torpedo shot in four years, and the hastily installed anti-aircraft guns did not play a role during combat. The medium guns could only be used against light craft during long-range artillery duels. The raised end-mounting of the heavy guns proved advantageous by reducing smoke and gas obstruction. The German guns proved equal or superior in penetrating power to British guns of the next higher calibre, owing to higher muzzle velocity. They were also more durable. Berlin had changed over to the built-up as opposed to the British wire-wound gun, and this weapon had almost double the life (200 rounds) of the British gun. In terms of broadside, the Admiralty could boast of a decided advantage : 15,600 lb for *Queen Elizabeth*, compared with 8,600 lb for *Kronprinz* (both laid down in 1912).

In terms of gunnery control, Admiral Sir Percy Scott had in 1911 brought out a director system whereby all guns could be trained, laid and fired by a master sight in the foretop, high above the smoke. A single telescopic sight electrically connected to each gun aimed broadsides on the enemy ship and was fired by pressing a single key. In August 1914 only eight ships with the Grand Fleet had been fitted with the director sight. The German counterpart, the *Richtungsweiser*, was very similar except that it was mounted not in the foretop but on the conning bridge. Berlin had also come up with Zeiss turret-mounted "stereoscopic" range-finders, and a trigonometrical computer (Dumaresq) and range-rate clocks allowed greater accuracy during the opening salvos; guns were still laid on target, however, by the individual gunlayers.

There was little to choose between the two fleets in terms of tactics. The hallowed rigid line of battle was sacrosanct and manoeuvres were still carried out upon a signal from the flagship, much in the fashion of a polonaise (Admiral v. Mantey). The idea was to form a long line of battle in the shortest possible time from cruising formation, and thereupon to attempt either to cross the line of advance of the enemy (crossing the "T"), or to concentrate on

9a. Armoured cruiser *Blücher* sinking off the Dogger Bank

9b. *Seydlitz* in Wilhelmshaven dockyard, 6 June 1916

10a. Light cruiser *Emden* destroyed on beach on North Keeling Island

10b. *Goeben* in the Bosphorus

his van, force him to come round and disorganize his fire. This not only deprived junior admirals of initiative, but the five-mile-long line of ships, surrounded at times by dense smoke, did not permit smart execution or sometimes even reception of battle signals (Jellicoe, in particular, distrusted wireless). Only in night fighting did the Germans have a clear advantage as Jellicoe equated this with "pure lottery".

A final Admiralty advantage lay with personnel. British seamen signed on for twelve years while their German counterparts were three-year draftees. This gave British crews closer unity and greater practice time. And there was the psychological edge of being part of a proud tradition. The German novelist Theodor Fontane summed up the German position as follows: "We do not have a trace of this confidence. . . . We are not mentioned in the Old Testament. The British act as though they *had* the promise." And Vice-Admiral Scheer said it all: "The English fleet had the advantage of looking back on a hundred years [*sic*] of proud tradition which must have given every man a sense of superiority based on the great deeds of the past."

The opening days of hostilities were to reinforce this psychological impediment. All flag officers from Admiral v. Ingenohl, Chief of the High Sea Fleet, downwards expected an immediate British descent upon the Helgoland Bight and the naval Armageddon that Tirpitz had predicted for so long. In retrospect, nothing is perhaps more hotly debated than the first few weeks of the war. Tirpitz later claimed that the "politicians", that is, the Kaiser, Chancellor, Chief of the Admiralty Staff, and Chief of the Navy Cabinet, had deprived Germany of a certain quick victory over the Grand Fleet with their argument that the fleet should be maintained as a bargaining counter at the peace table rather than hurled against either the British cross-Channel troop transports (about thirty per day) or Scapa Flow. On the surface, there is some merit to this. At one point in October 1914, repairs and the need to counter German ships at Falkland had reduced the British superiority in Dreadnoughts to a slender 17 : 15 ratio.

But the overall situation was not this simplistic. A sortie into the Channel in August 1914 would have achieved little. The High Sea Fleet would have arrived there dangerously low on fuel, without supply bases or repair facilities, and in danger of being cut off from home by the Grand Fleet – given that Ingenohl would have had no difficulty in disposing of the 19 elderly battleships and 20 cruisers that made up a joint Anglo–French Channel Fleet. In fact, nothing would have pleased the Admiralty more, especially if one keeps in mind that, thanks to Prince Louis' actions, the Grand Fleet was at full battle readiness. Moreover, confusion reigned supreme at German headquarters. It appears that Tirpitz had not been apprised of the Army's attack on Belgium (Schlieffen Plan), and Moltke had coolly informed the Navy that he desired no actions in the Channel, preferring instead to mop up Sir John French's Expeditionary Force along with the French Army. And what if the British landed in Flanders or Denmark? Or the Russians in the Baltic along the coast of Pommern? And had not the naval attaché in London warned as late as 30 July to expect an *"immediate attack . . . at the moment* of the outbreak of war"? German ships were designed to fight within 100 nautical miles of Helgoland, and who could shoulder the responsibility for attacking Jellicoe on *his* terms? Certainly not Tirpitz – despite his repeated calls for "action".

The opening days of the war fully revealed the bankruptcy of the "risk" theory. Nor did the "alliance value" of the fleet manifest itself; there were no allies to "value" it. Moreover, Berlin squandered its reconnaissance dirigibles on senseless bombing raids against the east coast of Britain, which at one point prompted both Fisher and Churchill to consider executing one German hostage for every life lost. Totally senseless was the decision in October to send four minelaying torpedo-boats into the Channel; they were intercepted and destroyed near Texel with the loss of over 200 men. Above all, the early days of the war revealed the utter fiasco of German strategic planning. The burning question of 1912, "what if they do not come?", was now at hand. With a total disregard for history, German planners had placed their hopes in an offensive "Trafalgar" mentality by the Admiralty. But had not Hawke as well as Nelson waited for years before he got his opportunity against the French in 1794? To be sure, the British public quickly criticized the naval impasse, and Churchill made his unfortunate statement that the Royal Navy would dig the Germans out "like rats from a hole", while Vice-Admiral Beatty wished "the beggars" to be "a little more enterprising". Yet Jellicoe stood firm in the correct belief that the Germans could only attempt "tip-and-run" operations in the North Sea.

Britain in 1914 at once seized control of the seas, hunted down the isolated German cruiser squadrons, transported eight Army divisions to France without loss, and gave range to her light craft around the globe (save the Baltic and Black Seas) by the presence of the Grand Fleet at Scapa Flow (the classic "fleet in being"). German maritime trade, except for the Baltic, had ceased on 4 August: 287 steamers (795,000 tons) had been destroyed, captured, or detained by Britain, and on 2 November Admiral Fisher had placed tight controls upon all neutral shipping in European waters. What naval commander would risk these gains for sheer glory? As Churchill later put it, "Jellicoe was the only man on either side who could lose the war in an afternoon." Subsequent hair-brained schemes by Admirals Fisher and Wilson as well as Churchill for assaults against Helgoland, Flanders, Borkum, and Brunsbüttel, or landings in Pommern, Schleswig-Holstein and Denmark, must be seen against this overriding consideration. Such notions reflected more the impatience of the men involved than official Admiralty policy.

Surface actions in the North Sea in 1914 did little to raise German expectations. When the British finally "came" on 28 August, Rear-Admiral Leberecht Maass's light cruisers *Ariadne, Mainz* and *Köln* were literally blown out of the water surrounding Helgoland by Beatty's battle-cruisers. Ingenohl showed no inclination to take the High Sea Fleet out that day, and low tides precluded egress from Wilhelmshaven in time to catch Beatty. This dreadful start persuaded Ingenohl not to risk a major fleet engagement but to concentrate instead on small surprise attacks by light units, and prompted Wilhelm II to place even greater restrictions upon the High Sea Fleet's freedom of action. But the British continued to offer the Germans battle, partly in order to distract them from the Channel transports. On 10 September, the Grand Fleet stood twelve miles off Helgoland ("bighting the Bight"), but again Ingenohl chose to remain in his anchorages. The fears of Admirals Fisher and Jellicoe as well as Field-Marshal Lord Kitchener concerning a possible German invasion (the bogey of 1900–10) remained utterly groundless – although the German Navy was approached by the former director of the Treptow Observatory with a scheme to transport troops to Britain with underwater wagons across the sea bed.

Partly out of frustration that the British did not attack German naval facilities in the North Sea, and partly to offset the mounting criticism at headquarters as well as the boredom in the High Sea Fleet, Admiral v. Ingenohl on 3 November dispatched eight cruisers to shell Yarmouth and to lay mines in the waters off this port; the

High Sea Fleet was to support the action at a distance. The risk was out of all proportion to possible gains – as was evidenced when the armoured cruiser *Yorck* foundered on German mines in the Jade river upon return from Yarmouth. This notwithstanding, Ingenohl on 16 November ordered a raid on the British coast at Hartlepool, Scarborough and Whitby, partly because he knew that the battle-cruisers *Invincible* and *Inflexible* had been sent to the Falklands. But a stroke of good fortune on 26 August had provided the Admiralty with the German cipher and chart books (these "sea-stained priceless documents") when the light cruiser *Magdeburg* was destroyed by the Russians. A special secret "Room 40" under Sir Alfred Ewing (the "Sherlock Holmes of Whitehall") was now able to transmit most German ship movements to the Grand Fleet as the Germans freely used their wireless, suspecting that the British pos-sessed their cipher books, but apparently not knowing (until 1917) the use they were making of them.

Accordingly, the British knew not only that Ingenohl at the last moment cancelled the November raid, but also that he rescheduled it for 16 December with the battle-cruisers *Seydlitz, Moltke, Derfflinger* and *Von der Tann* and the armoured cruiser *Blücher*. What they did not know was that Ingenohl at the very last moment decided to bring fourteen Dreadnoughts and supporting craft. The so-called Scarborough Raid therefore presented the Germans with the longed-for chance at last to catch parts of the British forces : six of the most powerful Dreadnoughts of the Grand Fleet and four battle-cruisers as well as supporting craft, sent to spring the trap on Vice-Admiral Franz Hipper's scouting forces. But Scarborough proved to be a bitter disappointment for both sides. Ingenohl, dis-covering the approach of the Dreadnoughts, turned off to port at 5.30 am and again one hour later, believing that the entire Grand Fleet was bearing down on him. Hipper was thus left to his own devices. But confusion reigned equally on the British side. Beatty, who had steamed after the departing Ingenohl, not knowing that he was chasing almost the entire High Sea Fleet, was informed of the bombardment of Scarborough and turned back. The trap might still be sprung on the *Derfflinger* and *Von der Tann*. Six Dread-noughts and four battle-cruisers stood between Hipper and home. But fate intervened. The weather turned foul by 11 am and, worse yet, two British cruisers misread Beatty's signal and broke off con-tact with Hipper's screen. The latter's scouting forces were able to make good their escape round the Dogger Bank under cover of rain squalls. Lady Luck had saved Hipper, as it had earlier rescued Beatty from Ingenohl's battleships.

The Scarborough Raid aroused acrimonious debate on both sides. Not for two centuries had such action occurred near British shores, and not since 1667 had foreign ships killed residents of the British Isles. The loss of more than 100 lives prompted the First Lord to speak of "the baby-killers of Scarborough", and other epithets such as "assassin squadron" and "Scarborough bandits" were reserved for the German "butcher-and-bolt" tactics. And in Germany, Admiral v. Müller lamented that "a great opportunity" had been missed, while Tirpitz exploded that Ingenohl "had the fate of Germany in the palm of his hands" and had let it slip away. Ingenohl's alleged lack of aggressiveness was often traced to his English wife, but few dared to point out that the Scarborough Raid hardly justified the deployment of the High Sea Fleet. Beatty's vessels were now moved from Cromarty to Rosyth in order to be closer to the sites of the German raids.

Subsequent British sorties into the German Bight on 24 November and Christmas Day 1914 again failed to lure the German heavy units from their anchorages, and the first major phase of the war in the North Sea came to an end with the encounter at the Dogger Bank on 24 January 1915. Admiral Jellicoe's forces had, in the meantime, been beefed up with five new Dreadnoughts, and on the line of battle his ships more than doubled those of the enemy. It was estimated that within two months he would possess a crushing capital-ship advantage of 32:21 over Germany. Ingenohl, on the other hand, managed to wring from the Kaiser greater freedom for fleet sorties, and on 23 January 1915 dispatched Hipper's four battle-cruisers (*Seydlitz, Moltke, Derfflinger, Blücher*) along with a screen of four light cruisers and eighteen torpedo-boats in the hope of surprising British light forces near the Dogger Bank. Hipper's chief of staff was Lieutenant-Commander Erich Raeder, destined to command the navy of Adolf Hitler.

The Admiralty once more knew of the raid beforehand and decided to spring a trap, as it had at Scarborough. This time there would be no battleships supporting Hipper. But again muddling ruled the day : Jellicoe was not given sailing orders in time, with the result that when Hipper and Beatty tangled at 9 am on 24 January, the Grand Fleet was about 140 miles away. The opposing battle-cruisers opened fire for the first time at the then unheard-of range of twenty kilometres. As the two squadrons closed on each other,

Beatty at once gained the advantageous lee side, forcing Hipper to a south-easterly course that obscured his sight with dense smoke, but Captain Pelly on *Tiger* botched Beatty's order that each ship should concentrate on her opposite number from right to left. As a result, *Moltke* remained unmolested and seized this rare opportunity to pound *Lion* severely. Matters turned worse thereafter. *Lion*, with Beatty on board, had to fall back owing to shell damage, and Beatty mistakenly spied periscopes and ordered his four light and four battle-cruisers eight points to port, thereby putting them astern of the Germans, who were heading for home. Yet this was not all. Beatty's subsequent signal, "Attack the rear of the enemy", was misread as an attack on the blazing *Blücher*, which was now mercilessly pounded by *Indomitable, New Zealand, Princess Royal*, and *Tiger* as Beatty on *Lion* crawled north with a list of ten degrees. Hipper, who was at about a five-knot speed disadvantage not because of the slower *Blücher* but because of his slow torpedo-boats, was therefore able to escape with his three battle-cruisers, leaving the *Blücher* to her fate. She went down after three hours and seventy hits. But her heroic stand was not in vain. A shell had pierced *Seydlitz's* aftermost turret, instantly killing 165 men and knocking both turrets out of action. Salvos racked her every ten seconds and only the heroic action of flooding the magazine spared her at this moment. She managed to limp home, to fight another day.

The Dogger Bank engagement produced mixed feelings in Britain. It was officially celebrated as a victory, but Beatty privately expressed his "disappointment" at the "terrible failure" to annihilate the German battle-cruisers. For the second time in three months the Grand Fleet had failed to spring its trap and to deal the Germans a crushing blow. Yet some lessons had been learned : the ships were given more rigorous gunnery practice (*Lion* had never fired upon a moving target), the introduction of director systems was stepped up, clearer fleet signals were adopted, and Jellicoe was more determined than ever not to permit Beatty's "cavalry of the sea" to engage heavy enemy units without full support from the Grand Fleet.

In Germany only the heroic action of the *Blücher* vitiated the mood of utter despair. Ingenohl was replaced by Admiral Hugo v. Pohl. The Kaiser was quickly dissuaded from distributing decorations on his birthday, simply because the action had taken place on Frederick the Great's anniversary, and he placed even greater restrictions upon the High Sea Fleet. Wilhelm, according to Admiral v. Müller, blamed Tirpitz "entirely for our cruiser losses". Pohl, for his part, was not to appear in the North Sea in force for over a year, limiting his operations to several minor "tip-and-run" sorties. And Tirpitz, slippery as an eel, now informed Müller that "successes" against the Grand Fleet were "hardly probable" and promised "an unqualified success from a cruiser war". It was a perfect *volte face* for Mahan's staunchest disciple, and it undermined the state secretary's credibility at headquarters.

The Reich, like Britain, made several technical changes. Planners had been severely shaken by the unprecedented range of the artillery duels, and the angle of maximum elevation of the heavy guns was increased from 13.5 to 16 degrees by cutting away some of the turret armour. Moreover, the *Seydlitz* experience prompted engineers to install "anti-flash" doors at the various levels of the loading cycle; the Royal Navy had to wait for this lesson until Jutland one year later.

During the course of the above-mentioned skirmishes in the North Sea, German surface vessels were also active in the Mediterranean Sea and the Pacific Ocean. War found the battle-cruiser *Goeben* and the light cruiser *Breslau* in the Mediterranean. Berlin ordered – and London correctly surmised – that the ships would either operate in the western Mediterranean as raiders or else break out into the Atlantic Ocean. But on 3 August, without the Kaiser's knowledge, Pohl and Tirpitz ordered Rear-Admiral Wilhelm Souchon to sail to Constantinople. Souchon's subsequent "escape" from Sicily (Messina) to the Dardanelles has long been blamed upon the ineptitude of the two British commanders in those waters, Admirals Sir Ernest C. T. Troubridge and Sir Archibald B. Milne. However, recent investigation by Ulrich Trumpener has shown that far greater blame lay with Whitehall and the Foreign Office for failing – despite clear evidence received during the early part of the opera- tion – to inform the two commanders that the "Mediterranean Squadron" was headed for Turkey. Milne in the process was so con- fused by conflicting reports from home that he even warned that *Goeben* would attempt to enter the Suez Canal.

In fact, the German battle-cruiser was beset with high fuel con- sumption caused by badly leaking boilers and lingered for sixty hours around the Greek archipelago taking on coal, where she might have been caught yet. Instead, Souchon entered the Dardanelles on

10 August. Churchill incredibly wired Milne that the German ships had now been "disposed of", and Prime Minister Herbert Asquith totally failed to appreciate the meaning of this move, arguing that after the departure of the German crews, "the Turkish sailors cannot navigate her except on to mines". He felt that even though the Turks were still "very angry at Winston's seizure of their battleships here", the Golden Horn would not be significantly affected by the arrival of the *Goeben* and *Breslau*. On the contrary, the vessels on 16 August were hastily "incorporated" into the Sultan's Navy as *Sultan Yawuz Selim (Goeben)* and *Midilli* after a bogus sale designed to maintain the fiction of Turkish neutrality. They flew the Turkish flag, Souchon became Chief of the Fleet at the Porte, and the crews stayed on, donning the Turkish fez. They were to raid the Black Sea – where the Russians under Vice-Admiral Eberhard maintained five battleships and two cruisers – and to tie down Allied naval forces off the Straits. Admiral Guido v. Usedom also arrived overland in August 1914 with a force of 27 officers and 521 men to bolster the German presence in Turkey.

The German holdings in Africa, on the other hand, fared much worse. On 7 August, the very day that French's forces crossed the Channel, British troops invaded Togoland; the latter fell three weeks later. The Cameroons were occupied by an Anglo–French contingent by 27 September 1914, although the remnants of the German garrison escaped into Spanish Guinea only in February 1916. German South-West Africa, according to Colonial Secretary Lewis Harcourt, turned into "nothing less than an Imperial disaster". From the start, inter-Allied wranglings and downright desertion rather than stiff German resistance brought chaos and almost disaster. On 9 October, the South African force under Colonel S. G. Marwitz rebelled and joined the Germans in what has been described as the "most important colonial event of the First World War". Only rigorous action by Generals Louis Botha and Jan Smuts saved the day, and in July 1915 the German garrison of 3,370 officers and men surrendered to 43,000 South African troops.

The Navy managed to play a part in the defence of German East Africa. In August 1914, the survey vessel *Möwe* was destroyed during the British shelling of Dar Es Salaam, as was the German dry-dock there. The light cruiser *Königsberg* put up a struggle: in September she destroyed the British light cruiser *Pegasus* off Zanzibar and, when caught by British forces in July 1915, placed her crew and supplies at the disposal of General Paul v. Lettow-Vorbeck for the latter's struggle against overwhelming British, Indian, Boer, and native troops. Lettow-Vorbeck's heroic troupe of 300 Germans and 11,000 native soldiers suffered severe hardships and surrendered only after the Armistice in November 1918; their success was due in no small part to premature Anglo–Belgian wranglings over the anticipated spoils in East Africa.

The Pacific theatre initially proved equally disastrous. Kiaochow fulfilled Schlieffen's nightmare. On 15 August 1914, Japan presented the German governor, Captain Alfred v. Meyer-Waldeck, with an ultimatum to surrender the leasehold by 15 September. When no answer came by 23 August, Japan declared war on Germany. Berlin attempted to circumvent impending surrender of the colony by offering it first to China and then to the United States, but to no avail. Within four days, Japanese warships had sealed Kiaochow off from the world; the garrison of about 3,500 German troops was surrounded by October by over 20,000 Japanese troops. The final assault came on 31 October, and on 7 November 1914 – precisely twenty-seven years after Wilhelm II had ordered its seizure – Kiaochow fell. China belatedly declared war on Germany in August 1917, but Japan refused to surrender its newly obtained base until 1922.

Germany's other Far East possessions fared even worse: within three months, the black-white-red imperial banner had been swept from the Pacific. On 30 August, about 1,000 New Zealand troops, aided by two battle-cruisers, took Samoa without serious resistance. New Guinea fell after heavy fighting to Australia on 13 September. Finally, in October 1914 Japan "for strategic reasons" occupied the Caroline, Marshall, Mariana, and Palau islands.

The outbreak of war in August 1914 had found the German Cruiser Squadron in the Far East at Ponape in the Caroline Islands, and Japan's belligerency made it clear to Vice-Admiral Maximilian v. Spee that he could tarry there no longer. Accordingly, he decided to strike out for Chile with the armoured cruisers *Scharnhorst* and *Gneisenau* and the light cruisers *Emden* and *Nürnberg* in order to intercept and destroy British shipping and, if possible, engage the three cruisers stationed there. However, Commander Karl v. Müller of the *Emden* had on 13 August persuaded Spee that failure to inflict losses upon British shipping in the Far Eastern theatre would be detrimental to future naval expansion in Germany as well as to the Reich's prestige at sea. Spee had agreed and dispatched *Emden* to raid the North Pacific and Indian Oceans – after he had fortified his squadron with the light cruisers *Dresden* and *Leipzig* from the Reich's erstwhile American naval station.

Emden became a legend in her time. She destroyed or captured seventeen British merchant ships of 68,000 tons, shelled the oil tanks of the Anglo–Persian Oil Company at Madras, sank the Russian light cruiser *Zhemtchug* in Penang harbour as well as the French destroyer *Mousquet* just outside that port, and overall cruised 30,000 sm while an armada of fourteen warships desperately searched for her. Müller had fitted his ship with an additional fourth (dummy) funnel to resemble the British *Yarmouth* class light cruisers, and his exploits appealed to British sporting instincts. At home he became a symbol of German superiority. The French septuagenarian ruler of Dago Garcia, not having been apprised of the outbreak of war, welcomed and dined Müller. One shore station even wired : *"Emden,* where are you?"

But the outcome was inevitable. Somewhere, someone, at some point was destined to spot Müller. It proved to be the Australian cruiser *Sydney* at Cocos (or Keeling) Island. Müller had stopped there to destroy the wireless station, but its wily operator signalled his presence. *Sydney's* eight 6 in guns were superior to *Emden's* armament and at seven kilometres, out of the German's range, *Sydney* raked her until Müller surrendered. His losses amounted to 134 men killed and 65 wounded. Lieutenant v. Mücke, who had been left on the island, boarded the elderly sloop *Ayesha* with a crew of forty-four and managed to reach Yemen and, overland from there, to join Souchon and Usedom at Constantinople in June 1915. Müller's chivalrous behaviour and feats of seamanship earned from the *Daily Telegraph* the comment : "It is almost in our heart to regret that the *Emden* has been destroyed. . . . The war at sea will lose something of its piquancy, its humour and its interest now that *Emden* has gone."

Meanwhile, Admiral v. Spee's actions were not quite as romantic but equally deadly. Rear-Admiral Sir Christopher Cradock with the armoured cruisers *Good Hope* and *Monmouth*, the light cruiser *Glasgow* and the antiquated auxiliary cruiser *Otranto* ("the floating haystack") was to intercept Spee in the South Atlantic. Cradock was eventually sent the pre-Dreadnought *Canopus* and the armoured cruiser *Defence*, but he feared the slow speed of the former and somehow failed to wait for the latter. With raw recruits for crews and heavily outgunned, the British commander, fearing that he would "suffer the fate of poor Troubridge in the Mediterranean", decided to engage Spee. Around 5 pm on 1 November, both admirals were surprised to face one another. Spee used his superior speed to keep the range at eighteen kilometres, and he opened fire. two hours later at twelve kilometres. The outcome was never in doubt. *Good Hope*'s magazine blew up after receiving thirty-five direct hits from *Scharnhorst*; *Nürnberg* at point-blank range demolished *Monmouth*; the other two ships escaped under the cover of darkness. Britain lost 1,600 men including Cradock, in what the First Sea Lord termed "the saddest naval action of the war".

The two elderly cruisers constituted the first losses in a hundred years "inflicted on a British squadron in a fair fight". It was, above all, a loss in prestige. Admiral v. Müller not surprisingly reported Wilhelm II to be "in good spirits", and the Kaiser ordered 300 Iron Crosses to be distributed among Spee's men. Vice-Admiral v. Spee was feted in Valparaiso by German residents, but when given roses by a woman, commented acidly that they should be kept for his funeral. He decided to steam to the Falkland Islands in order to destroy the British wireless station at Port Stanley before attempting to reach Germany via the English Channel.

Admiral Fisher was livid. Within six hours of news of Coronel, he ordered Jellicoe to release the battle-cruisers *Invincible* and *Inflexible*. The commander's pleas that this would seriously deplete his cruiser force were brushed aside. When workmen at Devonport failed to outfit the ships for duty in the tropics within the prescribed three days, the irate Fisher ordered them to sea with workmen still on board. Vice-Admiral Sir Doveton Sturdee, whom Fisher had once denounced as a "pedantic ass", was placed in charge of the ships, reinforced by the armoured cruisers *Defence*, *Kent*, *Carnarvon*, and *Cornwall* as well as the light cruisers *Glasgow* and *Bristol*. It was a classic example of overkill, quite in keeping with Fisher's dictum that he desired not to defeat but to annihilate Spee's squadron.

This time luck was with the British. Sturdee arrived at Port Stanley, despite several delays, on precisely the right day; a difference of twenty-four hours in either direction would have caused him to miss Spee. Nature also favoured Sturdee: there was plenty of sea-room, visibility was perfect and eight hours of daylight remained when he sighted the Germans at 9.40 am. Spee, whose ships had travelled 16,000 sm without repairs, had not been warned by Berlin that Fisher had dispatched the two battle-cruisers and, according to Marder, was probably the only person in South America not aware of their presence there. The Germans therefore must have been greatly surprised when they saw the British tripod masts over Port Stanley. Around 1.20 pm on 8 December, the battle-cruisers opened fire at about fourteen kilometres. Two hours later, *Scharnhorst* was listing badly and soon went under; *Gneisenau* was severely pounded at close range and received over fifty hits before also going down with three cheers for the Kaiser. *Nürnberg* and *Leipzig* were tracked down and destroyed; *Dresden* was later caught at Juan Fernandez island. Germany lost 2,200 officers and men, including Spee and his two sons.

Reaction in London was predictably jubilant. Sturdee became the first commander to be rewarded with a baronetcy in this war – even though neither Churchill nor Fisher could bring themselves round to congratulate him on account of personal animosity. The First Lord perhaps best summed up the strategic significance of Falkland when he wrote later that with it "the clearance of the oceans was complete, and soon, except in the land-locked Baltic and Black Seas and in the defended area of the Helgoland Bight, the German flag had ceased to fly on any vessel in any quarter of the world".

In Germany there was widespread consternation. On 11 December, Wilhelm II received Admiral v. Müller in bed and was "very depressed". Loss of the cruisers (as at the Dogger Bank) was blamed on Tirpitz, and the latter was subjected to a "tirade" about "unfortunate warship designs".

Falkland and Dogger Bank clearly indicated that a change in tactics and strategy was needed. These stultifying losses hotly renewed the *Grosskrieg* versus *Kleinkrieg* controversy, with the adherents of the former (the "blue water" school) at least until Jutland maintaining the upper hand. Of course, *guerre de course* tactics had not been ignored in and after August 1914, and it is to this issue that attention must now be turned.

Grand Admiral v. Tirpitz's policy during 1914–15 concerning submarine warfare (the so-called "third dimension") is difficult to follow as it is shifty and marred by the most odious personal character assassinations. Admirals Ingenohl, Pohl, Müller, Holtzendorff, and others were singled out at various times for Tirpitz's verbal abuse – buttressed by that of the group of loyal supporters that the state secretary had over the years cultivated: Eckermann, Hopman, Levetzow, Trotha, Schulze, among others. New titles were invented to smear the so-called "enemies of the fleet" : "Müller – Rasputin, Holtzendorff – the father of the lie, Capelle – Judas Iscariot!" The royal family was recruited by Tirpitz. Crown Prince Wilhelm, Empress Augusta Viktoria, Queen Viktoria of Sweden, and the Grand Duchess of Baden (the Kaiser's aunt) were asked to support Tirpitz's position at Court. Captain Magnus v. Levetzow tried to enlist the Grand Duke of Sachsen-Weimar-Eisenach for similar purposes, caustically complaining : "We are living from hand to mouth, we are playing at war [but are] not directing it." Levetzow's colleague, Captain Adolf v. Trotha, encouraged Lieutenant-Commander Prince Adalbert, Wilhelm's third son, to counsel his father not to rule out a "heroic sacrifice" of the High Sea Fleet. Tirpitz lamented to Trotha that with regard to surface action the Kaiser "completely buries his head in the sand", and Lieutenant-Commander Ernst v. Weizsäcker, hardly a "hawk", sadly noted that fellow officers felt "ashamed" because they had not gone into battle. The upshot of this disquietude was that in the autumn of 1915 Wilhelm II twice sharply reprimanded his naval officers' "detrimental criticism" and repeated "indiscretions" in this issue. "I have created and trained the Fleet. Where, when and how I wish to use it is *exclusively* the Supreme War Lord's business. Everybody else will have to remain silent on this matter and obey." Such language had never before been heard by *Seeoffiziere* from their beloved War Lord.

Tirpitz's position, of course, is critical for a number of reasons. He had given the Navy about seventeen years of uninterrupted leadership and had, with only a small band of loyal aides, decided construction policies almost alone. Moreover, in his bitter fights to prevent the emergence of an Admiralty Staff analogous to that of the Prussian Army's General Staff, Tirpitz had assumed the right to decide German naval strategy, that is, the reliance on the *Entscheidungsschlacht* in the North Sea. At the outbreak of the war, Tirpitz was permitted advisory rights in Admiralty Staff decisions and was invited to join the Imperial Headquarters on the Western Front along with Admirals v. Pohl (Admiralty Staff) and v. Müller (Navy Cabinet). Here the grand admiral from the start clamoured for action against the British. Müller's diary contains numerous references to Tirpitz's insistence that the High Sea Fleet be used for what Müller derisively called "prestige tactics".

Tirpitz had good reason to demand fleet action. His life's work was wrapped up in a fleet that now rusted in port. His position at headquarters was seriously undermined by the Navy's inaction at a time when the German armies were marching through Luxembourg and Belgium into France. Wilhelm II was becoming disenchanted with Tirpitz's pre-war construction policies, especially with regard to overseas cruisers, torpedo-boats and heavy guns. In addition, Tirpitz had lost priority in German armaments to the Army in 1912, and the present predicament was hardly likely to reverse that situation if allowed to continue. "If . . . we come to a peace agreement without the Fleet having bled and achieved something, then we will not get anything more for the Fleet. All the very scarce funds still available will go to the Army."

The continued idleness of the fleet was blamed by Tirpitz on the machinations of Pohl, Müller, Bethmann Hollweg and Wilhelm II. The initial "Fleet Order Nr 1" of 30 July 1914 had instructed Admiral v. Ingenohl to attempt to engage only portions of the enemy by surface encounters, "ruthless mining", and "if possible, also by a submarine offensive". But already by 6 August, when it became clear that the British were not "coming", Admiral v. Pohl and Chancellor v. Bethmann Hollweg managed in conjunction with Wilhelm II and Admiral v. Müller to restrict the fleet's operative freedom "in order to use it as a security at the peace table". It was, after all, to be a short war, over by Christmas. This was to become the official attitude at Imperial Headquarters.

Tirpitz was furious at this development. He attempted to counter it by removing Admirals Ingenohl, Pohl and even Hipper from positions of responsibility, hoping to take over as Chief of the Admiralty Staff himself. On other occasions, Tirpitz even suggested that he be entrusted with the High Sea Fleet, but his age as well as lack of front command (since 1897) militated against such a step. When Ingenohl was replaced as Chief of the High Sea Fleet by Pohl on 2 February 1915, Admiral Gustav Bachmann and not Tirpitz succeeded Pohl at the Admiralty Staff. In jockeying for office, Tirpitz had once more marshalled all possible support: Admiral Prince Heinrich, Crown Prince Wilhelm, General v. Plessen, and General v. Hindenburg.

The loss of the cruisers at Helgoland, the Dogger Bank and the Falkland Islands prompted Tirpitz early in 1915 to speak out against *Kleinkrieg* strategy and to demand instead "a fleet as strong as that of England". To Trotha he confided his unflinching belief that the battleship remained "the main thing for sea power". These ideas were to receive a rude shock in September 1914 and especially in January 1915, when Vice-Admiral Wilhelm v. Lans, head of the First Squadron, concluded in official reports that a battle in the North Sea constituted sheer "madness" and would result in "annihilation" of the German fleet. Tirpitz, naturally, was livid. He described Lans' reports as "poison for the fleet". But Lans' opinion only fortified the determination of Pohl, Müller, Bethmann Hollweg and Wilhelm II not to risk the fleet, and when Pohl in January 1916 succumbed to cancer of the liver, he was replaced not by Tirpitz but by Vice-Admiral Reinhard Scheer. Moreover, according to both General v. Plessen and Admiral v. Müller, Tirpitz in 1914 and again in 1915 had refused command of the High Sea Fleet. The Kaiser would not hear of such an appointment because Tirpitz "had not remained consistent on the subject of engaging the fleet".

Indeed, Tirpitz had not. The above-mentioned instances of Tirpitz's call for fleet action must be balanced against General v. Lyncker's (Chief of the Military Cabinet) diary entry for 19 August 1914: "Admiral v. Tirpitz, who sat next to me at lunch today, found it necessary to justify the passive waiting game played by the fleet." In addition to the reasons already stated, Tirpitz called for action partly to maintain morale in the High Sea Fleet as many young officers were asking for transfers to the Army, the submarine command and the air wing in order to end their boredom. Yet in his heart of hearts Tirpitz must have known that a naval Armageddon in the North Sea would have entailed certain disaster. Therefore his vacillating stance on *Grosskrieg* versus *Kleinkrieg* must be seen as an attempt to keep a foot in either camp until events forced him to choose between the two.

What was Tirpitz's attitude towards submarine warfare? We have seen that in 1913–14 he had opposed Admiral v. Pohl's *guerre de course* plans, had objected to U-boats participating in winter fleet manoeuvres, had limited the submarine budget in 1913 to 15 million GM, had placed these craft under a low-ranking (lieutenant-commander) officer, and had rejected a vast submarine offensive against Britain as late as June 1914. The state secretary repeated his opposition to submarine warfare to Pohl on 8 August and again on 9 November 1914, as well as on 6 January 1915. Twenty-one days later, he informed Bethmann Hollweg that he favoured postponement of any submarine offensive until the summer of 1915, when Germany would possess sufficient U-boats.

Others seconded this policy – though obviously for different reasons. Admiralty Staff, Foreign Office and chancellor in November–December 1914 feared "severe violation of international law" in the event of unrestricted submarine warfare. Weizsäcker described an underwater offensive as a *va banque* gamble, to be used only as a last resort. But events at the front worked against such restraint. On 5 September 1914, *U 21* sank the British cruiser *Pathfinder* off the Firth of Forth, raising hopes that the submersible might play a major role in the war.

In the meantime, Lieutenant Otto Weddingen's elderly *U 9* had unsuccessfully attempted to intercept and destroy British troop transports across the Channel. Malfunction in the gyrocompass and a severe storm had driven Weddingen off course, and when he surfaced on 22 September to recharge his batteries, he suddenly saw the masts of three armoured cruisers. They turned out to be the *Hogue, Cressy* and *Aboukir* of the *Bacchante* class, referred to in the Royal Navy as the "live-bait squadron". The storm and a missed Admiralty signal had deprived the vessels of destroyer escort in the "Broad Fourteens". At 6.20 am Weddingen fired a single torpedo almost at point-blank range at *Aboukir*. The ship began to list and her captain, believing that he had struck a mine, called the other two ships over to rescue his crew. Weddingen submerged to reload, and at 6.55 am he fired both bow torpedoes at *Hogue*, which began to sink so fast that *U 9* had to veer off in order to avoid a collision. Though her batteries were now almost exhausted, *U 9* again submerged and manoeuvred into position to fire the two stern torpedoes at *Cressy*. The latter's skipper managed to avoid only one of the torpedoes aimed at him, but Weddingen had taken care to reload one of his bow tubes and now delivered the *coup de grâce* to the third armoured cruiser. It was the most spectacular action in the annals of submarine warfare : three, albeit elderly, armoured cruisers had been destroyed in about one hour with the loss of 1,459 men. Britain was shocked, and for Germany the stigma of the Helgoland Bight disaster was partly erased. Admiral v. Müller reported the Kaiser to be "in seventh heaven".

Nor was the success of *U 9* an isolated case. In October 1914, *U 26* destroyed the Russian armoured cruiser *Pallada* in the Gulf of Finland, while *U 27* on the last day of that month torpedoed the British seaplane-carrier *Hermes* off Calais; early in January 1915, *U 24* sent the British battleship *Formidable* to the bottom off Portland. German submarine losses, on the other hand, amounted to seven boats in the North Sea during the first six months of the war.

These U-boat successes greatly encouraged the adherents of *guerre de course*. Pohl re-opened the U-boat question, and on 7 November recommended to Bethmann Hollweg that a blockade of Britain be established. London's decision to close the Dover–Calais Straits, to patrol the Atlantic traffic along the Hebrides – Faeroes – Iceland line and thereby to transform the North Sea into a "dead sea", prompted submarine commander Hermann Bauer in October and again in December to call for undersea raids along the British coast. He received endorsement especially from Vice-Admiral Scheer, chief of the Second Squadron, in two memoranda of 20 November and 7 December 1914. In the first of these, Scheer envisaged submarine warfare primarily as a means of luring the Grand Fleet from its northern lair; the second report, however, stressed the submarine's importance as a commerce raider. Albert Ballin, director of the Hamburg–America Line, demanded "the most brutal . . . submarine blockade", and a group of Berlin university professors added their prestige to the clamour for this type of warfare.

Fleet and Admiralty Staff in January 1915 supported similar proposals, and at a conference at Pless on 1 February 1915, it was decided to commence undersea warfare. Admiral v. Tirpitz was also coming round because the U-boat might take attention away from the recent surface disasters. As early as November 1914, he had sounded out the European representative of the American Hearst newspaper empire (Wiegand) on United States reaction to a possible German undersea offensive ("If pressed to the utmost, why not?"). And in a dramatic *volte-face* on 25 January 1915, Tirpitz informed Müller that "successes" against the Grand Fleet "are hardly probable", and instead called for airship attacks on London, cruiser warfare in the Atlantic ("I can promise an unqualified success from a cruiser war"), and submarine warfare against Britain's vital maritime commerce.

Germany placed its confidence in an incredibly small force. A mere twenty-nine U-boats were available for front duty early in 1915; most of these were armed with only six torpedoes, not all had been fitted with deck guns, fourteen were elderly petrol boats, and the *UC 1* series of minelayers had neither torpedo tubes nor guns. German construction was slow. Only fifteen boats came to the front in 1915; by May the U-boats had received deck guns. During the course of that year, Germany lost twenty-seven vessels through various causes, and by the end of 1915 a mere fifty-four U-boats were in service. It should also be remembered that not even in 1917 did the Reich manage to achieve a ratio of 1:3 in terms of submarine service as opposed to maintenance. The larger submarines were able to stay on station at most twenty days (by the end of the year, thirty-five days), with a cruising radius of 2,000 to 2,500 sm (later 3,600 sm). Moreover, torpedo hits amounted to but 40 per cent in 1915 and 50 per cent in 1917. Therefore it is not surprising that during the months of relatively unrestricted submarine warfare (March and April 1915), only 115,839 tons of Allied shipping were destroyed. And as, in the following period, monthly sinkings amounted to about 130,000 tons, Bethmann Hollweg and Müller in particular returned to the idea of submarine warfare according to prize regulations (*Prisenordnung*).

The undersea campaign, started on 28 February 1915 in waters around the British Isles and in April in the Baltic, encountered its primary opposition not from the Royal Navy but from powerful neutrals, especially the United States. During the course of 1915, there were no less than six major incidents of U-boats attacking vessels carrying passengers from neutral countries: *Falaba* (*U 28*), *Katwijk* (*UB 10*), *Lusitania* (*U 20*), *Arabic* (*U 24*), *Belridge* (*U 16*), and *Admiral Canteaume* (*U 24*). In particular, the sinking of the *Lusitania* on 7 May with the loss of 1,200 passengers, including 128 Americans, caused a rift between Bethmann Hollweg and Müller, on the one side, and Tirpitz and Bachmann on the other. Whereas the British denounced unrestricted submarine warfare as "a procedure hitherto limited to savage races making no pretence at civilization as understood in Europe", the Imperial Navy regarded it as "the only effective weapon against England". When the Berlin government on 5 June ordered all U-boat commanders not to sink large passenger liners on sight, Tirpitz and Bachmann angrily submitted their resignations. Wilhelm II, "in a towering rage", talked about "felony" and "downright military conspiracy initiated by Tirpitz". He accepted Bachmann's resignation immediately, replacing him with Admiral Henning v. Holtzendorff, a known opponent of Tirpitz.

The submarine offensive brought a new crisis in August when *U 24* torpedoed the British liner *Arabic* off Ireland with the loss of forty passengers, including three Americans. A sharp protest note from Washington on 30 August resulted in virtual cancellation of unrestricted undersea warfare by 18 September 1915, after what Müller termed "a battle royal". Tirpitz's position continued to decline: the state secretary had already been removed from Imperial

Headquarters and his advisory rights to the Admiralty Staff were now rescinded. Throughout the winter of 1915–16, however, Tirpitz worked tirelessly for resumption of U-boat warfare. The submarines had in 1915 destroyed 748,000 tons of British shipping, but new construction in Britain and the Empire in that year amounted to 1.3 million tons. Admiral v. Holtzendorff, who in 1914 had believed that the High Sea Fleet would reduce the Empire "to rubble", and who had come to the Admiralty Staff with the statement: "Believe me, gentlemen, you will not scratch the whale's [Britain] skin with your U-boat war", now recanted and joined Tirpitz. On 30 December he informed the state secretary and General v. Falkenhayn that in 1916 the U-boats would be able to sink 600,000 tons of shipping per month and that, were the undersea campaign to commence in March, it could bring a victorious end to the war in 1916. Holtzendorff repeated this argument in a discussion with Bethmann Hollweg on 7 January 1916, and in an Admiralty Staff paper of 12 February 1916. Such a campaign would restore "the wavering belief of the German people in the necessity of a strong Navy", and spread the hope of "victory in the next war". In particular, the argument that Germany's allies, Austria–Hungary and Turkey, could not conduct the war beyond 1916, won the day; unrestricted submarine warfare was resumed on 23 February 1916.

However, the Kaiser desired to avoid a repeat of the *Lusitania* incident and accordingly ordered that only *armed* freighters were to be torpedoed without warning. Tirpitz, who was no longer consulted on major policy decisions, tendered his resignation on Kaiser Wilhelm I's anniversary. It was accepted on 10 March 1916 by Wilhelm II with the caustic comment: "He is leaving the sinking ship." That same day, a weary Wilhelm confided to Müller: "One must never utter it nor shall I admit it to Falkenhayn, but this war will not end with a great victory." And the monarch's worst fears were soon realized: on 24 March, the small coastal submersible *UB 29* sank the French liner *Sussex* off Boulogne, again with loss of American life. A sharp protest from Washington on 20 April prompted the Berlin government to end the undersea offensive, and Scheer, believing that nothing could be accomplished under the rules of prize law, recalled all Fleet submarines. Herewith unrestricted submarine warfare ended ("catastrophic submission to America") to all intents and purposes. Only the Flanders boats and those in the Mediterranean (since June 1915 based at Cattaro) continued to operate *à outrance*. The total bag during the five months of 1916 had been 131 ships of 442,000 tons; the Reich lost 7 U-boats, while 34 new ones were completed.

The high figure of 141,000 tons destroyed in April 1916, of course, fell far short of Holtzendorff's promised 600,000 tons. In fact, it proved to be a monstrous psychological mistake to set a final victory deadline, and Holtzendorff quickly came to regret it. Max Weber at Heidelberg in March warned the Admiralty Staff that the figure was too high. Careful checking revealed that Holtzendorff had erred in believing that Britain possessed only 11 million tons of shipping by counting only British vessels; with her Empire and Dominions, Britain in reality had 11,328 ships of over 21 million tons. The roughly 2.5 million tons of German shipping seized in 1914 should have been added to this, as well as United States ship-building for Britain. Therefore, Holtzendorff's calculations that if Germany could destroy an average of 600,000 tons per month for a period of six months, and if about one-third of the 3 million tons of neutral shipping could be frightened off the seas, then Britain would lose 39 per cent of her tonnage – and thus the war – proved to be greatly in error. Bodo Herzog has shown that Britain's daily needs of 15,000 tons of cereals could be delivered by four ships, that not even the supply of oats for racehorses was jeopardized, and that mild rationing was introduced only in 1918, when the corner had been turned in the U-boat war. Finally, of the sixty-three German submersibles available in January 1916, only ten were large craft attached to the High Sea Fleet and available for service west of the British Isles.

The unrestricted submarine campaign had been blunted primarily by United States reaction to the indiscriminate sinking of passenger liners rather than to British antidotes. It was only in December 1914 that the Admiralty formed the Submarine Attack Committee, transformed in September 1915 into the Submarine Committee. Speed and zigzagging had been viewed as the best protection against submarines, but additional means were now sought. Some of these bordered on the fantastic: sea-gulls trained to perch on periscopes in order to make them visible; strong swimmers armed with sharp hammers to pierce U-boat hulls; ships armed with hammers to smash periscopes and canvas bags to "blind" the submarine. However, more realistic proposals also emerged: single sweeps, paravane sweeps, indicator nets, mines, and the like. These, in turn, prompted Berlin in April 1915 to order U-boats to reach western waters by way of rounding Scotland, which added seven days to the time required to reach the Irish Sea. As the U-boats carried relatively few torpedoes, they destroyed early in 1915 about one-half of their victims with deck guns which, in turn, prompted London to arm merchants usually with two 4.7 in guns. By April 1916, over 1,100 Allied ships had been thus armed and results were quickly discernible : between January 1916 and January 1917, among unarmed ships, 68 per cent of those attacked were destroyed; among armed ships, 3.9 per cent were sent to the bottom by submarine gunfire.

About 180 tramp steamers were also fitted with concealed guns to serve as "special service vessels" designed to lure a U-boat to the surface because they were too small to waste a torpedo on. These "Q-ships" were later highly romanticized, but they accounted for only eleven submarines (7 per cent of those destroyed); 27 "Q-ships" were lost to submarines at sea. More promising was the hydrophone designed to detect the U-boat's propeller beat, and the depth charge filled with TNT or Amatol. However, neither of these devices reached the front in sizeable quantities until mid-1917. Convoy, as we shall see, was introduced only after Germany again resumed unrestricted submarine warfare on 1 February 1917.

Among the "Q-ships", the *Baralong* gained notoriety in August 1915 when, flying the United States flag, she surprised Lieutenant-Commander Wegener destroying the freighter *Nicosian*, and killed eleven of *U 27*'s crew including her skipper. However, the principal British weapon in the war at sea remained the long-distance blockade; neutrals were submitted to search in the Downs and at Kirkwall. Differences between absolute (military) and conditional (fuel, food, clothing) contraband had been erased by 1915; all neutral goods having an ultimate enemy destination were seized; and imports to countries bordering on Germany were rationed. Lord Robert Cecil in February 1916 became head of the new Ministry of Blockade. As the First Sea Lord, Admiral Sir Henry Jackson, crudely put it, "this war will make history and we need not be too particular about precedents". For the Grand Fleet, the process of slow strangulation of Germany's civilian populace was a poor substitute for a "second Trafalgar", but both government and Foreign Office remained adamant in maintaining the "anaemic blockade".

Denied operative freedom in the North Sea and barred from the Atlantic, Germany undertook several raids into the Baltic Sea between 1914 and 1916. Grand Admiral Prince Heinrich commanded 9 cruisers and 11 torpedo-boats against Vice-Admiral Nikolai v. Essen's Russian flotilla of 5 elderly battleships, 6 battle-cruisers, 6 armoured cruisers, 77 destroyers, and 20 submarines. According to Bernd Stegemann, Germany did not place a high value on the Baltic Sea as a major theatre of war – other than to assure continued deliveries of Swedish iron ore. However, Prince Heinrich hoped to entice isolated units of the Russian Fleet into annihilation by "keen sorties" – a policy similar to that adopted for the North Sea. This proved to be a costly enterprise owing to the heavy mining of these waters. The armoured cruiser *Friedrich Carl* and the light cruiser *Magdeburg* had been lost in the Baltic in 1914; a raid into the Gulf of Riga in May 1915, on the other hand, netted German torpedo-boats several draft-eligible males as well as the mirrors of the lighthouse on Runö Island. The general advance of the German armies into Courland, and specifically the capture of Libau (Liepaja) in the same month, forced the Navy to assume administration of Libau and Memel (Klaipeda). Admiral v. Pohl in February 1915 thought briefly of reopening the Sound and Belts off Denmark and stationing modern battleships in the Baltic Sea in order to outflank the "easily guarded angle of the Helgoland Bight", but the mounting danger in the Baltic quickly dispelled this notion.

British submarines were by now in the Baltic, and German sorties against the Russian coast became increasingly dangerous. In October 1915, the armoured cruiser *Prinz Adalbert* fell prey to *E 8* off Libau; in November the light cruiser *Undine* was destroyed by *E 19*; and in December the light cruiser *Bremen* sank after striking mines off Windau (Ventspils). These losses, in turn, forced Prince Heinrich to withdraw from the Baltic the five battleships of the *Wittelsbach* class – which had been temporarily assigned to him – as well as the armoured cruiser *Roon*. As a parallel to the recent successful raid against the Dover patrol, eleven of the newest torpedo-boats were sent in November against Reval (Tallinn) – despite their inadequacy as assault batteries and the absence of military targets within their range. The upshot was that seven of these vessels were lost on minefields. There were to be no further "tip-and-run" operations in the Baltic Sea until October 1917.

A number of contingency operations plans were developed during this period, but never carried out. A possible occupation of the Netherlands (Case K) was ruled out so long as Germany received the Belgian coast for future use. Denmark, on the other hand, offered a more suitable venue. Rumania's entry into the war on the side of the Allies in August 1916 aroused some fears in Berlin that Denmark might follow suit, and Holtzendorff, Prince Heinrich and

Scheer at once drafted plans to seize all of Jutland as well as the islands up to the line Isefjord–Stigsnäs in case of war. This was formally adopted as "Case J" in May 1917. A blockade of the Swedish coast (Case S) was also worked out in the event of her joining the Entente. Finally, "Case N" called in 1916–17 for the possible occupation of Norway. Prince Heinrich, in particular, desired this position – along with Jutland – as "the necessary elbowroom" in order "to keep the passages to the Ocean open in the future". Cases "J" and "N" in particular reflected the growing German awareness that ready access to the Atlantic could alone provide the Reich with sea power in the true meaning of the term. These two plans are obviously the forerunners of Operation *Weserübung* in April 1940.

The Flanders theatre of war should not be overlooked. The Imperial Navy on 29 August 1914, acting on Tirpitz's recommendation, created a special Navy Infantry Division under Admiral Ludwig v. Schröder in occupied Flanders. Schröder's force was placed under Army Supreme Command (OHL), and in November 1914 added a second, and in June 1917 a third division of infantry, while headquarters for the Corps were situated in Brügge (Brugge). The first German U-boat arrived in Zeebrügge (Zeebrugge) on 9 November, and a naval air station and shipyard were established there in December; additional yards were centred round Brügge and Ostende (Oostende) in the fall of 1916, and Ghent in the spring of 1917. Especially the small UB and UC craft were stationed in Flanders, where they were assembled after overland transport from Germany. Schröder also had to defend the 50 km strip in Flanders against British sea assaults; most spectacularly, Rear-Admiral Keyes in April 1918 attacked Zeebrugge and Ostend to make them unusable by German U-boats, and although three block-ships were sunk at Zeebrugge, it was not possible to block the harbour channel completely.

By May 1915, heavy navy guns ranging between 15 cm and 38 cm calibre were installed in Flanders. The 38 cm guns had a range of 138 kilometres at optimum elevation, but took about six weeks to be installed either on concrete battlements or on railway carriages. Moreover, they could easily be spotted from the air and their detonation could be heard as much as ten kilometres away. This notwithstanding, during General Ludendorff's vaunted "Michael" offensive in the spring of 1918, seven 21 cm guns fired

on Paris from Laon (125 km). However, the Allied counter-offensive
forced the Navy Infantry Corps into action, and on 15 October
1918 the Army ordered the evacuation of Flanders. Admiral v.
Schröder's troops had suffered 10,000 casualties, but the "Lion of
Flanders" was ready in November 1918 to march against rebellious
sailors in German ports.

There remained the Mediterranean Sea. In February 1915, Britain
and France (with Russian support in the Black Sea) decided upon
a naval assault against the Dardanelles. This was later changed to
an amphibious landing in this region – despite Lord Nelson's dictum
that "any sailor who attacked a fort was a fool". It was a brilliantly
conceived plan by the First Lord and the "Easterners" against the
"soft underbelly" of Europe in order to force Turkey out of the
war, relieve the Serbs and the Russians, exert pressure upon the
Austro–Hungarian armies, and end the dreary "slogging match" on
the Western Front. And while this is certainly not the place to
analyse the Dardanelles campaign of 1915–16, a few words are in
order upon Germany's role in it.

The German military adviser to Turkey, General Liman v.
Sanders, who had come to the Porte in 1913 and who now com-
manded the Fifth Turkish Army, had developed an intricate defence
system : ten lines of about 300 mines between Chanak and Cape
Helles Narrows, intermediate artillery batteries on land consisting
of about 100 pieces, and mobile howitzers at the main forts (Kum
Kale, Sedd el Bahr, Orkanie, and Cape Helles). The battle-cruiser
Goeben was kept in the Sea of Marmora as a last defence owing to
the crushing naval superiority of the Anglo–French coalition; the
Turkish Fleet consisting of 3 dated battleships, 2 cruisers and 10
destroyers would have to bear the brunt of any naval assault, including possible attack by the 7 pre-Dreadnoughts and 2 armoured
cruisers of the Tsar's Black Sea Fleet. On paper, the German–
Turkish position was hopeless.

The initial Allied attack on the Straits was set for 19 February
1915, the anniversary of Admiral Sir John Duckworth's costly
passage of the Dardanelles in 1807. As is well known, five major
naval bombardments by the Dreadnought *Queen Elizabeth*, the
battleships *Lord Nelson* and *Agamemnon*, and the battle-cruiser
Inflexible by early March failed to reduce the forts. Admiral Sir
Sackville Carden was replaced by Admiral Sir John De Robeck,
who on 18 March decided to have a "real good try" at the

Dardanelles. Lord Kitchener and the "Westerners" in London had meanwhile agreed to release 18,000 men, the French a further 18,000, and the Australian and New Zealand governments 34,100. The Russians, for their part, not only refused to permit three Greek divisions to attack Gallipoli, but also declined to send their own detachment of 47,600 men until Constantinople had fallen. A paranoid fear of the *Goeben* and *Breslau* in the Sea of Marmora partly evoked this response.

A task force of twenty-three Allied battleships and fifteen cruisers opened the attack on the Narrows – the tenth – at 11.15 am on 18 March 1915, and before the day was over the battleships *Bouvet, Irresistible, Ocean, Gaulois* and *Suffren* and the battle-cruiser *Inflexible* were rendered *hors de combat*. The Turkish Navy lost two battleships, including the *Heireddin Barbarossa* (formerly *Kurfürst Friedrich Wilhelm*). The Germans played an important role in the defence of the Straits. In addition to Admiral v. Usedom's forces manning the coastal batteries and mines, machine-gun detachments from the *Goeben* and *Breslau* in May 1915 bolstered the German–Turkish defence; German crews had also been placed on the gunboat *Muavenet* which, on 13 May, torpedoed the battleship *Goliath*. At various times, between six and eleven German and Austro–Hungarian submarines were in Turkish waters; three small UB boats had been brought to Pola on the Adriatic by land, assembled there, and then towed by Austro–Hungarian cruisers through the Straits of Otranto on their way to the Dardanelles. It was not in vain. Lieutenant Otto Hersing's *U 21* on 25 May torpedoed the battleship *Triumph*, and two days later the battleship *Majestic*.

The ill-fated Gallipoli campaign brought about the dismissals of both Churchill and Fisher ("it's like Beethoven deaf"), and the establishment of a coalition government in London on 25 May 1915. Allied losses, in addition to the six battleships mentioned, amounted to 20,000 assault troops, and in December 1915 the entire project was liquidated.

Nor were Allied prospects elsewhere in the Mediterranean and contiguous waters commensurate with their crushing battleship superiority (roughly 40:12). Allied jealousy and petty rivalry prevented success against the small Austro–Hungarian Fleet under Admiral Anton Baron v. Haus. Italian naval forces were stationed in the south at Otranto (battleships) and at Brindisi (light craft), and the obvious strategy was to block the Straits of Otranto through a combined Anglo–French–Italian effort – after Rome declared war against Vienna on 23 May 1915. Yet nothing of the sort happened. Instead, the Austrians destroyed two Italian cruisers and three torpedo-boats in the first months of the war, prompting the Italians to issue orders forbidding heavy ships to leave port. Not only were no raids on Cattaro and Pola undertaken, but the so-called blockade of the Straits proved to be a sieve. German U-boats easily slipped through the indicator nets or dived below them, even though at the narrowest point the Straits were only forty-five miles wide and patrolled by over 300 craft. The three Allies operated their ships as independent units despite the appointment of the French Vice-Admiral Dartige du Fournet as Allied commander. The British Admiral Sir Herbert Richmond unleashed his anger to the Admiralty : "These folks [Italians] deserve to lose, for by Heaven they do nothing towards trying to win." At another trying moment, Richmond advised that "they had better sell their Fleet & take up their organs & monkeys again, for, by Heaven, that seems more their profession than sea-fighting". His colleague, Admiral Sir Arthur Limpus at Malta, shared this attitude and, while he deplored the inability of the French to do "hard, practical, dogged sea patrol work", he wrote of the Italians that "they are *children* at the game of the sea compared to the French". The Allies paid the price for this disunity : Admiral du Fournet lost the armoured cruiser *Léon Gambetta*, and the Italian Vice-Admiral Prince Luigi di Savoya the armoured cruisers *Amalfi* and *Giuseppi Garibaldi*.

German submarines first came to the Adriatic in June 1915, with five craft based at Pola. They were officially attached to the Austro–Hungarian Navy and flew the red-white-red ensign. After Italy's declaration of war against the Reich on 28 August 1916, Berlin increased its submarine forces at Pola and Cattaro to 29 units, and to 39 in 1917. In all, 55 German submersibles were stationed in the Mediterranean theatre; 16 were lost in the Great War (11 in 1918). As in Flanders, the small boats were shipped overland in sections and assembled at Pola. There were neither proper docks nor repair facilities available at Pola, Cattaro or Constantinople, yet sinkings in the autumn of 1915 alone amounted to 92 Allied ships, while 75 were added to this during the first five months of 1916. The most successful single sortie of either world war was undertaken by Lieutenant Lothar v. Arnauld de la Perière with *U 35* between 26 July and 20 August 1916 in the Mediterranean. He destroyed 29 enemy steamers and 25 sailships of 90,350 tons, and returned to

Cattaro out of torpedoes and shells, and almost on the last drop of diesel fuel. Other famous German commanders in the *Mittelmeer* included Lieutenants Karl Dönitz, Wilhelm Canaris and Martin Niemöller.

The German submarines preyed primarily upon the huge tonnage required to maintain 400,000 British troops in Egypt and Gallipoli as well as 200,000 Allied soldiers stationed in Salonika in order to stem the collapse of Serbia after Bulgaria joined the Central Powers in October 1915. The success of the U-boats is even more surprising if one remembers that at any given time only six or seven craft were on station over more than one million square miles of seas, and that not until June 1917 did Berlin create a centralized command for its forces in the Mediterranean. It was strictly on account of these twenty or thirty submarines that Britain – despite the presence of an Allied armada of about 490 ships – in March 1916 had to reroute her Far Eastern shipping from the Suez Canal round the Cape of Good Hope.

These accomplishments in the south were not generally appreciated in Berlin. Admiral v.Müller's diary contains only tangential allusions to affairs in the *Mittelmeer*. Perhaps the entry of three European nations (Italy, Rumania and Bulgaria) into the war overshadowed Gallipoli, but in any event the North Sea remained the focal point of the war at sea to a generation of naval officers raised in the Tirpitzean tradition. Moreover, the art of generalship had by February 1916 reached its nadir with General v. Falkenhayn's penetrating analysis that Germany, with a population of almost 25 million more than France, could "bleed" the latter "white" with a kill ratio of 1 : 1 before Verdun.

The German High Sea Fleet, in the meantime, was expected to undertake some sort of action in order to pin down British forces at home. Vice-Admiral Scheer ventured between 5 and 7 March 1916 with a force of thirty heavy units to the most southerly position in the Hoofden that the fleet ever attempted. Net gain : two fishing smacks. The Grand Fleet had been out at sea, but no contact was made. The British, in turn, on 25–26 March launched a seaplane raid against Zeppelin bases at Tondern. The sortie was supported by Beatty's battle-cruisers and behind them stood the Grand Fleet, but even though Beatty tarried in German waters for twenty-seven hours, there was no response other than a tardy scouting sweep by Vice-Admiral Hipper that did not advance beyond Sylt.

It was now Scheer's turn once more. On 24–25 April he put out
to sea with twenty-two capital ships and twelve light cruisers in the
direction of Lowestoft and Yarmouth. It is not clear what his intentions were, but the raid was designed to coincide with a planned
uprising in Ireland on Easter Sunday. The scouting forces were
under Rear-Admiral Friedrich Boedicker as Hipper was ill, and
were soon without the *Seydlitz* which struck a mine near Norderney.
At about 3.50 am, Boedicker's ships sighted Commodore Tyrwhitt's
Harwich Force of three light cruisers and eighteen destroyers.
Scheer stood about seventy miles off near Terschelling; Beatty's
battle-cruisers had left Rosyth at midnight, heading south in heavy
seas. Tyrwhitt failed to draw the Germans into action (having sent
Beatty and Jellicoe urgent signals), and Boedicker proceeded to shell
Lowestoft and then Yarmouth as planned. By about 4.50 am,
Boedicker rejoined the Second Scouting Force with four light
cruisers that had mauled Tyrwhitt's flagship *Conquest* during a
brief skirmish. It was a heaven-sent opportunity. The "tip-and-run"
raid now promised to turn into a turkey-shoot: Boedicker's four
battle-cruisers and four light cruisers, supported by two flotillas of
torpedo-boats and submarines, had cut off Tyrwhitt's weaker force
of three light cruisers and eighteen destroyers. The German Navy
had sought such an opportunity ever since "Fleet Order Nr 1" of
30 July 1914. The Helgoland Bight action of August 1914 loomed
in reverse. Instead, lamely arguing that Tyrwhitt's force possessed
greater speed and probably suspecting that Beatty's "sea cavalry"
was behind the screen, Boedicker at 4.55 am turned away and
headed home. Scheer proceeded to do the same with the fleet about
thirty minutes later. Tyrwhitt doggedly maintained contact with
the German scouting forces until the Admiralty recalled him at
8.40 am. Professor Marder aptly summed it up: "The raid was
hardly a brilliant exploit, whether from the point of view of strategy,
tactics, or results."

The Royal Navy on 4 May attempted once more to lure the High
Sea Fleet out of its Jade basin. The "bait" consisted of two seaplane-carriers and four light cruisers as well as supporting craft.
The Grand Fleet by dawn steamed off the Skagerrak, with the
battle-cruisers further south; mines had been strewn across Scheer's
most probable route, and seven British submarines lay in wait for
him off Horn Reefs (southern Jutland). All but one of the eleven
seaplanes failed to take off from the choppy seas, but the vital issue
was whether Scheer would leave port. Jellicoe was to be sadly

disappointed once more. He waited in vain for Scheer from dawn until early afternoon. With fuel supplies running low, and adamantly opposed to any fleet action at night, Jellicoe and Beatty ("with a sad heart") headed home. Scheer finally appeared at 3 pm, and swept the seas as far north as Sylt, but the British had departed.

There reigned utter frustration and depression in the Grand Fleet after this futile sortie into the Skagerrak. Jellicoe agreed as a result of Scheer's two raids against the British coast to detach eight capital ships to Sheerness. First priority was now given to the outer defences of the Firth of Forth in order to make Rosyth a primary base for the Grand Fleet (which it became in April 1918). In the meantime, boredom in the northern anchorages was partly relieved by scheduling films, plays, concerts, lectures, and sporting events such as golf, soccer, boxing, fishing, and the like. The Royal Navy's *matériel* was also enhanced : thirteen Dreadnoughts had been added since the outbreak of war, elevating the total to thirty-three; one battle-cruiser raised Beatty's force to ten. In terms of strategy, Jellicoe was slowly and grudgingly accepting the slow-starvation principle of the distant blockade, thereby curbing the burning desire for a "second Trafalgar". He would not, as he wrote to the Admiralty in April 1916, "risk unduly the heavy ships of the Grand Fleet in any attempt to hasten the end of the High Sea Fleet" under unfavourable conditions. The commander may well have consoled himself with Admiral George Rodney's comment after he had been accused of not having pursued the French with sufficient vigour in April 1782 : " 'Tis provoking, but never mind it; their fate is only delayed a short time, for have it they must and shall."

Vice-Admiral Scheer's predicament across the North Sea was much more critical. Only five Dreadnoughts had been added to the fleet since 1914, raising it to eighteen, while the battle-cruiser force had been increased by one unit (another compensated for the loss of the *Blücher*). Moreover, only one battle-cruiser (*Hindenburg*) was being built in May 1916. And pressure for naval action mounted steadily at a time when the Army was making incredible sacrifices before the Verdun salient. Baron Curt v. Maltzahn summed up the prevailing mood of many Germans : "Even if today large parts of our battle fleet . . . [were lying] at the bottom of the sea, our fleet would have accomplished more than it does now by lying well preserved in our ports." Even Vice-Admiral Hipper, who had earlier opposed Tirpitz's frenzied calls for action as a crass attempt to placate parliament in this matter, on 27 May 1916 warned that the

SWEEPING THE NORTH SEA.

CHORUS OF GERMAN ADMIRALS. "STILL NO SIGN OF THE BRITISH SKULKERS!"

fleet would have to pay the price for its lack of action. "For this reason alone, I wish that we may soon be able to do battle." The unkindest cut of all was a popular slogan scrawled upon walls in Wilhelmshaven : "Dear Fatherland, you may rest assured; the Fleet lies in the harbours – moored" (*Lieb' Vaterland, magst ruhig sein, die Flotte schläft im Hafen ein*).

Perhaps to overcome this mood, Scheer planned yet another raid against England for 17 May 1916. Submarines had been recalled from unrestricted undersea warfare on 25 April, and were available to the fleet. Scheer decided to send his scouting forces against Sunderland as bait : U-boats would lie off the Firth of Forth and wait for Beatty to race out to meet Hipper, while the latter would, in turn, attempt to lure Beatty's remaining forces into Scheer's arms about fifty miles off Scarborough. Dirigibles would accompany the sortie in force in order to warn Scheer before Jellicoe could arrive at the scene with the Grand Fleet (which the Germans had absolutely no desire to test).

On 17 May, the German commander ordered nineteen U-boats into the waters between Norway and Rosyth (*U 74* sank on the way out), but delays in repairing the *Seydlitz* forced postponement of the sortie to 23 May. Yet further delays in getting the battle-cruiser ready caused Scheer to call off the operation until 29 May. Time was now of the essence. The U-boats had a maximum endurance of twenty days at sea, and Scheer had given them orders to leave their stations on 1 June, if no fleet action had resulted by then. *Seydlitz* was finally ready on the 29th, but heavy gales precluded the egress of the five airships, the "eyes" of the fleet. The winds continued unabated on 30 May, and Scheer was faced with an indefinite postponement of the operation. Instead, he came up with an alternative plan that did not depend upon aerial reconnaissance. Rather than shell the British coast, he decided to send Hipper's Scouting Forces up the Danish coast into the Skagerrak as the requisite bait. This would almost certainly bring out the Grand Fleet, which had to pass the U-boat lines in these waters and engage Scheer (should he decide to accept battle) near his bases and minefields. The airships would join his task force should the weather clear up. Finally, an operation near home waters would permit Scheer to take the slow *Deutschland* class ships along.

At 2.00 am on 31 May 1916, the German Scouting Forces with Vice-Admiral Hipper on *Lützow* put out to sea; Scheer on board *Friedrich der Grosse* followed at 3.30 am. In all, 16 Dreadnoughts, 5 battle-cruisers, 11 light cruisers, and 61 torpedo-boats left their Jade and Elbe sanctuaries that morning.

IX

Jutland 1916

Missed Opportunity or
Fortunate Escape?

Admiral Jellicoe left Scapa Flow on *Iron Duke* at 11.30 pm
(German time) on 30 May 1916 – 180 minutes before Hipper
weighed anchor in the Jade river – with 24 Dreadnoughts, 3 battle-
cruisers, 8 armoured cruisers, 12 light cruisers, and 51 destroyers.
Thirty minutes later, Vice-Admiral Beatty on *Lion* steamed out of
the Firth of Forth with 4 Dreadnoughts, 6 battle-cruisers, 14 light
cruisers, 27 destroyers, and the seaplane-carrier *Engadine*. The
two forces had been ordered out by the Admiralty, which again
had intercepted and deciphered the German special code word, to
a point about 100 miles east of Aberdeen and 90 miles west of the
Naze at the entrance to the Skagerrak, "ready for eventualities".
This time, however, Jellicoe decided not to concentrate his forces
and to have Beatty about 70 miles south-east of the Grand Fleet.
Nor did the Admiralty deem it necessary to order Commodore
Tyrwhitt's Harwich Force out to sea that morning, for fear of the
German torpedo-boats in Flanders.

The two fleets steamed at right angles to, and unaware of, each
other until 2.00 pm on 31 May. The Grand Fleet possessed a
numerical advantage of 37:27 in heavy units – 37:21 in modern
capital ships – and 113:72 in light support craft. The British
advantage in heavy guns is clear, if not precise: Marder claims a
272:200 ratio; Peter Padfield 324:196. In addition, Jellicoe's ships
had a 2:1 superiority (400,000 lb against 200,000 lb) in weight of
broadside. But there was little excitement evident among the Grand
Fleet; there had been too many disappointing sorties since 1914.
As one of Jellicoe's officers on *Iron Duke* put it: "Just another
b—— useless sweep".

By about 3.15 p.m., Beatty and Hipper were roughly fifty miles

11a. *Der Tag.* Surrender of the High Sea Fleet, 21 November 1918. HMS *Queen Elizabeth* leading the way

11b. Interned German ships at Scapa Flow

12. Scuttled *Bayern* at Scapa Flow

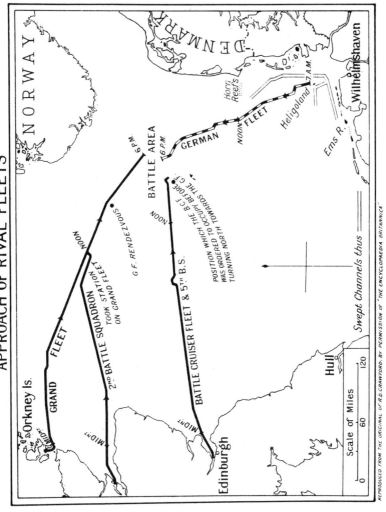

APPROACH OF RIVAL FLEETS

NORWAY

DENMARK

Wilhelmshaven

Orkney Is.

GRAND FLEET

2ND BATTLE SQUADRON TOOK STATION ON GRAND FLEET

G.F. RENDEZVOUS

BATTLE AREA

GERMAN

NOON FLEET

Horn Reefs

Heligoland

Ems R.

7 A.M.

6 P.M.

16 P.M.

NOON

NOON

BATTLE CRUISER FLEET & 5TH B.S.

POSITION WHICH THE B.C.F. BEFORE WAS ORDERED TO OCCUPY THE TURNING NORTH TOWARDS THE G.F.

Edinburgh

Hull

Swept Channels thus

Scale of Miles

0   60   120

180

"Luxury" Fleet

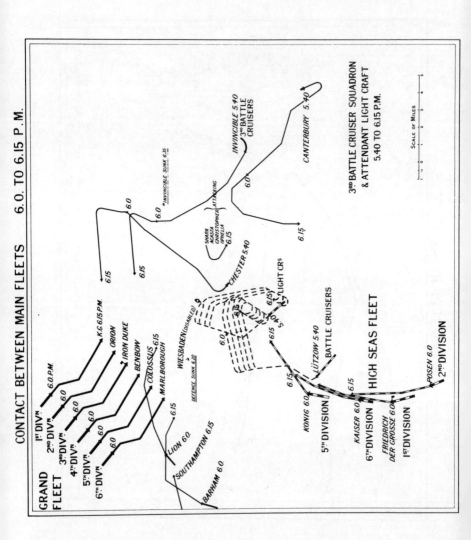

apart. Midway between them lay the Danish steamer *U. Fjord*. The Germans dispatched two large destroyers to investigate the neutral; the latter halted and blew off steam. The British cruisers *Galatae* and *Phaeton* on the right wing of Beatty's Battle-Cruiser Force spotted the action, reported it, and then engaged the two German destroyers as well as the light cruiser *Elbing*. The latter managed to land a shell under the bridge of *Galatae*, thereby drawing first blood on 31 May 1916.

Hipper and Beatty now altered courses. The British Battle-Cruiser Force – save the four powerful battleships of the *Queen Elizabeth* class, which misread the signal – wheeled and steamed east to cut off the Germans from their home ports. Hipper, in turn, charted a course south-east in order to fall back on the High Sea Fleet, about fifty miles to the south. Beatty, chasing Hipper, was now unknowingly running at about twenty-five knots into Scheer's waiting arms. Intelligence available to him suggested that the main German battle fleet was still anchored in the Jade basin. In addition, the *Engadine* could not maintain Beatty's breakneck speed and was hampered by low visibility, so that she was utterly unable to provide accurate aerial reconnaissance.

The two scouting forces were rapidly converging on one another. Hipper enjoyed the lee gauge, and Beatty's ships were silhouetted against the clear western sky. At 4.48 p.m., with both fleets running on a parallel south-east course, an artillery duel commenced at roughly 15,000 metres. Hipper's fire was devastating. Within two minutes, German shells struck the centre turret of *Lion,* exposing it "like an open sardine tin". Only the heroic action of flooding the magazines by her mortally wounded turret commander saved the ship.

Indefatigable was not so fortunate. Within five minutes of the first salvo, she received two rounds from *Von der Tann*. Sheets of flame lept toward the sky and dense smoke enveloped her. Internal explosions reverberated within her for a full thirty seconds. She went down with over 1,000 men. The British Fifth Battle Squadron (*Queen Elizabeths*) now joined the action. *Moltke, Von der Tann* and *Seydlitz* had all been hit, but the anti-flash precautions taken by the Germans after the Dogger Bank saved at least *Seydlitz*.

British destroyers steamed up the engaged side of Beatty's ships and thereby substantially reduced his visibility. Nevertheless, the pitched artillery duel continued unabated. Range was down to 14,000 metres, and the noise of battle deafening. The naval grey paint of the gun barrels was blistering into shades of yellow and brown. Thick smoke belched from the funnels and, surging through the seas at twenty-five knots, both sides fired salvos about every seven seconds. It was too hot to last. The two commanders turned several points away from each other, but rounds from *Derfflinger* (which had strangely been left unmolested by yet another signal error) and *Seydlitz* now found the *Queen Mary*. At 5.27 p.m., the German fire opened the battle-cruiser's centre turret. Bright red flames shot up from within. Internal explosions rocked her as the magazines caught fire. The *Queen Mary* quickly broke in two and, stern high with propellers slowly turning, disappeared beneath the waves in a 1,000-feet-high cloud of smoke. Almost 1,300 men found a watery grave with her. Beatty at this juncture rendered his incisive observation : "There seems to be something wrong with our bloody ships today." A pitched battle was simultaneously conducted between British and German destroyers in the waters between the two battle-cruiser forces at ranges sometimes as low as 600 metres.

Despite the destruction of the two British battle-cruisers, Hipper's situation was becoming a matter of some concern. He was now outnumbered 9:5, and an overwhelming volume of shells was raining down on his ships. The glorious destroyer *mêlée*, fought at speeds up to thirty knots, had forced Hipper to turn eight points away from the British, yet his heroic feat of continuing on a generally southern course was about to bear fruit. At roughly 5.30 p.m., British light cruisers spotted the High Sea Fleet on the southern horizon, steaming north-west in single line.

The complexion of the battle now changed radically. Beatty the hunter became Beatty the hunted. He was from this point on to exchange roles with Hipper. At 5.40 p.m., the signal went up for the Battle-Cruiser Force to steer first north-west and then north. Beatty's primary mission was to lure both Hipper and Scheer onto the Grand Fleet, which was steaming on a southerly course at about twenty knots. As Beatty had initially been ignorant of Scheer's presence, so now Hipper was to chase Beatty towards the unknown. In fact, the German might have guessed what awaited him : Jellicoe's six columns of four battleships each. As there were no British bases to the north and as Beatty would have had to turn west in order to head home, it was probable that Beatty was, in fact, now playing the erstwhile role accorded to Hipper.

With the Grand Fleet only sixteen miles to the north, Beatty altered course from north-north-west to north-east in order to regain contact with Hipper, and to prevent the latter from sighting the Grand Fleet. In the ensuing artillery duel, the sun was directly against the Germans. In addition, the British 3rd Battle-Cruiser Squadron fell upon Hipper, who was forced to turn east and finally south-west. The battleship *Wiesbaden* was severely mauled as were the light cruisers *Frankfurt* and *Pillau*. More important, Hipper had been denied sight of Jellicoe's armada by Beatty's brilliant manoeuvre; the Grand Fleet was now only ten miles to the north. Finally, Hipper had mistaken the 3rd Battle-Cruiser Squadron for the Grand Fleet and this realization, compounded by erroneous U-boat reports as to the whereabouts of Jellicoe's battleships, totally clouded Scheer's view of the situation. Hence the German commander was utterly unaware of his dangerous position when, at 7.10 p.m., he rallied his battle-cruisers and battleships and, with Hipper in the lead, steered a north-east course.

Hipper, on the other hand, was more apprehensive. He informed his flag officer around 7.00 p.m. : "Something lurks in that soup. We would do well not to thrust into it too deeply." Jellicoe, for his part, was bearing down on the entire German armada at twenty knots, unaware of Scheer's precise position but knowing of his presence. "I wish someone would tell me who is firing and what they are firing at", he caustically remarked as the deafening boom of heavy guns became discernible.

Admiral Jellicoe had to make the decisive move to engage the Germans. The two fleets were approaching one another at almost thirty knots, and every second counted. Finally, at 7.15 p.m., Jellicoe ordered deployment to port, that is, to form a single line of battle eastward and away from the Germans. As Marder points out, this masterly stroke of bringing all his ships in a line by a ninety-degree wheel to port brought him the advantage of the light, cut the enemy off from his home bases, and allowed him to cross the "T" as the enemy came upon him from the north-east. However, during the wide arc required by the turn to port, *Warspite,* which had lost her helm, came under intense German attack. *Defence* suffered a worse fate, drawing the fire of *Derfflinger* and four battleships of Scheer's van; she blew up "in an immense column of smoke and flame, hundreds of feet high". *Warspite* was also badly damaged and had eventually to be abandoned owing to heavy seas.

At this point the British suffered the loss of a third battle-cruiser. Hipper was under intensive bombardment by the Grand Fleet, a

mere 9,000 metres away and showing a ring of gun flashes from the
north-east to the north-west horizon. Jellicoe's flagship *Iron Duke* in
six minutes scored as many hits on Vice-Admiral Paul Behncke's
leading battleship *König*. The German battle-cruisers finally made
a complete circle in an effort to escape the heavy pounding, but
four of Hipper's vessels plus a battleship took the *Invincible* under
fire at 10,000 metres. A fate similar to that of the other two battle-
cruisers befell her : the third salvo from *Derfflinger* struck the centre
turret and *Invincible* "blew up exactly in half with a magazine
explosion amidships". More than 1,000 men plunged to their deaths
in the North Sea.

But now the Grand Fleet found the range. Hipper's battle-
cruisers in particular were in for a terrible punishing. His flagship
Lützow was hit repeatedly, and listed heavily with her bow deep
in the seas. She was forced to leave the line. Captain Johannes
v. Karpf on *Moltke* commented on the British hail of fire : "The
enemy's salvos lie well and close; the salvos are fired in rapid succession, the fire discipline is excellent !" Hipper was able to take his flag
onto the *Moltke* by 10.50 p.m., having first ascertained that neither
Derfflinger nor *Seydlitz* nor *Von der Tann* was fully serviceable.

The British were in the midst of their first naval battle with a
major sea power in a century. Scheer was in for a fight, and he
knew it. Morale in the High Sea Fleet was high, and many a ship
cleared her guns that day with shouts of "revenge for the
Gneisenau" and "revenge for the *Scharnhorst*". Scheer reportedly
remained calm throughout the encounter. As Jellicoe crossed his
"T", the German commander allegedly stated : "If one wants to
throw me out of the Navy for this, it is indifferent to me." By about
7.30 p.m. at the latest, whatever nonchalance he may have had
turned to recognition of danger and possible annihilation. The
official German history of the war at sea notes : "Suddenly the
German van was faced by the belching guns of an interminable
line of heavy ships extending from north-west to north-east, while
salvo after salvo followed almost without intermission."

Scheer had but one chance, and that was to leave the scene of
battle. At 7.33 p.m., he gave the signal for a battle turn away : each
battleship, beginning with the rear, turned sixteen points to
starboard (eastward) and formed a single line ahead in the opposite
direction. A heavy smokescreen and a desperate torpedo-boat attack
against British capital ships permitted Scheer to slip off towards the
south. Jellicoe steamed on a generally southern course in the hope

of cutting Scheer off from Wilhelmshaven. The Grand Fleet was deployed in a wide arc some ten miles north of Scheer's apparently retreating forces. But at this very moment, the German admiral radically altered the situation by once again reversing his position 180 degrees.

It is highly unlikely that we will ever know why Scheer executed this manoeuvre. According to Marder, Scheer intended to slip astern of the British and to make for his bases under the cover of darkness. Padfield, on the other hand, argues that Scheer, being just as blind as Jellicoe, decided to press to the east for more concrete information of his opponent's whereabouts. This he soon received.

By 8.15 p.m., the entire German van was under fire. The Grand Fleet, on southerly course, was again crossing the "T". The Germans could only make out the British gun flashes like red searchlights on the horizon. The modern *Königs* and the battle-cruisers, in particular, took a severe pounding at 10,000 metres. Already over twenty hits had been scored on Scheer's heavy units; the battleships in his van slowed down in the confusion, causing his line to bunch in the rear. Within five minutes, Scheer realized that he was rapidly steaming towards annihilation. The German commander at once ordered his battle-cruisers, save the *Lützow*, on a "death-ride" against the British line. His torpedo-boats were like-wise ordered to launch an all-out attack and to lay a heavy smoke-screen for the capital ships. While the *Derfflinger* led the suicide charge and the torpedo-boats laid their screens, Scheer ordered the third sixteen-point turn for his line. The daylight phase of the battle was over by 8.59 p.m., when Scheer recalled the battle-cruisers. His torpedo-boats had forced Jellicoe two points off course.

But the Germans were not out of danger yet. By 9.00 p.m., the entire Grand Fleet in seven columns on a westerly course some 12,000 metres east of the High Sea Fleet stood between Scheer and his bases. Had the German admiral continued towards the south-west, the two fleets might have met in the last remaining light about nine miles ahead. But because every mile that he steamed west meant more than a mile's extra cruising to get back to Horn Reefs, Scheer altered course. As a result, the two columns of the High Sea Fleet were now crossing ahead of Jellicoe's forces, twelve miles away. Night fall was Scheer's principal hope. Although Beatty's units managed at 9.23 p.m. to launch an attack on the already damaged *Seydlitz* and *Derfflinger,* a counter-attack by six pre-Dreadnoughts sufficed to prevent any pursuit of the German van. Thus ended the last engagement between capital ships during the war. By 10.00 p.m., the *King George V* and the *Westfalen,* leading ships of both lines, unknowingly were only five miles apart on converging courses. Few objective observers could fault Jellicoe's claim that "if it had only been about 6 p.m. instead of nearly dark and clear instead of thick, we should have had a second Trafalgar".

Nothing better demonstrates the inability of the fleets to engage at night than the ensuing six hours. Scheer believed the British to be off to the east for good, while Jellicoe thought the Germans to be far ahead and to the west. The British commander desired no night encounter for fear of torpedoes and inability to distinguish friend from foe; nothing remained but to maintain course in order to keep between Scheer and the Ems estuary. It was estimated that daylight would break by about 3.00 a.m.

Both Jellicoe and Beatty believed that Scheer would attempt to reach home via the southern route that ran along the North Frisian shore from the Ems to the Jade. The German commander instead opted for the route along the Schleswig-Holstein coast from Horn Reefs down the Amrum Channel and Helgoland to Wilhelmshaven. Scheer undoubtedly feared the possible arrival of the British Harwich Force off the Frisian Islands. Only two of his battle-cruisers – as opposed to six with Beatty – were operational, and Jellicoe had twice nearly closed the trap on him. Nothing remained but to take the shortest route home. Just after 10.00 p.m., Scheer changed course to south-south-west. One hour later he was in night formation : *Westfalen* led the undamaged First Squadron, followed by the mauled Third Squadron, with the Second Squadron and the battle-cruisers *Derfflinger* and *Von der Tann* bringing up the rear. *Seydlitz, Lützow* and *Moltke* were badly damaged, proceeding independently. Scheer was determined at any cost to break through possible British forces obstructing his path home.

There had, in the meantime, been seven separate phases of night action. The severity of close combat under cover of darkness has been attested by Commander Corbett : "In a moment all was a roar of passing and exploding shell and a wild confusion of gun-flashes, dazzling searchlight beams and rapid changes of course. It was work in the old style at point-blank range, with missing hardly possible on either side." The Germans lost the light cruisers *Frauenlob, Rostock* and *Elbing* (the latter rammed by the battle-ship *Posen*) in the *mêlée*; the *Nassau* was rammed by the destroyer *Spitfire*. Nor did the old battleship *Pommern* fare better : British destroyers torpedoed her at about 3.00 a.m., with the loss of all hands. The British lost one light cruiser and five destroyers. The latter's black paint was particularly visible at night, and the German grey was hereafter adopted by the Royal Navy. Miraculously, both *Seydlitz* and *Moltke* managed to limp through the nocturnal chaos – despite having been sighted by several British warships.

Most incredible to the modern reader, the two main fleets managed to pass one another at a distance of less than nine miles without sighting each other. By midnight, the two vans were steaming down the sides of a long, slender "V". Inexplicably, Scheer ordered the Second Squadron to the rear of the line, while Jellicoe brought his rear up to form the spear of his group. The Grand Fleet enjoyed a speed advantage of one knot over the High Sea Fleet. As a result, Jellicoe arrived, according to Gibson and Harper, at the junction point at the bottom of the "V" at 12.30 a.m., minutes ahead of Scheer. The "V" thus became an "X", and the first traces of dawn at 2.45 a.m. found Scheer safely east of the Grand Fleet, less than thirty miles from Horn Reefs. *Lützow* had to be sent to the bottom at about the same time by a German destroyer escort.

Although Scheer brazenly claimed in his memoirs that he was ready by 4.30 a.m. at Horns Reef to resume battle, he was in fact in no condition or mood to tackle Jellicoe. Ernst v. Weizsäcker noted at 4.00 a.m. that the Germans were still unaware of their success at Jutland, and that the murky weather perfectly suited their plans. Only after intercepted British signals revealed to Scheer almost at the entrance to the Jade river that the encounter had not been lost, did he order champagne to the bridge. Of his battle-cruisers, only *Von der Tann* was fit for action, as were a mere three light cruisers. The pre-Dreadnoughts were utterly unprepared to resume battle, and even the newest units of the Third Squadron were in need of repair; *König* was drawing over ten metres of water. Scheer's U-boats had missed the signal to remain at sea for an additional twenty-four hours, and many were unaware that the British were out to sea. It was hardly the setting for a glorious engagement.

Jellicoe, on the other hand, had by 4.30 a.m. taken up a battle formation stronger than that during the initial encounter on the night of 31 May. His twenty-four untouched Dreadnoughts and battle-cruisers were ready to challenge Scheer's ten battle-ready heavy units. Nothing better illustrates the outcome of the battle at

Jutland than the respective positions and conditions of the two
main fleets on the morning of 1 June 1916. The High Sea Fleet
did not venture out to meet the Grand Fleet. Jellicoe headed for
Scapa Flow shortly after 11.00 a.m.; on the evening of the following
day, he reported that the Grand Fleet was ready for sea at four
hours' notice.

The Germans, not surprisingly, attempted to exploit their
quantitative success. Scheer claimed that he had destroyed
4 capital ships, 4 cruisers and 13 destroyers. He failed to inform
the German people of the loss of the *Lützow,* an omission that later
backfired when word of her loss leaked out. Scheer hereafter was
celebrated as the "Victor of the Skagerrak", received the *Ordre
pour le Mérite,* and was promoted to the rank of admiral. Hipper
received the same decoration and was awarded a knighthood by the
King of Bavaria. Wilhelm II visited the fleet on 5 June, showering
Iron Crosses on the crews and kissing most captains, including
Scheer. The monarch preferred the name "the North Sea Battle
of June 1st", aping Howe's "the Glorious First of June" of 1794,
but finally yielded to the "unhistorical" name of "Battle of the
Skagerrak".

The overall euphoria extended from the Kaiser ("The magic of
Trafalgar has been broken") to the Social Democrat Eduard David
("for centuries the first hammer-blow against British naval
supremacy"). On the other hand, Bethmann Hollweg allegedly
condemned the "incredibly frivolous manner" in which Scheer
had risked the fleet at Jutland. This notwithstanding, Scheer was
widely celebrated as a master naval tactician. Yet one must agree
with Marder that "he had a very bad off-day at Jutland, since
every time he came within sight of the British fleet, he did so by
accident and was so completely taken by surprise that on each
occasion he found the British battle line across his 'T' ". Scheer
might have been of similar mind. During a candid conversation
with several senior German admirals shortly after Jutland, he
commented on his "strategy" during the battle : "I came to the
thing as the virgin did when she had the baby."

To be sure, the statistics point to a clear German victory. The
British lost 14 ships (3 battle-cruisers, 3 cruisers and 8 destroyers)
of 111,000 tons to Germany's 11 ships (1 battleship, 1 battle-cruiser,
4 light cruisers, and 5 torpedo-boats) of 62,000 tons. Moreover,
British casualties amounted to 6,784 officers and men, as against
3,058 for Germany. Yet the *Seydlitz* remained under repair until

September and the *Derfflinger* until December; the Dreadnoughts *König, Grosser Kurfürst* and *Markgraf* also required extensive refits.

The British after 1 June made substantive alterations. Safety doors were installed in magazines. New armour-piercing shells were sent to the fleet. Ship protection was enhanced. Fire control was improved. Director-finding systems were fitted to secondary batteries. German night tactics and searchlights were adopted. Aircraft were assigned to the heavy ships to compensate for the overall low level of surveillance during all stages of the battle.

The Germans also realized that all had not gone well. Rear-Admiral v. Trotha, Chief of Operations Division, High Sea Fleet, lamented on 18 July that the battle-cruisers "were no longer operational". He pointed out that the best ships of the Third Squadron had been badly damaged, and that the copper-steel barrels of the heavy guns of the *Nassau* class vessels and of *Von der Tann* had jammed during the battle owing to the stress of rapid-firing. Moreover, Trotha acknowledged that the torpedo-boats lacked range and possessed insufficient torpedo storage.

It is superfluous here to recapitulate the many areas of contention concerning this naval encounter. It is generally accepted that Hipper outskirmished Beatty during the initial phase of the battle, and that Jellicoe outmanoeuvred Scheer badly on two occasions. During the latter, the Germans received seventy hits while scoring twenty against the Grand Fleet. British shells managed to pierce Krupp 11 in steel at 17,000 metres, while German shells penetrated British 9 in plates without great difficulty.

What is crucial about this titanic confrontation involving about 250 ships and 100,000 men, is that it brought the Reich no strategic relief. Jutland was as decisive as Trafalgar, even though Russia continued to be cut off from urgently needed British supplies through the Baltic Sea. The Germans had been driven home, and all thoughts about a renewed encounter with the Grand Fleet were equated with a suicide sortie. In fact, the High Sea Fleet put out to sea only three times more: in August and October 1916, and in April 1918. And, like the French after Trafalgar, the Germans now turned to *guerre de course* in a final attempt to throw off the steel yoke of British naval supremacy.

Admiral Scheer realized the fruitless nature of renewed surface operations perhaps better than any other naval officer in Germany.

On 4 July 1916, he presented Wilhelm II with his evaluation of the war at sea in the wake of the battle of Jutland. The crux of the matter was that "there can be no doubt that even the most successful outcome of a fleet action in this war will not *force* England to make peace". Scheer pointed to the Reich's "disadvantageous military-geographical position" and to "the enemy's great material superiority" in arriving at this conclusion. Instead, he returned to a theme that he had already aired in December 1914 : "the defeat of British economic life – that is, by using the U-boats against British trade". The German commander stated that he recognized the possible danger of a conflict with the United States arising out of unrestricted submarine warfare, but argued that only "full determination" to play out the U-boat "trump" could bring the desired result.

Scheer's sober synopsis of Germany's naval dilemma in July 1916 fully revealed the bankruptcy of Admiral v. Tirpitz's "risk" theory. The master planner of the Navy had from the start expected the British in case of war to attack the Germans in the Helgoland Bight, or at least to institute a close-in blockade. But as early as 1908, the Chief of the Admiralty Staff, Vice-Admiral Count Friedrich v. Baudissin, had cautioned that the British would be content to sit back and guard the distant exits to the Atlantic Ocean; it would remain for Germany to force access to the world's maritime arteries. One year later, Baudissin's successor, Admiral Max Fischel, put it well :

In the final analysis we are fighting for access to the ocean, whose entrances on that side of the North Sea are in England's hands. However the war may be fought, we are therefore basically the attacker, who is disputing the enemy's possession.

As we have seen repeatedly, such opposing views were not tolerated in the "Tirpitz" Navy and their proponents were turned out of office.

The basic issue raised by Baudissin and Fischel, among others, could not be laid to rest – especially after the British in 1912 formally adopted precisely such a "distant" blockade. Perhaps the most famous discourse on German naval strategy was written in the summer of 1915 by the First Admiralty Staff Officer with the First Battle Squadron of the High Sea Fleet, Lieutenant-Commander Wolfgang Wegener. His treatise was read by at least the Chief of the High Sea Fleet, Admiral v. Pohl, the Chief of

Operations, Captain Hans Seebohm, Captain v. Levetzow, and perhaps Trotha.

Wegener argued in 1915 that at sea, as opposed to on land, the destruction of enemy forces was not the primary objective; the naval battle was merely the means to achieve command of sea routes. Annihilation of the opposing fleet, so fervently taught by Tirpitz, was "to a certain degree an incidental goal". Wegener suggested that the British superiority in pre-Dreadnoughts would always accord Britain a dominant role *vis-à-vis* the Reich. Moreover, Germany's maritime geographic position with regard to Britain was "approximately as Helgoland Island is to Helgoland Bight", that is, "England blocks us merely by her geographical position". In effect, Wegener here underscored Tirpitz's incorrect reading of Mahan, who had taken free access to the world's major maritime arteries as the precondition for sea power.

Given the Reich's inferior geographic position, Wegener suggested territorial expansion as the only solution. German possession of the Flanders coast would sever the English Channel trade, while in the north, occupation of Denmark was termed a "necessary military action". German domination of the Skagerrak would interrupt British trade with Scandinavia as well as provide "the exit to the Atlantic". Nor was this Wegener's entire programme. He further clamoured for German occupation of the Faeroe Islands in order to outflank and encircle Great Britain from the north; possession of the French Atlantic coast (Brest and, to a lesser degree, Cherbourg) as well as the Portuguese islands, the Azores and the Cape Verdes, would outflank Britain in the south.

Here, in essence, was Admiral Erich Raeder's blueprint for the seizure of Norway and the French Atlantic ports during the Second World War. Yet Wegener realized that the present war was only the initial stage of a long struggle, perhaps the "First Punic War" between Berlin and London. He bemoaned past naval building, calling the High Sea Fleet a "rider without a horse", and claimed that the "one-sided" concentration on "the battle" between Helgoland and the Thames had adversely "affected the dislocation of our naval forces and even the construction of our ships". More than Scheer, Wegener demanded faster capital ships with greater fire power.

Other naval commanders also turned to the issue of possible naval war aims in the event of a victorious outcome of the war. Admiral Henning v. Holtzendorff, Chief of the Admiralty Staff, in

November and December 1916 at the request of Bethmann Hollweg drafted the Navy's first comprehensive war-aims programme. It left no doubt that Germany remained firmly wedded to *Weltpolitik*. Holtzendorff defined five areas in which the Reich would have to acquire new territory. In Europe, he sought to annex the Belgian coast with the harbours of Brugge, Oostende and Zeebrugge, the Courland coast with Libau and Windau, the Baltic islands Moon and Oesel, and the Danish Faeroe Islands, which would "open up the way to the free ocean for us [and] *form the first breach in England's dominant maritime geographic situation"*. Had Holtzendorff also read Wegener's treatise? In the Atlantic area, Holtzendorff cherished naval bases at either Dakar or the Cape Verde Islands, and at the Azores. These *Stützpunkte* would serve especially as supply depots for the forward bastions of Germany's Central African colonial empire, which was eventually to be created. In the Far East, the admiral hoped to acquire Tahiti, while in the West Indian Ocean he sought Madagascar and in the East Indian Ocean he wanted one of the large Dutch islands. Finally, in the Mediterranean Sea he desired the harbour of Valona on the Albanian coast, along with a land connection to the Austro-Hungarian Empire. Admiral v. Tirpitz endorsed this platform, calling German retention of Belgium "the cornerstone on which one can build a German world power equal to that of the Anglo-Saxons and the Russians". Field-Marshal Paul v. Hindenburg as well as General Erich Ludendorff incorporated Holtzendorff's points into their own war-aims programmes.

But first Britain had to be defeated. Admiral Scheer decided on 19 August 1916 to take the High Sea Fleet out for what Marder has termed "blind man's buff". Since Jutland, Scheer had retired the elderly *Deutschlands* and, there being only the battle-cruisers *Moltke* and *Seydlitz* available, attached three of his Dreadnoughts, including the new *Bayern,* to the First Scouting Squadron. Finally, Scheer was determined never again to rush blindly onto the Grand Fleet, and hence he vowed not to sally forth without his Zeppelin aerial scouts.

The operations plan for 19 August was basically that of May 1916, "to bombard Sunderland, to force the English Fleet to come out and show the world the unbroken strength of the German Fleet". Twenty-four U-boats were to take part in the action while ten airships would constitute the "eyes" of the fleet. But once again, on 18 August, Room 40 in London intercepted the German signal and the Grand Fleet was out to sea several hours before the Germans. Jellicoe this time commanded 29 Dreadnoughts and 6 battle-cruisers, against 18 Dreadnoughts and 2 battle-cruisers for Scheer.

Early on 19 August, Scheer's reconnaissance brought nothing but confusion. At 7.30 a.m., Zeppelin *L 13* reported Commodore Tyrwhitt's Harwich light units 120 miles to the south, bearing south-west. Twice thereafter *U 53* reported capital ships heading north. Worse yet, by 10.50 a.m. airship *L 31* informed Scheer that the Grand Fleet was steaming north-east. All these conflicting reports indicated to Scheer that the British were moving away from him instead of, as in reality, converging on him from the north as well as the south. Thus the German commander continued on course for Sunderland, and around noon of 19 August stood about 100 miles off Whitby.

At 1.03 p.m., Scheer received the electrifying news from *L 13* that a large enemy force "of about 30 units" was coming up from the south. Once again, expectations ran high among German fleet commanders that isolated units of the Grand Fleet were about to be caught out in the open. Scheer quickly abandoned his plans to bombard Sunderland, and at 1.15 p.m. ordered the fleet on a south-easterly course in order to intercept the British heavy units.

In fact, Scheer was now chasing a "phantom squadron" as the Harwich units had no battleships with them. Moreover, at about the same time Tyrwhitt had given up sighting the Germans and had turned for home. Hence Scheer was ploughing into open seas, heading south-east. And when at 3.13 p.m. he received the accurate news from *U 53* that the Grand Fleet was bearing down on him from the north, about sixty-five miles away, Scheer's surprise must have been immense. There remained nothing but to head for home as quickly as possible, before Jellicoe could position the Grand Fleet between Scheer and his bases. Only *U 66* and *U 63* managed to establish contact with the British, dispatching the light cruiser *Falmouth* with four torpedoes.

Providence had once more smiled upon Scheer. Had airship *L 13* not sent the incorrect signal reporting the approach of heavy units from the south, the Germans would have been trapped off Sunderland by Jellicoe.

Undaunted, Scheer attempted in September to stage another raid on the English coast, but foul weather all through that month

as well as the resumption of unrestricted submarine warfare on 6
October militated against this undertaking. Finally, at midnight of
18–19 October, though deprived of covering U-boats, Scheer set
out yet again for the British coast east of the Dogger Bank; ten
airships covered his advance. And again the British got wind of the
planned German sortie the day before the High Sea Fleet left port,
but this time Jellicoe opted to remain at anchor and to await the
German plan of action.

Scheer reached the Dogger Bank by noon of 19 October, but
sighted no enemy surface units. The light cruiser *München* was
damaged by the British submarine *E 38,* there was no enemy in
sight, and intelligence available to Scheer convinced him that the
British knew of his position. He turned for home. The High Sea
Fleet as a whole was not to venture out again until April 1918.
Even Lady Luck seemed to have deserted Scheer. On 3 November
1917, when he dispatched five capital ships to rescue two U-boats
stranded in fog off North Jutland, Scheer courted disaster as two
of his battleships were hit by British torpedoes in the foul sea.
Wilhelm II was irate, chastising his fleet chief for "risking a
squadron . . . in order to save two U-boats". There apparently
remained only the U-boat "trump".

The debate concerning resumption of unrestricted submarine warfare became acute in the summer and autumn of 1916. Scheer
remained adamant in his belief that undersea warfare should be
conducted either all-out or not at all; in the latter case, the U-boats
would be freed for use in conjunction with the fleet. Perhaps most
tortuous was the role played in this by Admiral v. Holtzendorff.
On 10 June 1916, Holtzendorff managed to persuade Wilhelm II
to commence submarine warfare by 1 July, but the monarch once
again could not remain firm in his decision. Three days later,
Holtzendorff agreed with Bethmann Hollweg that the undersea
offensive was not in Germany's best interests, yet within a fortnight
the head of the Admiralty Staff again counselled Imperial Headquarters to seize the initiative and to inaugurate an all-out undersea
offensive. By July, Holtzendorff favoured unrestricted submarine
warfare only in the English Channel, and finally on 6 October he
announced the resumption in nine days of undersea warfare
according to "cruiser" or prize laws.

This decision pleased no one. Scheer, Trotha and Levetzow
intrigued in the most despicable manner against the vacillating

Holtzendorff, and did not shrink from rallying the Empress and Count Eulenburg, Wilhelm's Royal House Marshal, to their banner. Above all, the fleet's leaders fervently courted the favour of Hindenburg and Ludendorff in their endeavours on behalf of unrestricted submarine warfare. Even selected Reichstag deputies and members of the right-wing press were provided with top-secret information in order to win the public for the new tactic.

Perhaps the strongest argument in favour of the proposed radical conduct of the undersea war was the low yield and accompanying high risk of the U-boats in the prize warfare now being conducted. German estimates of all enemy shipping destroyed during the last four months of 1916 rested optimistically at around 400,000 tons, that is, a net loss to the British of 2 million tons (18.5 per cent) of their shipping, or about the same amount as the London regime had seized from neutrals or purchased from foreign governments since 1914. Moreover, while losses over the last quarter of 1916 amounted to less than 2 per cent per month, the vital statistic is that British imports during 1916 did not decline from the 1915 level of 46 million tons. Only in the Mediterranean was there cause for consternation : Allied losses were estimated in the second half of 1916 at 62 per cent, while 32 per cent of all ships traversing the *Mittelmeer* were sent to the bottom. During the last half of that year Germany lost fifteen U-boats.

While most senior naval leaders argued that only the submarines could bring "perfidious Albion" to her knees, several prominent junior officers with front experience as well as civilian leaders warned against such a course. Most argued that there simply were not enough U-boats on hand to fulfill the Navy's promise of starving Britain into submission in six months. Lieutenant-Commander v. Weizsäcker cautioned against the "stupidity" of unrestricted submarine warfare, and warned Admiral v. Trotha that such a step 'remained a *va banque* gamble of Germany against half the world". Weizsäcker in the fall of 1916 penned the following home :

> The executive officers sit around, eat, drink, politicize, intrigue, and even believe that they are being patriotic in trying by sordid means to bring about the adoption of unrestricted submarine warfare. Submarine warfare is supposed to cover up the stupidities in the fleet construction and in the wartime deployment of the fleet. The bad conscience [of the executive officers] emerges in this forbidden propaganda for it.

Bethmann Holweg's son-in-law, Count Julius v. Zech v. Burckers-roda, seconded this view, expressing the hope that the undersea offensive would not mark "the death of the German Empire". And the chancellor's intimus, Kurt Riezler, referred in his diary to the "terrible fate" that awaited this "leap in the dark". Riezler above all feared that most of the Continent would be brought to the verge of starvation by 1918 through Britain's long-distance blockade, while Britain with American succour would triumph in that same year despite the U-boats. It proved to be a good guess.

Of far greater import for the subsequent course of events proved to be several lengthy memoranda prepared under the guidance of Captain Kurt Grasshoff and Lieutenant-Commander Ernst Vanselow in the Admiralty Staff. The most famous of these was drafted by a Dr Richard Fuss, a banker from the Magdeburger Discontogesellschaft. It was Fuss who, at the behest of Holtzendorff, calculated in December of 1916 that Britain could only resist unrestricted submarine warfare for six months before she collapsed owing to lack of vital imports. A fellow co-worker, Professor Hermann Levy, concurred, pointing out that wheat imports were the Achilles heel of the British economy. The findings of these two alleged experts were passed on to Bethmann Hollweg, who asked that they be kept top secret. However, Admiral v. Müller distributed them to no less than 228 military posts; in all, almost 500 copies of these reports were circulated among military and naval leaders.

On 22 December 1916, Admiral v. Holtzendorff incorporated the views of Fuss and Levy, among others, in the famous document that led to the declaration of unrestricted U-boat warfare. The two crucial points were the ultimate tonnage of merchant shipping controlled by Great Britain, and the percentage of the total world production of wheat available to that island nation. Holtzendorff estimated that the world production of wheat in 1916 was 9 per cent below normal yield; the British supply of this vital grain on 1 December 1916 was estimated to be sufficient for fifteen weeks, while between February and August 1917, about 2.2 million tons of wheat would have to be imported on 1.1 million tons of merchant shipping. It was decided that while Britain possessed about 20 million tons of shipping, only about 10.65 million tons were deployed to provision Great Britain.

Accordingly, the German analysts calculated that if, over the first two months of unrestricted submarine warfare, 600,000 tons per month could be destroyed, and about 500,000 tons per month over the next four months, the British tonnage available for food imports would decline by "a final and irreplaceable" 40 per cent. Incredibly, the United States was dismissed as either an economic or a miltary factor. Wheat rust would seriously deplete the American harvest, the U-boats would prevent any landing of American troops in Europe, and the thirty-nine United States Navy capital ships were passed over as a negligible quantity. Reports from envoys in neutral countries warning that the all-out U-boat offensive would prompt these to curtail food shipments to Germany or even to consider hostile actions against the Reich, were negated by Captain Grasshoff as "defeatists of the *first* order".

The decision to resume unrestricted submarine warfare was reached on 9 January 1917 at Imperial Headquarters in Pless. Holtzendorff reiterated the basic points contained in the memorandum of 22 December, and Captain v. Levetzow "guaranteed with good conscience for the fleet" that the U-boats could destroy 500,000 tons of shipping per month. Hindenburg and Ludendorff stressed that the naval initiative would curtail American munitions deliveries to the Allies. Bethmann Hollweg, although deeply concerned over the diplomatic consequences of the decision, voted for the new naval tactic. However, the chancellor clearly anticipated "the entry of America into the war", an eventuality that Levetzow dismissed as being "of no importance to the fleet". Ludendorff also counted upon American belligerency, but was prepared "to accept this risk". The issue was decided when Wilhelm II agreed with his military and naval paladins, adding that he "fully expected America's entry into the war" but that this was "irrelevant" to the outcome of the struggle.

Admirals v. Tirpitz, v. Hipper and Souchon enthusiastically endorsed the latest naval action, believing that the massive undersea offensive against commerce would end the war before the United States could intervene with sufficient force to affect the outcome decisively. Of course, none of them could have guessed that the Russian Empire would collapse within a few weeks (12 March) of the commencement of the undersea campaign (1 February), or that the United States would declare war against the Reich a few weeks later (6 April).

We know today that the German calculations ignored several important political factors, and that they also had a narrow focus in their analysis of economic determinants. German naval leaders failed to appreciate the enormous ship-building potential of the

United States in particular. They ignored, as Karl Helfferich pointed out as early as 1916, the total shipping tonnage available to Great Britain. They had no clear notion of precisely how many ships per month England required to sustain her industry and to feed her subjects. They over-emphasized the importance of wheat, failing to note that other grains could be substituted. They never imagined that rationing would be instituted owing to their conception of the British "national character". They did not foresee that Britain could increase her output of foodstuffs by bringing into production land and resources not yet fully tapped. They did not realize that the London government would rigidly regulate prices, believing that international food prices would skyrocket until Britain could no longer afford to pay them. They also felt certain that shipping and insurance rates would become unaffordable especially to neutral nations. Finally, they did not take into consideration the available grain reserves – the United States, for example, possessed sufficient supplies to cover the Allied deficiencies owing to the poor harvest of 1916.

Despite the obvious errors, the Reich on 9 January 1917 opted for a massive undersea attack against all commerce, designed to bring Britain to her knees by August 1917 through monthly merchant shipping sinkings of 500 to 600,000 tons. Naval leaders purposely opted for a tactic certain to antagonize the world's major neutrals in the slender hope of victory over Britain within six months. Such was the German blueprint for victory early in 1917. Under the leadership of the "Victor of the Skagerrak", *Kleinkrieg* apparently had triumphed over *Grosskrieg* in the fourth year of the war.

Across the North Sea, the year 1916 ended with a number of major personnel changes. On 22 November, Jellicoe accepted the post of First Sea Lord; that same day, Beatty was given command of the Grand Fleet. And on 7 December, a new coalition government headed by David Lloyd George assumed the reins of power in London. Balfour was replaced as First Lord of the Admiralty by the volatile Sir Edward Carson. Hence the year 1916 closed with fresh political as well as naval leadership in London, and a new naval tactic in Berlin. But before we see how these events were to shape the course of the war in 1917–18, it is useful to redirect the narrative in order to analyse the *matériel* with which the Reich hoped to turn the tide against the Allies in the Great War, and to ascertain to what degree German planners managed to cling to Tirpitz's master plan.

X

"Museum of Experiments"

The End of the
Battleship Era, 1914-1918

The Great War, as we have seen, caught the German Navy woe-fully off-balance and unprepared. Three ships of the *König* class were still under construction in August 1914, and joined the fleet by November as *König, Markgraf* and *Kronprinz,* thereby giving Germany seventeen Dreadnoughts in commission. The picture was even bleaker with regard to battle-cruisers. Only three vessels of this type, *Moltke, Von der Tann* and *Seydlitz,* were available in home waters; the fourth, *Goeben,* was irretrievably lost in the Mediter-ranean. Three ships of the *Derfflinger* class were also being built: *Derfflinger* joined the fleet in September 1914, *Lützow* in August 1915, and *Hindenburg* in May 1917. Moreover, only four armoured cruisers were available for duty in the North Sea (*Blücher, Prinz Adalbert, Roon,* and *Yorck*), while two others (*Gneisenau* and *Scharnhorst*) were overseas. Of the full fleet strength of 41 battle-ships and 12 battle-cruisers envisaged under the *Novelle* of 1912, only 17 Dreadnoughts and 3 battle-cruisers were available against the Royal Navy by the end of 1914.

The war at sea proved to be cruel. The pre-Dreadnoughts in particular showed a high casualty rate because of their vulnerability underwater. The elderly battleship *Pommern* was lost at Jutland – along with the battle-cruiser *Lützow* – and between 1914 and 1915 Germany lost six armoured cruisers (*Blücher, Friedrich Carl, Gneisenau, Prinz Adalbert, Scharnhorst,* and *Yorck*). Thirteen light cruisers also perished during the first two years of the Great War.

In addition to the three *Königs* and three *Derfflingers*, Germany in July 1914 also had on the slipways three units of the *Bayern* class (*Württemberg* was to be laid down in January 1915), while orders were placed for four battle-cruisers of the *Mackensen* series between August 1914 and April 1915. Moreover, replacements were now required for the armoured as well as light cruisers lost at sea as well as for a host of torpedo-boats and minesweepers needed to clear the approaches to Wilhelmshaven. The need for dirigibles and seaplanes for reconnaissance purposes was clearly displayed by bold British raids into the Helgoland Bight in 1914–15. Nor could the mounting cry for U-boats be ignored – especially in view of the inactivity of the High Sea Fleet. Finally, the monstrous expenditure required to equip and supply an Army of almost 2 million men – particularly after the inauguration of the so-called "Hindenburg Programme" in 1916 – forced naval planners constantly to re-examine their wartime building policies.

The Navy Office as well as the High Sea Fleet were fully aware that any decision made during the war would weigh heavily upon future building programmes. On the basis of the Supplementary Bill of 1912, they calculated that the Navy for the years 1913 to 1917 would require one Dreadnought as well as one battle-cruiser per annum, in addition to an extra battleship in 1913 and in 1916. By February 1915, when the expectation that the war would be over by Christmas 1914 had proved false, Berlin decided to proceed with the replacement of five armoured cruisers and seven light cruisers that had been lost to date. This decision was reinforced in October of that year when the British submarine *E 8* torpedoed the armoured cruiser *Prinz Adalbert* in the Baltic. Wilhelm II at once ordered battle-cruiser replacements at a projected unit cost of 72 million GM (compared with *Prinz Adalbert*'s original cost of 16 million GM in 1900–4). Whereas the Kaiser desired a change-over to the British 38 cm heavy gun, the Chief of the High Sea Fleet, Admiral v. Ingenohl, favoured the customary 30.5 cm cannon. A compromise solution, the 35 cm gun, was finally worked out.

But neither party had counted on the chancellor. Bethmann Hollweg now renewed his opposition of 1912 to naval expenditure, and found an ardent supporter in the State Secretary of the Treasury, Hans Delbrück. Both men countered naval arguments by citing the general disappointment among the German people with naval developments, and especially with the inactivity of the High

Sea Fleet. Admiral v. Holtzendorff in December 1915 also informed Wilhelm of the "wavering belief of the German people in the need for a strong Navy". Moreover, the head of the Admiralty Staff apprised the Kaiser of the fleet's lack of confidence and uncertainty over naval building to date. "Either the ships of the Navy Office are fast, and then they have insufficient fire power. Or they have good artillery on board, and then they are not fast!" The monarch, not surprisingly, opted to reactivate his long-standing pet project of a "fast diesel-operated battle-cruiser hybrid", in other words, the "fast battleship" of the later *Panzerschiffe* ("pocket" battleships). Above all, he demanded greater imagination from Navy Office planners.

"Imagination" came instead across the North Sea from Admiral Fisher, who had been recalled as First Sea Lord in October 1914. Fisher developed the shallow-draft "hush-hush" battle-cruisers *Glorious, Courageous* and *Furious* (dubbed "Spurious", "Outrageous", "Uproarious") for his pet scheme of a landing along the coast of Pommern only ninety miles from Berlin – a repeat of the Russian action of 1761. Even Beatty harboured doubts about these "Gallopers", while they were generally regarded as "white elephants" in the Grand Fleet. Yet Fisher had even a "one bigger, one better" class, the *Incomparable*, in mind. German submarine sinkings of four cruisers had infuriated him. *"More men lost than by Lord Nelson in all his battles put together!"* The new ships were to be fitted with 50.8 cm (20 in) guns and given a best speed of thirty-five knots, but Fisher's fall from office in May 1915 laid this project to rest. The last major British battle-cruiser class (*Hood*), planned in 1915, consisted of ships displacing 36,000 tons, with a best speed of thirty-one knots and eight 38 cm heavy guns.

Admiral v. Tirpitz was greatly disturbed by official as well as public reaction to further naval building. In January 1916 he informed Captain v. Trotha that no political party in Germany would grant one capital ship if the Fleet remained inactive. However, Tirpitz was not willing to assume responsibility for a sea battle *à outrance* with the Grand Fleet in the North Sea.

Nor would anyone in a position of authority decide the burning question of what type of ship to build. It was generally agreed that a ratio of two-thirds coal to one-third oil was to be maintained, because the side bunkers would afford indispensable protection, especially for the battle-cruisers. The imperial dry-docks could not hold ships with a draft over nine metres, which meant that any increase in displacement would have to be compensated for in terms of increased length and beam. Such increases, in turn, entailed new problems. The locks at Wilhelmshaven permitted a beam of only 30–31 metres at high water, while a draft of 10 metres, according to Admiral Scheer, precluded navigation on the Elbe river as well as other river estuaries. Finally, Holtzendorff compounded the entire building dilemma by raising the valid question whether money, time and energy should be spent at all on capital ships when only U-boats seemed capable of defeating Great Britain. Thus the thorny issue of *Grosskrieg* versus *Kleinkrieg,* of Mahan versus Aube, was brought out into the open once more.

Nagging financial problems also recurred. It was estimated that any increase in displacement would necessitate expenditure of about 50 million GM to enlarge existing canal and harbour facilities. On the other hand, the Navy still expected the war to end before 1917 and hence the brakes continued to be applied to the construction programme throughout 1916. Whereas Britain maintained a force of 3,000 to work on a ship's hull, Germany had only 1,000 in the same trade.

The Battle of Jutland gave testimony to the great durability as well as excellent fire power of German heavy ships. It did not, however, alter one iota the strategy of either combatant. Early in July 1916, Scheer reported to Wilhelm II that only improvements in terms of capital ship best speed (Dreadnoughts twenty-eight knots, battle-cruisers thirty-two knots), heavy guns (over the 43 cm cannon of the *Furious* class), and better citadel armour would permit him to accept battle with the Royal Navy in the future.

Confusion and doubts continued to plague German naval planners. Admiral Hebbinghaus in the Navy Office clung to the "risk" theory and demanded greater armour in place of Scheer's call for superior speed. Hebbinghaus likewise rejected Scheer's general offensive strategy and termed sorties in the North Sea off the British coast "daring feats of horse cavalry". Admiral v. Capelle, who replaced Tirpitz as State Secretary of the Navy Office, in August 1916 at a staff meeting decided to retain both battleships and battle-cruisers, but ruled against keeping any ships older than the *Nassau* with the High Sea Fleet; he refused to go above the 38 cm navy gun. Finally, he ordered capital-ship building at the rate of two per annum, first eight battle-cruisers, then four Dreadnoughts, and thereafter battle-cruisers only. This decision, of course, discarded Tirpitz's sixty-ship master plan. In addition, it did not sit well with Scheer, who once again demanded greater speed, a

42 cm gun and priority for battle-cruiser building. In October 1916 neither High Sea Fleet nor Admiralty Staff was consulted on the deliberations in favour of 38 cm or 42 cm heavy guns, and Capelle unilaterally ruled that Germany would not build any capital ships over 41,000 tons displacement, or 235 metres in length, with a beam of 31 metres and a draft of 9.8 metres. Expansion of harbours, locks and canals was ruled out once and for all.

The battleship *Baden* joined the fleet in October 1916. Apart from continued work on the last two *Bayern* class units (*Sachsen* and *Württemberg*), German yards for the rest of the war concentrated in terms of capital-ship building on the *Mackensen* class of battle-cruisers. These continued along the lines initiated with *Derfflinger*, except that their armament was raised to 35 cm guns in answer to the British change-over to 18 in guns with *Queen Elizabeth*. The heavy guns were to be mounted as in the *Derfflinger*, and secondary battery was to consist of fourteen 15 cm and eight 8.8 cm (anti-aircraft) guns. And despite the fact that in the first two years of the war not one capital ship managed to get off a single decent torpedo shot, it was nevertheless decided to retain five submerged 60 cm torpedo tubes.

Mackensen was launched in April 1917 and destined for internment at Scapa Flow. However, she was not seaworthy in November 1918 and *Baden* took her place; *Mackensen* was sold to breakers in 1921. "Ersatz Freya", to be named *Prinz Eitel Friedrich*, was launched in March 1920 and dubbed "Noske" by dock workers after the SPD Defence Minister Gustav Noske; she was broken up in 1920–2. The *Graf Spee* was launched in September 1917 and sold to breakers in 1921. "Ersatz Friedrich Carl" was intended to be named *Fürst Bismarck*, but was scrapped on the slipway in 1922. The ships were at best twelve, at worst twenty-six months from completion at the end of the war. The heavy guns, as far as they were ready, were deployed in Flanders, some mounted on railway carriages as movable heavy batteries. According to Breyer, the ships of the *Mackensen* class marked the first step on the road towards the "fast battleship" (Table 26).

The final planned battle-cruisers ("Ersatz Yorck") were initially intended as part of the *Mackensen* class. However, once it became known that Britain in the *Renown* series had changed once again to a higher calibre, the 15 in (38 cm) heavy gun, it was decided to follow the British lead, and orders were placed for the ships in 1916 even before design changes were completed. Work was started on

the "Ersatz Yorck", "Ersatz Gneisenau" and "Ersatz Scharnhorst"
in 1916, but at the end of the war these ships were at least twenty-
six months away from completion; all were scrapped on the slipways.

The specifications for these three battle-cruisers were much the
same as for *Mackensen* – with the exception of the heavy guns, a
price tag of 75 million GM, and parity between coal-fired and oil-
fired naval boilers. It is of interest that this was the first German
design of single-funnel ships. The diesels that had once again been
designed for a single ship ("Ersatz Gneisenau") were built into the
large merchant submarines (*U 151–U 154*).

German capital-ship building and planning in 1917–18 sputtered
and finally came to a halt. At first, despite the resumption of
unrestricted U-boat warfare on 1 February 1917, work continued
on three battle-cruisers. Future ship designs were arrived at in the
Navy Office without the advice or consent of the High Sea Fleet.
The Kaiser in January 1918 renewed his twenty-year-old call for a
uniform "fast-battleship" class, and Admiral v. Holtzendorff two
months later even considered a change-over to the Krupp 50 cm
gun. But German industry simply was in no position to deliver the
requisite supplies for capital-ship building and, with ever-increasing
Army needs, the Navy by the fall of 1916 had to cease work on the
"Ersatz Scharnhorst". The ready dates for *Sachsen* and *Württemberg* remained "unknown", and only the *Graf Spee* had a crew of
1,500 workers preparing her for completion. Incredibly, by June
1918 the Navy Office was once more ready with a major capital-
ship programme in the wake of the Army's victorious advance in
France ("Michael" offensive), fearing that the British might attempt
a desperate sortie against the High Sea Fleet in order to offset
the reverses suffered on the Western Front. However, the Allied
counter-offensive in France quickly dispelled such notions, and by
October 1918 the situation was to be reversed. Moreover, Wilhelm II
in an "unrestrained" rage now opposed the fleet's demands as "too
big, too expensive".

Generally speaking, the German naval officer corps during the
Great War was divided roughly into four different factions in the
debate over battleship building versus *Kleinkrieg*. First, there were
those who supported Tirpitz to the bitter end in clinging to Mahan's
battleship strategy. Then there was a diametrically opposed group of
primarily young officers who saw the U-boats as Germany's only hope
against British superiority in surface ships. The rest were divided into

two compromise factions, with one wanting both capital ships and submarines developed simultaneously, while the other desired only a temporary wartime emphasis on submarines and a return to battleship building after the war.

There could, on the other hand, be no argument concerning the Reich's need to build more light cruisers. Thirteen of these craft were lost during the first two years of the war and, given the Navy's continued fear of torpedo attack, their absence posed a danger to the High Sea Fleet by severely reducing its anti-torpedo screen.

Between 1915 and 1916, two light cruisers, *Bremse* and *Brummer*, were built specially as minelayers; they carried four 15 cm and two 8.8 cm guns, two deck 50 cm torpedo tubes, and 400 mines. They joined the fleet in 1916 and were interned at Scapa Flow.

The last major series of German light cruisers was the *Königsberg II* class, built between 1914 and 1917. They were larger than their predecessors with a displacement of 5,440 tons, and were fitted with twice the number of 15 cm guns but only half the number of mines. They were all assigned to fleet duty and were interned at Scapa Flow, save the *Königsberg* which was turned over to France (Table 27).

A final series of light cruisers (*Cöln*) was designed in 1914, but only two ships (*Cöln II, Dresden II*) were completed. They differed little from the *Königsberg II* class. Both vessels were assigned to the High Sea Fleet and later interned at Scapa Flow. Eight others were sold for scrapping in 1920–21.

The exigencies of submarine warfare and the need to clear vital channels of British mines in the waters near Helgoland prompted the Imperial Navy to continue building light as well as large torpedo-boats. Including the boats on slipways in 1913–14, the Reich built 234 of these craft (174 alone during the actual war years). Blohm & Voss, Hamburg, in 1914 had on the slipways six large *Novik*-type destroyers for the Russian Navy. They became the first true destroyers of the Imperial Navy, and altogether twelve large "T" boats being built for foreign powers were seized by Berlin at the outbreak of war. The Russian vessels, *B 97–B 98* and *B 109–B 112*, were all scuttled at Scapa Flow.

By the end of the war, the typical German torpedo-boat, displacing between 500 and 600 tons and armed with two 8.8 cm guns, was on the way out. Perhaps because they had not fulfilled the extremely high expectations placed on them in fleet engagements by the Navy Office, larger boats became the vogue and the

Reich followed the British lead. Howaldt in Kiel in 1917 laid down the *H 145* series, displacing 1,147 tons, turbine-powered, purely oil-fired, and armed with three 10.5 cm guns, six 50 cm torpedo tubes, and forty mines. Schichau in Elbing in 1916, and Vulcan in Stettin developed the *S 113* and *V 116* respectively. These were 2,400-ton leader boats armed with four 15 cm guns, four 60 cm torpedo tubes, and forty mines. These were at the time the largest and most powerful "destroyers" in the world. However, they proved to be top heavy, rolling badly in high seas, and failed by a wide margin to reach contract speed during trials.

The mounting demands of the submarine campaign also prompted Berlin by 1915 to order about 200 minesweepers. Britain had by the autumn of 1917 dropped about 51,000 mines into the North Sea, and during the last quarter of 1917 alone added 10,000 new "H" mines. This saturation was felt by the High Sea Fleet. In November 1914, the armoured cruiser *Yorck* sank in Schillig Roads on German mines, taking 300 men down with her. The armoured cruiser *Friedrich Carl* was lost off Memel that same month, while in 1915 the light cruisers *Danzig* and *Lübeck* had to be towed home after striking mines in the Baltic Sea; *Bremen* was not this fortunate, going down with heavy loss of life. At Jutland, mines found the battle-cruiser *Seydlitz*, which had already been badly mauled by the Grand Fleet, as well as the light cruiser *Graudenz*; however, both ships managed to limp back to port. The light cruiser *Stralsund* in January 1918 also struck a mine and eventually reached port. Generally speaking, the British mines prior to the introduction of the "H.II" – copied "nut for nut and bolt for bolt" from a captured German "egg" mine – in the autumn of 1917, were not as good as the German model. A Berlin estimate claims that almost 67 per cent of British mines failed for various reasons to detonate upon impact; German ships frequently mounted captured British mines on deck as souvenirs. German superior underwater protection and more complete watertight hull-subdivision (afforded by greater beam) accounted for the high rate of survival among German ships after striking mines.

Great Britain early closed the Dover Straits with the Channel Fleet as well as with a barrage of 9,500 mines. The waters between Scotland and Norway, about 250 sm wide and approximately 180 m deep, required about 400,000 "H" mines to seal off, but introduction of the superior United States' "antenna" mine in 1917 reduced this figure to 100,000 – or only 70,000 of the new type for the

Norway–Orkney Islands stretch. Overall, mines of all nations accounted for 23 per cent of the 78 battleships and cruisers lost between 1914 and 1918, 57 per cent of the 120 destroyers lost, and 27 per cent of the 170 submarines.

German mines laid in British waters during the first year of the war were deposited primarily by the High Sea Fleet during two raids in November and December. *Stralsund* laid about 120 mines off Yarmouth, which found the submarine *D 5*; *Kolberg* dropped 100 mines off Scarborough, claiming about twenty small craft; *Berlin's* 200 mines off north-western Ireland found the battleship *Audacious* near Lough Swilly as well as two auxiliary cruisers and some freighters. Beginning in the summer of 1915, German auxiliary cruisers and U-boats entered the picture, while the light cruisers *Brummer* and *Bremse*, specifically built for minelaying, were never properly deployed in this manner. The High Sea Fleet disengaged from minelaying, placing only a few belts around the Helgoland Bight and as far west as the Dogger Bank. Only torpedo-boats were stationed in Flanders to lay mines in British waters. Commodore Tyrwhitt regarded mines as "distinctly barbaric" and in August 1914 lamented : "It will be months before the North Sea is safe for yachting !"

Of special note are the minelaying "UC" submarines operating out of Flanders. These 170-ton boats held twelve mines each in front holds, and from June 1915 to the end of the war managed to place nearly 1,000 barriers in British waters. The auxiliary cruiser *Meteor* in August 1915 dropped 374 mines off the Firth of Moray, netting one destroyer and several minesweepers. Ironically, the Firth was devoid of anti-submarine devices and by clearing only side channels, Jellicoe used *Meteor's* mines as protection against U-boats. *Möwe* in January 1916 laid 252 mines in the icy waters west of Scapa Flow; the elderly battleship *King Edward VII* fell victim to this deposit. The armoured cruiser *Hampshire*, with Lord Kitchener on board, also foundered in a minefield in June 1916 off the Orkneys, and in that same year the cruiser *Arethusa* likewise went down in British waters. France lost the armoured cruiser *Kléber* off Brest in May 1917 as a result of German mines; the United States in this manner lost the armoured cruiser *San Diego*, while the battleship *Minnesota* was damaged by German "eggs". Most of the British submarines lost in the North Sea were claimed by mines; possibly the last victims in August 1918 were the destroyers *Vehement* and *Ariel*.

The Mediterranean Sea also took its toll of warships sunk by mines. The Allied attempt to force passage of the Dardanelles in March 1915 proved to be extremely expensive in terms of pre-Dreadnoughts: Britain lost the battleships *Irresistible* and *Ocean*, while the battle-cruiser *Inflexible* had to retire from battle after running on to a mine; France lost the battleship *Bouvet*, which took 600 men to their death in about one minute. The Italian battleship *Regina Margherita* foundered in December 1916 on her own mines off Valona, and early in 1917 the Russian Navy lost the battleship *Peressvjät* off Port Said to a mine laid by a German UC boat; in April the British battleship *Russel* was lost off Malta from similar causes. The Russian armoured cruiser prototype *Rurik* in November 1916 ran on to mines in the Baltic Sea.

Germany facilitated this incredible mine contagion with some converted merchant ships. Only three of these (*Kaiser*, *Königin Luise* and *Preussen*) were used in the North Sea; the *Königin Luise* was destroyed in the Thames estuary by the cruiser *Amphion* on only the second day of the war, having left Germany with her deadly cargo even before war was officially declared. In the Baltic Sea, where there was less danger from hostile surface craft, *Deutschland*, *Hertha*, *Odin*, *Prinz Adalbert*, *Prinz Sigismund*, *Prinz Waldemar*, *Rügen*, *Senta*, *Silvania*, and *Wotan* laid between 80 and 320 mines each, and helped to perfect Germany's mine barrages off her major rivers. The Helgoland barrage in the North Sea was eventually extended along the line Horn Reefs to the Frisian Islands.

Captain Magnus v. Levetzow estimated after the war that German mines had accounted for 8 battleships, 3 armoured cruisers, 2 light cruisers, 44 destroyers and 207 auxiliary ships; also over 1.1 million tons of merchant shipping. In all, the Reich laid nearly 50,000 mines, which necessitated a staff increase at home from 900 to 4,000 during the Great War. British statistics support the magnitude of this effort. The Royal Navy's monthly minesweeps retracted 178 mines in 1916, 355 in 1917, and 159 in 1918. It was estimated in Berlin that about 3 or 4 per cent of the mines laid found targets. At the height of the mine war, Britain deployed nearly 1,00 minesweepers in European waters, and it took several years after the end of the war to sweep up the more than 200,000 mines that had been laid by Britain, Germany and the United States, especially in the North Sea.

As previously mentioned, Germany converted a number of fast merchant ships to act as auxiliary cruisers. In all, seventeen of these vessels were used during the war while another ten were prepared for this task but never deployed, and a further four considered but not converted. The ships were requisitioned chiefly from the North German Lloyd, the Hamburg–America Line and the Hamburg–South Line; about six enemy prize ships were also used as surface raiders. The craft were disguised as neutral freighters and armed with either 10.5 cm or 15 cm concealed guns. Three raiders, *Möwe*, *Wolf* and *Seeadler*, earned particular notoriety at the Admiralty. *Möwe*, the old banana steamer *Pungo*, has already been cited in her minelaying capacity where she claimed the battleship *King Edward VII*. She conducted Atlantic raids in 1915–16 and 1916–17, during which she bagged thirty-four Allied ships totalling 161,000 tons. *Seeadler* was the old United States three-master *Pass of Balmaha* (1878), seized by *U 36* in 1915 and fitted with two 10.5 cm guns. She eventually destroyed ten hostile ships totalling 30,000 tons, and from the Atlantic passed round Cape Horn and operated in the South Sea before being beached on Mopelia Island in August 1917. *Wolf* was the former steamer *Wachtfels*, fitted with five 15 cm guns and 465 mines. She also carried a single seaplane (*Wölfchen*) for reconnaissance. At the end of 1916, she embarked on a trip that was to take her into the South Atlantic Ocean, through the Indian Ocean and into the Pacific Ocean off Australia. She sent to the bottom twelve enemy ships totalling 38,400 tons, and her mines accounted for another 74,000 tons of quarry. *Wolf* survived the war, returning from her exploits to Kiel in February 1918.

Merchant ships were also converted for other uses as the Navy slowly became aware of the possibility of deploying seaplane-carriers in the North Sea. Little had been done along these lines before 1914 owing to Admiral v. Tirpitz's firm belief that such craft had no military value whatsoever. The British, on the other hand, under Churchill's prodding, already proved surprisingly willing to experiment in naval aviation.

The Royal Naval Air Service was born in July 1914, and on 1 April 1918 merged with the Royal Flying Corps to form the Royal Air Force; by the end of the war, it operated about 2,950 aircraft. After a modest start, the RNAS quickly converted four Channel packets (*Campania, Empress, Engadine,* and *Riviera*) as seaplane-carriers. They each carried three Short aircraft below decks and hoisted them to and, it was hoped, from the water by derricks. On Christmas 1914, the *Empress, Engadine* and *Riviera*, escorted by two cruisers and eight destroyers, carried out the first carrier strike

in history. Steaming to a position only twelve miles north of Helgoland, they placed seven seaplanes in the water in order to raid the
Zeppelin sheds at Cuxhaven. It was indicative of the pioneering
stage of this weapon that only three craft managed even to complete
the flight to the target, doing little damage but greatly scaring the
Germans and causing them to lose one seaplane. The three British
planes buzzed the High Sea Fleet anchored in Schillig Roads, and
in the ensuing confusion the battle-cruiser *Von der Tann* rammed
another warship. The British seaplane-carriers safely tarried off
Helgoland for three hours and then returned to Harwich. Also
during that autumn, British flying craft successfully raided the
Zeppelin sheds at Friedrichshafen on Lake Constance – the first
completely successful air raid upon Germany (21 November). On
the other hand, German U-boats in December torpedoed the first
seaplane-carrier, *Hermes*, off Dover.

The RNAS by 1915 had built up its forces to 11 dirigibles, 118
seaplanes and 236 aeroplanes. *Campania* was assigned to the Grand
Fleet, and *Engadine* to Beatty's Battle-Cruiser Force. *Ark Royal,
Ben-my-Chree* and *Vindex* were added as seaplane-carriers during
that year; the first two went to the Dardanelles, where *Ben-my-
Chree* unsuccessfully attempted to bomb the *Goeben* and *Breslau*
from the air. *Campania* proved to be beset with bad luck : she was
home during Jutland because she had missed the signal to put out
to sea, and later that year engine trouble forced her to remain in
port during a German raid on Sunderland. *Engadine*, which had
been at Jutland with Beatty, was frustrated at Sunderland because
her seaplanes could not lift off the heavy seas. Early in 1917,
Manxman joined the Grand Fleet, giving Jellicoe three seaplane-
carriers with twenty-four aircraft.

Jutland had shown the Admiralty that there existed a need for
proper aeroplane-carriers that could send their craft aloft even in
mist and heavy seas. Experiments during 1917 were encouraging.
A Sopwith Pup not only took off from the deck of the cruiser
Yarmouth, but also managed to down the Zeppelin *L 23*. Another
Pup was launched from the gun turret of the battle-cruiser *Renown*,
and each squadron of the Grand Fleet now received one light cruiser
specially fitted with a flying-off platform. In addition, the converted
battle-cruiser *Furious* in March–July 1917 was given an 86 m by
21 m flight deck as well as protective guns; she carried between
eight and ten planes below decks and, following the example of the
Pennsylvania in 1912, was provided with arrester wires on deck;

her planes received special hooks on their undercarriage axles. Sopwith Pups could land on the forward flying-off deck of *Furious*, and the modern aircraft-carrier had arrived. The Admiralty at once decided to convert two more ships into seaplane-carriers : the *Argus* and *Eagle* were given completely flush decks with offset island super-structures, thereby taking on the appearance of the aircraft-carrier of later days.

There could now be no retarding naval aviation. In June 1918, escorted by the First Cruiser Squadron, *Furious* managed to send seven Sopwith Camels against the German airship base at Tondern. It was the first carrier-launched strike against a land target and, according to John Killen, the forerunner of Fleet Air Arm Sword-fish at Taranto in 1940. Two weeks before the armistice, the air-craft-carrier *Argus*, with twenty craft and with a flight deck of 565 ft, joined the Grand Fleet. Admiral Fisher fully appreciated the revolutionary nature of naval air power in 1919 : "All you want is the present naval side of the Air Force – that's the future navy." By war's end, each capital ship with the Grand Fleet carried one plane fore and one aft, a total of over 120 planes. Their value to the Fleet was never determined because the Germans did not test the Royal Navy in the North Sea after Jutland. Admirals Andrew Browne Cunningham and Isoroku Yamamoto were later to justify Fisher's somewhat hastily arrived-at faith in naval aviation.

The German Navy reacted quite differently to the potential of naval air power. Neither the six seaplanes at Helgoland, nor the four at Holtenau nor the two at Putzig, nor even the airship *L 3* had been included in mobilization orders in August 1914. In fact, only the dirigible and nine of the available thirty-six seaplanes were operable in 1914. Unlike their British counterparts, they carried no wireless sets. Moreover, the German aircraft did not have bomb-sights, bomb bays or a camera for aerial photography. The best model developed was a two-seater fighter armed with two fixed machine-guns and one mobile one. Nothing of substance had come of the long-range plan to build fifty seaplanes and aeroplanes by 1915, and the 1914–15 budget of 7.65 million GM for naval aviation was hardly likely to alter the sad state of affairs. The future, German naval planners argued, belonged to airships.

With the outbreak of war, the German Naval Air Service fell under the command of Rear-Admiral Hipper, Commander of Scouting Forces. Hipper expected an immediate British attack, and accordingly sent his aircraft on reconnaissance patrols. He also requisitioned five airships. When the Harwich Force appeared in the Helgoland Bight, in August 1914, *L 3* was fired upon by German warships and hastily left the scene, with the result that it failed to spot Beatty's battle-cruisers and perhaps to save three light cruisers. Possibly because of this, German air forces were reorganized towards the end of 1914. A special Commander of Navy Aerial Forces (BdL) was established with both dirigibles and aeroplanes under his command. The aircraft training centre was moved in October from Johannisthal to Putzig, and three naval aircraft divisions were created: I. Navy Flyer Division at Kiel-Holtenau, II. Navy Flyer Division at Wilhelmshaven, and III. Navy Flyer Division at Flanders. Additional smaller centres were also on Helgoland and later on Borkum, Sylt and Norderney. The Flanders contingent came under the command of Admiral v. Schröder, widely hailed as the "Lion of Flanders" but known to his friends as "Ludwig the Prickly". The Navy Office also established a new Department of Aerial Navigation (Ab. Lu.), and by the autumn of 1915 a special land station at Johannisthal began systematically to train pilots for the Navy.

These were modest beginnings, indeed. By the end of 1914, Germany had only six airships and less than twelve seaplanes on patrol in the North Sea – at a time when the RNAS had over seventy seaplanes. The purely reconnaissance function of air power, however, was terminated with construction of the Friedrichshafen 200 hp (Benz) craft. With a range of 130 sm, a crew of two, a wireless set, and machine-gun and bombs, they were deployed against enemy submersibles. German seaplanes initially had been armed only with carbines and pistols, but by 1915 a movable, air-cooled machine-gun for defensive purposes had been mounted near the observer's seat. At the end of 1916 this gave way to a model similar to that of the Army with machine-guns for attack fitted on the sides of the engine up front. And during the summer of 1918, Germany first mounted the 2 cm aircraft-cannon.

The Reich initially developed a single-seater fighter for the Navy, including the Hansa-Brandenburg W12 with 200 hp propulsion. Later, emphasis was placed on two-seater craft of 180 hp, with a best speed of 170 km per hour, three machine-guns aluminum pontoons, and fuel sufficient for an endurance of 210 minutes (Hansa-Brandenburg W29). Twin-engined torpedo-planes were also developed. These craft were fitted with two 100 hp motors and were designed to deliver a single torpedo. It was expected that the plane would be lost after it had discharged the torpedo. In addition to this highly unproductive trait, torpedo-planes proved to be too light for the job. Further structural strengthening only brought with it the need for stronger and hence heavier propulsion plants. The first torpedo-planes had been designed by Ernst Heinkel at Flensburg, using the basic twin-engined Hansa-Brandenburg GW type. A larger GWD model was designed to carry one 4,000 lb torpedo, and in November 1916 managed to destroy a British ship in the Thames estuary. However, by 1918 the Navy abandoned development of torpedo-planes because the heavy losses in craft did not justify the meagre results. On the brighter side, continued development of the two Hansa-Brandenburg types in 1917–18 gave the Imperial Navy virtual air superiority over the Channel; both the biplane W12 and the monoplane W29 were based at Zeebrugge and Oostende.

Perhaps because of the disappointing performance of the torpedo-planes, the Navy slowly turned to the idea of seaplane-carriers. As previously noted, tests with the cruiser *Friedrich Carl* in September 1913 had not impressed Tirpitz, and hence the Navy had to start anew during the Great War. Among German warships, only the light cruiser *Stuttgart* was converted to a seaplane-carrier. Her armament was reduced from ten to four 10.5 cm and two 8.8 cm anti-aircraft guns during February–May 1918, and in addition to 108 mines, she received three seaplanes which had to be lowered to and raised from the water by special davits on her aft deck. The armoured cruiser *Roon* in 1916 was also planned for service as a carrier for four seaplanes, but was not converted in time. Instead, Berlin decided between 1915 and 1918 to use five merchant ships as seaplane-carriers. The *Adeline Hugo Stinnes* was fitted with three seaplanes, *Answald* with two (later three), *Santa Elena* with three (later four), *Glyndwr* and *Oswald* – two British prizes – with four. It was at one time planned to convert the light cruiser *Stettin* along the lines of her sister-ship, but this never materialized.

Ernst Heinkel had developed the fast and heavily armed Hansa-Brandenburg *W12* biplane for these seaplane-carriers, and he later came up with the *W19* and *W29* monoplanes for use at sea. Apart from these Hansa-Brandenburg floatplanes, only Friedrichshafen entered the picture with the uninteresting *FF 33E* series of two-seater seaplanes. The latter, single and sturdy conventional biplanes, attained some fame because one, dubbed *Wölfchen*, was carried by the raider *Wolf*. Its success, in turn, prompted Heinkel to develop a small biplane flying-boat for the newly designed large ocean-going submarines (*U 139–U 141*), but assembly, dismantling and stowage problems remained unresolved by August 1918. On the other hand, both in Britain and in Germany, a mania for huge flying-boats developed. Claudius Dornier produced a gigantic craft made of a new duraluminum alloy and powered by Maybach engines, *Rs III*, but these did not see service at the front. However, the Gotha G.V. arrived in Gent in 1917 and, with endurance of four hours, was used as a bomber against British cities. A Zeppelin-Giant seaplane with four 260 hp engines was also used to bomb Britain between May 1917 and May 1918. In all, the German Navy placed orders in the Great War for 2,500 seaplanes.

German seaplanes and aeroplanes did not play a decisive role in the war at sea. At the Dogger Bank in January 1915, a seaplane from Borkum managed to bomb a British destroyer rescuing victims of the sinking *Blücher*. This sad incident marked the first participation of naval aircraft in fleet action.

Administrative changes were frequent in the Imperial Navy. At the beginning of 1916, the BdL was divided into a "Commander of Navy Flyer Department" (BdFlieg.) and a "Leader of Navy Airships" (FdL), the latter directly under the Chief of the High Sea Fleet. In June 1917, the "BdFlieg." was dissolved and replaced by a "Navy Fly Chief", who found support for aircraft development especially from the Admiralty Staff and, after August 1918, the Navy Supreme Command. By November 1918, the German naval air arm consisted of 16,122 men (including 2,116 flight personnel) distributed over thirty-two seaplane stations in the North Sea, Baltic Sea, Black Sea, and Mediterranean Sea, as well as seventeen land air stations with an overall strength of 1,478 seaplanes and aeroplanes. However, not a single ship similar to a modern carrier such as the British *Furious* had gone as far as the drawing-board. Nor had aircraft of any type been assigned to the High Sea Fleet – at a time when the Admiralty in London had fitted nearly all battleships, 11 battle-cruisers and 22 light cruisers with flying-off platforms; in all, over 100 aeroplanes, including many Sopwith 2F.1 "Camel" craft, with the Grand Fleet.

The Imperial Navy had rested its hopes on airships. This faith depended on an incredibly small force. In August 1914 the newly created Leader of Airships (FdL) commanded a single Zeppelin (*L 3*) based at Nordholz. His forces were to grow, however, in the course of the war by 9 airships in 1914, 16 in 1915, 18 in 1916,

23 in 1917 and 8 in 1918, as well as 3 taken over from the Army. Personnel climbed from 273 officers and men in 1914 to 6,000 by 1918. Dirigibles were delivered by three firms: 64 by Luftschiffbau Zeppelin for service over the North Sea, 9 by Schütte-Lanz for the Baltic Sea, and 3 by Parseval as well as the one "M" airship. The 77 dirigibles flew 1,148 reconnaissance missions and engaged in 200 attacks. Their initial task was to scout enemy warships, find mine-fields and search out hostile submarines; in 1915 the first raids on the British and Russian coasts were undertaken, but they were suspended in the winter of 1916–17 owing to heavy losses to British aircraft. A second wave of Zeppelin attacks was ordered in March 1917 with the arrival of larger and faster dirigibles, but attacks against freighters were called off because the latter had been armed with anti-aircraft guns.

Zeppelin reconnaissance started slowly. No dirigibles accompanied Hipper's battle-cruisers in raids against Gorleston, Hartlepool, Scarborough, Whitby, and Yarmouth in 1914 owing to bad weather. The Leader of Airships in January 1915 felt emboldened to launch the first airship raid. *L 3* and *L 4* attacked King's Lynn, Sheringham and Yarmouth, doing little damage – as did all subsequent Zeppelin raids – with only 3,000 kg of explosives; *L 6* had to turn back because of engine malfunction. The two ships that had attacked the British towns in January were lost the following month in Danish territory when strong snow gales forced them off course. In March and April 1915, three airships were deployed by Admiral v. Pohl for the first time for close tactical reconnaissance for the High Sea Fleet.

These early airships (*L 3*) were small craft with aluminum skeletons containing 23,000 cbm oxy-hydrogen gas, powered by four Maybach engines, and carrying three gondolas armed with machine-guns. They increased moderately by 1915 (*L 10*) to 32,000 cbm, and by 1916 (*L 31*) to 55,200 cbm displacement. The larger craft required a crew of twenty-three as well as ground personnel of twenty-four; all were volunteers from the High Sea Fleet, and many sought action here to relieve the monotony of life in the High Sea Fleet at home. Dirigibles were armed primarily with incendiary bombs, demolition bombs, and flares hand-thrown from the housing. The *L 10* class could reach Britain with two tons of bombs.

Zeppelins in 1915 conducted 297 scouting trips and 51 raids, including an attack of 5 airships on London in August; 2 were lost in aerial action and 4 through accidents. The airships caused great consternation among Admirals Fisher, Jellicoe and Beatty as the so-called "eyes" of the High Sea Fleet. Churchill, on the other hand, accurately evaluated their weaknesses and favoured aircraft development instead. The RNAS at first countered airships by stationing two paddle-steamers each with two or three Sopwith Baby planes sixty miles east of Great Yarmouth and Killingholme – a clear indication that Germany did not have a monopoly of muddling through.

The year 1916 proved to be decisive for the future of the airship. In March, L 7 became the first Zeppelin downed by ship fire from an ordinary 15 cm gun. The next month, three airships accompanied Hipper's battle-cruisers as scouting craft during a raid against Lowestoft. Admiral Scheer left port on 31 May 1916 in order to raid the British coast around Sunderland; five dirigibles were assigned to the fleet as scouts, but had to be left behind owing to foul weather. They arrived at the scene of battle only after the surface screens had made contact, and even then fog and mist restricted reconnaissance by the much-feared "eyes" of Scheer's fleet. Ironically, Hipper's Scouting Forces were discovered by British seaplanes commanded by Flight-Lieutenant F. J. Rutland, destined to go down in history as "Rutland of Jutland". Neither seaplanes nor dirigibles played a significant role during the first and only fleet encounter of the war.

In May 1916 the new "Super Zeppelins" of the L 30 class arrived at the front. They were powered by six engines and were able to reach Scapa Flow with impunity because anti-aircraft guns could not reach them at optimum altitude. That year, German dirigibles performed 283 scouting missions and 202 bombing raids. Losses amounted to sixteen craft, including five gunned down, and constituted the highest casualty rate of the war for a single year. When fourteen Zeppelins became available in 1917, they were deployed primarily as scouts for the submarine war – as were seaplanes – owing to the high attrition rate.

But the year 1917 brought no relief. In April and May, the United States made available several Curtiss flying-boats ("Large America"), and L 22 had the dubious honour of becoming the first airship destroyed by one of these craft. Mine-clearing by dirigibles now also had to be abandoned because British seaplane attacks became highly effective. In order to circumvent this new threat, Zeppelins climbed ever higher, from 3,000 to 6,000 metres, with the result that crews often lost consciousness and became sick because of lack of oxygen and extreme cold at high altitudes. Wind also continued to take its toll, driving four dirigibles off course to France, where they were downed by aircraft. Over the latter part of 1917, airships undertook only three raids against England, and during the last of these, five of eleven were lost. General Ludendorff attempted to halt all Zeppelin building, but Admiral Scheer managed to win the Kaiser's approval for naval use of them. At the end of that year, only eleven dirigibles as opposed to fifty seaplanes remained.

In 1918 the large *L 60* airships, displacing 68,500 cbm, arrived at naval stations, but failed to turn the tide in the air war. Five dirigibles burned at Ahlhorn in January, leaving only six for North Sea scouting. Foul weather in April also precluded airship reconnaissance for the High Sea Fleet's final sortie into the northern North Sea. And in August the last Zeppelin raid against Britain was undertaken. It proved to be a disaster as British aircraft shot down *L 70*, which took the Leader of Airships, Commander Peter Strasser, a pioneer of naval airship development, down with her. Raids were left in 1918 primarily to the large Gotha and Staaken Giant heavy bombers, which attacked London several times. Between 1914 and 1918, Germany dropped 355 incendiary and 567 explosive bombs on London, killing 670 people and injuring 1,962. On the lighter side, bombs dropped at Leith in April 1916 struck a whisky distillery causing the precious liquid to flow in the gutters; many citizens were soon found unconscious on their backs.

At war's end, Germany had only 16 airships in service for the Navy: 8 were surrendered to the Allies, 1 was dismantled, and 7 were sabotaged by their crews in June 1919. 53 airships were destroyed between 1914 and 1918, including 35 lost with their crews.

Obviously, the "lighter-than-air" dirigible did not prove itself to be a reliable *guerre de course* weapon. Neither as a scout nor as a raider did it live up to expectations. Submarine development, on the other hand, evoked a different response in Berlin. Here was a *Kleinkrieg* craft that could, indeed, seriously threaten Great Britain's vital overseas lifelines with relatively small expenditure of time and money.

The U-boat, as we have seen, had not been accorded a high place in Tirpitz's strategy prior to 1914. The Chief of the Admiralty Staff, Admiral v. Pohl, in October 1914 likewise opposed an all-out underwater offensive, informing the Leader of Submarines (FdU),

Lieutenant-Commander Hermann Bauer, that it constituted a "severe violation of international law". In fact, already in June 1914 the Chief of Submarine Inspection, Captain Hermann Nordmann-Burgau, and Admiral v. Tirpitz opted against a suggestion by a junior officer to build 222 submarines for use against British overseas trade.

The Royal Navy, for its part, before August 1914 dismissed the notion of sinking merchant ships without warning as "impossible and unthinkable"; the First Lord refused to believe that "this would ever be done by a civilized Power". This notwithstanding, warfare against merchants was inaugurated on 20 October 1914, when Lieutenant Feldkirchner's *U 17* stopped and then destroyed the British freighter *Glitra* in Stavanger. On 22 February 1915, Berlin declared the waters round Britain and Ireland to be a war zone, warning that all vessels found there would be treated as belligerents. It was the start of a new type of warfare, whose victims were to be civilian passengers as well as merchant crews.

But Germany needed a force greater than twenty-eight U-boats effectively to blockade the British Isles. In November 1914, Berlin had designed a new type, the UC minelaying boats. These were generally about 150 tons and carried twelve mines, loaded with 120–150 kg explosives, in six holds fore and aft. An additional UB series of small coastal craft was also developed, displacing about 125 tons and armed with two 45 cm bow torpedo tubes. They were primarily deployed in Flanders, where they were transported in three sections by rail and assembled for fear of their inability to make the long journey from Germany through the often treacherous North Sea.

The Imperial Navy between 1914 and 1918 built 139 UB craft (4 were completed after the war had ended). The initial *UBI* type (nos 1–17) was followed by a large *UBII* series (nos 18–47). These were 270-ton boats built at a cost of between 1.1 and 1.3 million GM; two 50 cm bow tubes could fire four (later six) torpedoes, and one 5 cm gun with 200 rounds completed their armament. A final *UBIII* series (nos 48–132, 148, 149) was built in 1916–17. These boats displaced about 500 tons, could dive in thirty seconds, and were armed with four bow tubes and one stern tube firing ten 50 cm torpedoes, and one 8.8 cm (later 10.5 cm) gun. Surface speed was 13 knots, submerged 7.5 knots. Underwater endurance was limited to 55 sm at four knots.

The pioneer *UCI* craft (nos 1–15) were succeeded in 1915–17 by the *UCII* series (nos 16–79). These were 410-ton boats armed with two bow tubes and one stern tube firing seven 50 cm torpedoes, one 8.8 cm (later 10.5 cm) gun, and six 100 cm shafts discharging eighteen mines. A final *UCIII* class (nos 80–105) was built in 1917–18. These were roughly 180-ton boats, armed with three tubes firing seven 50 cm torpedoes, one 8.8 cm or one 10.5 cm gun, and six shafts fitted for fourteen mines. Overall, ninety-five of these craft were delivered during the war. The first mines were laid on 31 May 1915 in the southern estuary of the Downs by UC boats stationed at Zeebrugge, and UC craft arrived at Pola in the Adriatic in 1915. The *UBI* and *UBIII* as well as the UC vessels were single-hulled; *UBIII* boats were double-hulled and became the basic *VII A-C* type used in the Second World War.

The customary six obliquely mounted bow shafts or tubes discharged a normal load of eighteen mines through the boat's bottom. The German mines operated as follows. Both mine and sinker went to the bottom, where the dissolution of a soluble plug allowed the partially air-filled mine to float up toward the surface until a hydrostatic device was activated at the desired depth. The line connecting the mine to the sinker was then snubbed. The sinker had arms that swung out when it reached the bottom in order to stabilize it. The drawback of this system was that the two ropes connecting mine to sinker allowed substantial swaying and variance in depth, while the soluble release mechanism at times dissolved as soon as the mine was released, with the result that it came up and struck the submarine. The so-called German "egg" mine was fitted with the Hertz horn, a lead tube containing sulphuric acid in a glass container. Impact with a ship broke the glass, allowed the acid to flow onto carbon/zinc elements and thus produced an electric current that fired the detonator attached to the explosives.

When unrestricted submarine warfare was first announced in February 1915, only two boats (*U 16, U 30*) patrolled British waters. Berlin simply could not build sufficient craft. In August 1914, 11 U-boats were behind schedule. This figure rose to 25 in April 1916, 36 in July 1917, 70 in April 1918, and 72 in October 1918. Throughout the war, only 12 vessels were delivered on time; 50 arrived at the front more than six months and 114 more than nine months behind schedule. In all, between 1908 and 1918, the Imperial Navy built 143 so-called large fleet boats, all of which save the large minelayers *U 71–U 80* were double-hulled craft. Their classification ranged from *U 1* to *U 165* (Table 28).

The fateful decision to resume unrestricted submarine warfare on 1 February 1917, after United States protests had twice halted the U-war in 1915 and 1916, greatly compounded the need for more submarines. Every available vessel was needed for the war effort, including the merchant submarines *U 151–U 157*. These were 1,503 to 1,880-ton boats, converted for naval use in 1917. They were armed with two bow tubes firing eighteen or twenty 50 cm torpedoes, two 15 cm and two 8.8 cm deck guns. Twin 400 hp Germania diesels (originally intended for the battleship *Sachsen* and the battle-cruiser *Ersatz Gneisenau*) provided a best speed of twelve knots on the surface; submerged speed was a dismal five knots. Unfortunately, in addition to being slow both above and below the surface, the boats were limited in torpedo power by having only two bow tubes, and almost entirely without manoeuvrability.

Germany had commenced unrestricted submarine warfare in 1917 with a total of 104 boats (45 with the High Sea Fleet, 22 in Flanders, 24 at Pola, 10 in the Baltic or Courland, and 3 at Constantinople). During 1917, the U-boat flotillas increased by 87 new vessels: 32 fleet, 42 UB and 13 UC units. The *U 96–U 98* series built by Krupp's Germania yard in Kiel at a unit cost of 4.4 million GM was fairly representative. They displaced 837 tons, had a best surface speed of almost seventeen knots, submerged eight knots, and a diving time of sixty-six seconds. They were fitted with four bow and two stern tubes firing twelve or sixteen 50 cm torpedoes, and one 10.5 cm deck gun with 140–240 rounds. Two MAN six-cylinder four-cycle diesels provided 2,300 hp and a range above water of about 8,000 sm at eight knots; underwater endurance remained relatively disappointing with 47 sm at five knots.

During July 1917, the submarines sighted their first convoys. Danger increased. Success diminished. While only twenty boats were destroyed during the first half of 1917, the toll by the end of the year had risen to sixty-three. Planners in Berlin reacted by enlarging the blockade zones around the British Isles, carefully training crews in the latest tactics at the U-boat School in Eckernförde, and stepping up production. To facilitate the latter, the Reich in December 1917 finally created a special U-boat Office under Vice-Admiral Ernst Ritter v. Mann, Edler v. Tiechler – ten months after the total commitment to unrestricted submarine warfare. One of Mann's first tasks was to place orders for 120 submersibles, followed over the next six months by an additional 200. As a result, 88 boats came to the front in 1918: 25 fleet, 47 UB and 16 UC craft. Losses that year amounted to 69 U-boats. It was computed that on an average day in 1918, Germany had 5,467 men out at sea in 160 submarines (Table 29).

Great strides had been made since 1914 in U-boat construction, especially with the introduction of the "shark's head" bows which mounted net cutters against enemy net obstructions. On the other hand, basic weaknesses concerning underwater propulsion in particular were chronic until the very end. The dependence upon heavy batteries (2 × 110 Afag mass-cell storage batteries) for submerged running prompted planners constantly to seek to increase battery power which, in turn, meant reduced fuel capacity for surface running as well as reduced armament. The larger U-boats could usually travel submerged for about 100 miles at three knots, or about thirty hours; evasive action underwater necessitated higher speed (eight knots) and considerably reduced endurance to 20 miles, or 150 minutes. Under these conditions, it is remarkable what commanders such as Arnauld de la Perière managed to get out of the primitive boats.

Germany's U-boat command was incredibly tangled. At the initial stage of development between 1905 and 1913, submarines were placed under the Inspection of Torpedo Development, and in 1914 transferred to a newly-formed Inspection of Submarine Development. Between August 1914 and November 1918, the U-boat force was badly divided among numerous command posts. Submarines attached to the High Sea Fleet to June 1917 came under a Leader of Submarines (FdU), and thereafter under a Commander of Submarines (BdU); both were accountable to the Chief of the High Sea Fleet. Flanders units were headed by the Leader of Submarines-Flanders from October 1917 to October 1918, while those in the Baltic came directly under the auspices of the Commander of Baltic Fleet (Admiral Prince Heinrich) from August 1914 to December 1917. The submarine-cruisers based on Kiel in 1917 were commanded by the Admiralty Staff, and in 1918 by the Commander of Submarines (Captain Andreas Michelsen) at Wilhelmshaven.

Most confusing of all was the situation in the Mediterranean and Adriatic Seas. At the start of the war, the boats in the western Mediterranean flew the Austro–Hungarian flag, and in the eastern Mediterranean the Turkish. In October 1915, Emperor Franz Joseph ruled that with the passage of the Straits of Gibraltar, the U-boats were to be carried in the lists of the Austro–Hungarian

Navy. When Italy entered the war, Berlin in August 1916 ordered
its forces in the *Mittelmeer* to wear German uniforms but to fly the
Habsburg red-white-red banner. Finally, in June 1917 a special
Leader of Submarines-Mediterranean (FdU Mittelmeer) was created
for Pola and Cattaro. Nominally under Austro–Hungarian command, this post nevertheless received orders from the Admiralty
Staff in Berlin. And if this tangled web of command posts in Berlin,
Kiel, Wilhelmshaven, Pola, Cattaro, Vienna, Flanders, and Courland was not enough, Admiralty Staff, High Sea Fleet and Navy
Office vied with the U-boat Office after December 1917 in ship-
building policies.

At least with regard to the latter, relief finally came on 1 October
1918 when Admiral Scheer became head of the new centralized
Navy War Command (*Seekriegsleitung*). This post at once drafted
the so-called "Scheer Programme" parallel to the Army's "Hindenburg Programme" of 1916, calling for an increased monthly production of U-boats from 13 in October 1918 to 22 by April 1919,
and to 33 by August 1919. At the end of the programme, Germany
would produce 37 boats in December 1919, and 33 per month
during 1920. This monstrous undertaking called for 376 to 450
submersibles and would have entailed a work force of 69,000 men
distributed over eleven shipyards. The "Scheer Programme", of
course, never really had a chance of success, given the Army's urgent
needs, and it remained a Utopian dream. Moreover, there exists
sufficient evidence to suggest that Scheer developed this programme
as a massive propaganda effort designed to have an effect at home
and abroad – it was officially announced in Köln, where a large
enemy spy-ring was known to exist.

By war's end, Germany had built 6 light cruisers, 174 torpedo-
boats, 346 submarines (115 fleet, 136 UB and 95 UC craft), and
196 minesweepers. The last Dreadnought (*Württemberg*) had been
launched in June 1917, the last battle-cruiser (*Graf Spee*) in
September 1917, and the last light cruiser (*Frauenlob*) in October
1918. Over the four years of the war, the Imperial Navy lost 2
battleships, 1 battle-cruiser, 6 armoured cruisers, 18 light cruisers,
17 gunboats, 110 torpedo-boats, 229 U-boats, and various other craft.

In conclusion, it should be pointed out that any attempt to render a
few prescient comments on the basic issue of *Kleinkrieg* versus
Grosskrieg can only scratch the surface. The subject deserves a full,
detailed treatment. Defenders of the Tirpitzean battle-fleet strategy

readily point out that the High Sea Fleet prevented the British from landing troops along the German coast or in Flanders, kept the vital sea lanes in the Baltic open for Swedish iron ore deliveries, held superior Russian Baltic forces at bay for four years, protected the egress and return of German submarines from North Sea bases, helped bring Turkey into the war on the side of the Central Powers in 1914, and tied down the world's largest fleet in its northern anchorages. Proponents of *guerre de course* quickly counter that the High Sea Fleet only engaged the Grand Fleet once in the North Sea, sinking three armoured cruisers and three battle-cruisers, without altering the course of the war significantly – while the submarines made 3,274 sorties against the enemy, destroying 6,394 ships of 11,948,702 tons.

There can be no question, however, that paralyzing indecision concerning capital-ship building developed in Germany during the war. As early as October 1914, Wilhelm II had recognized "that no more Dreadnoughts should be built". The Navy Office's renewed belief in capital ships in the spring of 1918, in the wake of the first successes of the "Michael" offensive in the West, was perhaps prompted by the realization that the submarine campaign had by then failed. But the later claims of many executive officers, from Scheer downwards, that only the High Sea Fleet in 1917–18 permitted the submarine offensive by securing the vital North Sea approaches against British submersibles and mines is an old bogey that needs to be dispelled. Admiral Jellicoe had decided already in 1916 to stay out of the south-eastern North Sea, *not* on account of the High Sea Fleet, but for fear of submarine attack. Therefore it was Jellicoe's strategic decision that permitted the relatively safe passage of U-boats; Admiral Beatty later opted for the same policy with regard to his battle-cruisers. Moreover, Scheer's argument in October 1918, that even after a defeat in the North Sea the High Sea Fleet would retain enough heavy ships to protect the U-boats, constitutes perhaps the most cogent counter to post-war claims that nearly all twenty capital ships of the fleet played an indispensable role in the submarine war.

Admiral Scheer realized fully after Jutland that the *Grosskrieg* could not defeat Britain. In addition, the Reich never managed to develop a happy synthesis of a uniform type of capital ship, a "fast battleship". The constant conflict between High Sea Fleet and Navy Office was never resolved. Scheer demanded greater speed (32 knots), heavier guns (42 cm) and thicker armour (350 mm belt), while Capelle countered with financial and technical arguments to show that a "fast battleship" could not be realized. Both men thus merely hoped to delay the basic decision between the "blue water" and the "young" school while the U-boat "trump" was played out. As Rear-Admiral Walther Baron v. Keyserlingk later put it: "It was a tragic picture of disharmonious energies, each individually capable of great performances but unable to achieve close co-operation." By the time the submarine campaign had failed, it was too late to attempt basic decisions. Nor did the Kaiser prove to be of assistance in resolving the tangled and competing naval commands. Levetzow bitterly commented after the war: "Our beloved Imperial War Lord at General-Headquarters was not a Frederick the Great."

Personnel considerations weighed heavily in the controversy between the competing schools of thought. Bethmann Hollweg's aide, Kurt Riezler, in February 1915 tersely recognized the basic issue: "Fear of the Navy's interest in battle fleets. U-boats and cruisers do not require admirals." The Navy Office (Rear-Admiral Karl Hollweg) in 1915–16 voiced similar trepidation among flag officers, noting that future concentration on small craft would "offer prospects for positions only to younger people, and not in sufficient numbers to persons in higher stations of life". The Navy Office also argued that too much attention was being paid to submarine skippers at the expense of officers in the High Sea Fleet. Many of the latter turned to parliamentary deputies such as Gustav Stresemann to plead for better promotion in the fleet. The derisive term "the war of ensigns and lieutenants" (*Der Krieg der Leutnants und Kapitänleutnants*) soon became fashionable. Tirpitz's successor, Admiral v. Capelle, while inspecting a new submarine model in Hamburg in January 1917, ominously warned: "We have already discussed in the Navy Office the possibility of creating after the war a special cemetery for our existing submarines." Three months later, he informed the Reichstag: "But you must take into consideration how organization and promotion will function in a Navy which has replaced its capital ships with dirigibles and submarines. This is a problem that has not been solved yet." In October, Capelle asked Holtzendorff to rescind what he termed "unlimited submarine construction orders" not only because this might precipitate "domestic crises" owing to labour's demands for higher wages, but also because promotion to flag rank would become superfluous except for a few administrative posts in Berlin. Such a drastic change would be tantamount to severing the head from the body, and the Navy Office wanted no part of such a radical innovation. It might be added that German naval leaders in the Second World War also never resolved this dilemma over *Kleinkrieg as* opposed to *Grosskrieg*. Erich Raeder's virtual removal from power in January 1943 in favour of the Leader of Submarines, Karl Dönitz, in the wake of Adolf Hitler's angry decision to pay off all existing capital ships and to use their heavy guns as shore batteries, was merely an outward symptom of the tragic repetition of an earlier period of indecision.

Grand Admiral v. Tirpitz's "Comments on the War at Sea 1918" sought merely to obfuscate the failure of German naval leaders to resolve the thorny issue of future naval building. Tirpitz recommended that only the German seizure of Jutland and Funen (Case J) could guarantee the Reich's future as a naval power by placing in her hands both the Skagerrak and the Kattegat, and with them at least limited northern access to vital Atlantic sea lanes. This memorandum, which was distributed to high-ranking fleet commanders by Rear-Admiral v. Trotha, recognized the validity of Commander Wolfgang Wegener's strategic considerations of 1916, but bore little resemblance to Germany's military situation in 1918. The failure of the submarine offensive, coupled with the continued idleness of the High Sea Fleet, established by the summer of 1917 a mood of despair and rebellion against authority among many petty officers and ratings.

XI

"Between the Thames and Helgoland"

German Naval Policies, 1917-1918

German submarine activity at sea in the spring of 1917 surpassed all expectations. In February 540,000 tons were torpedoed, an increase of about 170,000 tons over January. In March, Allied losses reached the target level of 600,000 tons. And April marked the best month of either world war: the available 107 U-boats conducted 133 raids, destroying 458 ships of 841,118 tons. Only the United States' declaration of war against Germany on 6 April 1917, a direct result of the resumption of unrestricted submarine warfare, marred the general euphoria of Germany's leaders. The Reich tried at first to maintain the fiction that it was not at war with the United States, but by 22 May the Admiralty Staff authorized attacks on American ships in the area around the British Isles. But Wilhelm II rejected the expansion of undersea operations to the east coast of the United States because he did not want to arouse what he considered to be the less militant regions of the American republic, the Midwest and the West.

On 10 May 1917, a new turn of events confounded U-boat commanders: the first British convoy of fifteen ships reached Plymouth from Gibraltar with no losses. In fact, on 25 April the energetic Prime Minister, David Lloyd George, had visited the Admiralty and ordered it to institute convoying of merchant shipping bound for England. Admiralty leaders initially feared that convoying would reduce the speed of all ships assembled to that of the slowest, thereby allowing the U-boats a better chance to attack. It was also believed that the requisite cruiser and destroyer escorts would deprive the Grand Fleet of its protective screen, and thereby cripple it in case of a sortie by the High Sea Fleet. The Admiralty also doubted whether merchant skippers possessed sufficient skills to navigate in convoy. Nor were they convinced that British ports could handle the congestion caused by the arrival and departure of so many vessels at the same time. But in the end, the prime minister's action proved to be correct; almost twelve months were to pass before the Germans even attempted to attack a convoy.

Several technical innovations developed earlier in the war against the U-boats were now fully adopted. These included for the Royal Navy depth charges, bomb howitzers and throwers, mine nets, explosive paravanes, flares, hydrophones, and even sea lions. One imaginative private developer suggested to Admiral Jellicoe that the North Sea be filled with barrels of Eno's Fruit Salt. They could be opened by shore control whenever a U-boat was spotted; the fruit salt would effervesce upon contact with the water, and the resulting bubbles would force the U-boat to the surface, where it could easily be disposed of. For merchantmen, the Admiralty produced a host of anti-submarine devices such as "dazzle" painting, the "Otter" mine-protecting device, zig-zagging, the "Actaeon" anti-torpedo net, and especially the arming of ships with small guns.

Convoying as well as anti-submarine devices rapidly reduced the effectiveness of the submarines. Sinkings in May dropped to 600,000 tons, rose in June to 700,000 tons, and fell by July to 550,000 tons. From this point on, monthly results levelled off around the 350,000 mark. The undersea war also took its toll of German submersibles. Whereas only twenty boats were destroyed in the first half of 1917, forty-three went to the bottom in the second half of that year.

Not surprisingly, optimism was no longer the dominant mood in German Army circles by the summer of 1917. Hindenburg's staff were beginning to show concern. The Army's head now regretted that the Admiralty Staff had announced a specific deadline (October) for the submarine victory over Britain. Bethmann Hollweg was also becoming apprehensive over the deteriorating course of the "last card", afraid that Austria-Hungary would not last out the year, and that the British would not yield by October 1917.

In the East alone was there a flicker of hope. In March 1917, a provisional government, headed by Prince George Lvov, replaced Tsar Nicholas II. Unfortunately, in July the new regime placed its hopes in a massive land offensive commanded by General Alexis

Brusilov against the Austrians, which, when halted by German
counter-attacks, caused Russian casualties to leap to 9 million as
German units mounted a relentless drive deep into the Ukraine and
the Caucasus.

October 1917 came and went without the predicted British surrender. Instead, U-boat sinkings were on a lower level than those
for May–July: in September the tonnage torpedoed was 352,000,
in October 460,000, in November 290,000, and in December
400,000. Something had to be done. The submarines attempted to
pool their information on merchant shipping sightings. They also
tried to intercept convoys near to shore, where the large escorts
left the freighters. At the U-boat School in Eckernförde, new crews
were trained to hunt convoys. And the war zones, in which all
shipping would be torpedoed without warning, were repeatedly
extended in order to provide the U-boats with more targets as well
as to force the enemy to disperse his escort craft. The original war
zone encompassed the English Channel, the western part of the
North Sea, and the western coasts of England, Ireland, Scotland,
and France, reaching approximately 400 miles west into the
Atlantic Ocean. The Mediterranean was also declared a war zone,
save for narrow shipping lanes south and east of Spain, the Balearic
Islands, and a safe channel for Greece. In March 1917 the Barents
Sea was incorporated into the German war zone, as were the Azores
in November. When Greece joined the Allied and Associated
Powers on 27 June 1917, her waters were freed for U-boat warfare,
and in January 1918 the Canary Islands and the Cape Verdes
were included in the German war zone.

The Germans also toyed with the idea of hunting convoys with
packs of submarines in order to enhance the effectiveness of the
undersea campaign. As the wireless range of U-boats was gradually
raised during the war from 140 sm in 1915 to almost 1,000 sm by
1918, some officers considered dispatching one large submarine to
the war zone to act as an information station. The Leader of
U-boats, Lieutenant-Commander Bauer, in 1916 persuaded the
fleet's leaders to send a U-cruiser to the west coast of England for
this purpose. Unfortunately, the Admiralty Staff, which commanded
U-cruisers, vetoed the notion and preferred instead to scatter its
units and to cover all zones. In fact, Admiral v. Holtzendorff
throughout 1917 opposed concentration of U-boats in so-called
"wolf packs" in favour of dispersing the submarines – and hence
also the enemy's escorts – as widely as possible. Bauer's successor,

Captain Andreas Michelsen, in November and December 1917 and again in April, May and July 1918 asked for permission to experiment with "wolf packs". To no avail. Not even the Kaiser, who was an enthusiastic proponent of this tactic, could persuade Holtzendorff to release U-cruisers for this purpose. Lieutenant Karl Dönitz later claimed that in the submarine service during the First World War there was not one successful joint operation of even two boats.

Several other factors militated against the success of unrestricted submarine warfare. As previously stated, the available units were spread out too thinly, from the Baltic to the Black Sea, and from the Mediterranean to the Barents Sea. Flanders was used as a U-boat base only after March 1915, for fear of British attacks. The submarine flotilla at Courland, by contrast, was maintained until December 1917, long after it had ceased to be useful.

Technical construction failures also plagued the campaign. The boats were too slow both submerged and on the surface. Air leaks from the torpedoes often provided ample warning to the intended victim, while similar air seepage from the submarine's tubes allowed enemy escorts to detect and attack the undersea raiders. The range of the submersible's wireless sets was insufficient at first, and no system of underwater wireless communications developed. German codes were frequently lost or broken.

The High Sea Fleet attempted to alleviate the mounting plight of the U-boats. Several minor sorties into the North Sea were conducted in the autumn of 1917 in yet another attempt to force the Allies to scatter their anti-submarine craft. Most notably, on 17 October the light cruisers *Brummer* and *Bremse* intercepted an Allied convoy of twelve vessels, destroying ten freighters and two escort destroyers (*Mary Rose* and *Strongbow*) on the route between Great Britain and Norway. Henry Newbolt roundly condemned the conduct of the Germans on that day :

Throughout the attack the Germans displayed a severity which is hard to distinguish from downright cruelty. They gave the neutral masters and crews no chance to lower their boats and get away, as though they had been armed enemies. . . . In the case of the destroyers the enemy's conduct was even worse; for to their everlasting discredit fire was opened and maintained upon the *Strongbow*'s survivors.

At least the Kaiser was ecstatic, toasting the deeds of the two light cruisers with champagne.

Two months later, on 12 December, one German light cruiser and four torpedo-boats raided another Scandinavian convoy of six ships; the latter were all sent to the bottom, as was one of the two British escort destroyers (*Partridge*). The Admiralty Staff hoped that these surface attacks might be implemented on a regular basis, but the Allies counteracted them by assigning heavier surface units as escorts and by reducing the number of convoys from Scandinavia to one every three days. Berlin thereupon refrained from committing its capital ships against convoys and instead concentrated on naval demonstrations in the Baltic Sea designed to assist the Army's capture of Riga. But large-scale disturbances in the High Sea Fleet quickly interrupted all tactical planning.

Morale on the big ships had reached deplorable levels by the summer of 1917. The last sortie by the entire fleet had been back in October 1916, and idleness, compounded by abysmal food, gnawed at the spirits of the men. In addition, the best junior officers were increasingly requesting transfers for service with the submarine branch; their replacements, inexperienced sea cadets and reserve officers, failed to provide the leadership requisite for maintaining morale and discipline among the ratings. While the submarine officers and crews received the undivided attention of the nation, those on the heavy ships felt neglected and forgotten. Routine duties such as coaling and painting failed to provide stimulation. The ships bobbed up and down at anchor and rusted while the war raged elsewhere. Sailors on shore leave came into contact with shipyard workers and political newspapers, mainly of the left-wing *genre*. Executive officers sought to counteract this development with still greater adherence to petty naval regulations pertaining especially to spit and polish. In short, the war became remote for the men of the fleet, while shore leave provided ample opportunity to indulge in political speculation and rumour.

Above all, the quality of the food served on the ships remained far below acceptable levels. Turnips, either boiled or dried, became the staple, along with what the men termed *Drahtverhau* – a nauseous concoction described by Seaman Richard Stumpf as consisting of 75 per cent water, 10 per cent sausage, 3 per cent potatoes, 2 per cent peas, 1 per cent yellow turnips, and small amounts of beef, fat and vinegar. Not surprisingly, the sight of better provisions in officers' messes incited the men to further complaints, and the isolated cases of officers who misused their privilege as members of the first estate especially embittered the stokers who toiled in coal bunkers and before blazing furnaces.

Idleness and boredom were not special preserves of the High Sea Fleet. The British capital ships were likewise affected by lack of action, and in addition were sequestered among the rocky crags and inlets of barren northern Scotland. To offset the lack of amenities, the British had organized rugby and soccer matches, golf, fishing, films, hikes, and a host of related activities designed to overcome boredom.

Across the North Sea, Admiral v. Capelle on 20 June 1917 at the behest of parliament had ordered the establishment of food supervisory committees (*Menagekommission*) on all ships in order to give the ratings a voice at least in the selection and preparation of their food. The Army had long ago introduced a similar measure. While such commissions were therefore hardly unique, the Navy command, from Scheer downwards, objected to what they considered to be "an infringement upon purely miltary matters". Ship captains, in fact, in most cases refused to appoint the food supervisory committees. When news leaked out through the press that the state secretary had ordered the creation of the *Menage-kommission* on each ship, the men in the fleet naturally felt deceived and even betrayed by their superiors.

Outright opposition to military orders or massive strikes would have constituted mutiny, and hence the enlisted men in June 1917 opted instead for passive resistance in order to force establishment of the food committees. The leaders of the movement were a mixed lot. Stoker Albin Köbis of the battleship *Prinzregent Luitpold* was a machinist from the working-class district of Pankow-Niederbarnim near Berlin, and an avowed anarchist. Another stoker on the same vessel, Johann Beckers, was also an anarchist and the son of a miner. Willi Sachse, stoker, and Max Reichpietsch, seaman, of *Friedrich der Grosse,* on the other hand, maintained contacts with Social Democracy, in particular, hoping that ties to the Independent Social Democratic Party (USPD) would provide concrete leadership for their efforts in the fleet. Sachse, born in Leipzig, had been a mechanic by trade, and had belonged to the Social Democratic Youth Movement; Reichpietsch came from the Berlin working-class suburb of Neukölln, and had bounced from job to job before enlisting in the Navy in 1912. By contrast, Seaman Conrad Lotter on the light cruiser *Bremse* was a devout Catholic and a German nationalist, who complained of conditions in the fleet simply to raise its combat-readiness.

Tempers began to boil on 6 June 1917, when the engine-room crew of the *Prinzregent Luitpold* refused to consume any more turnips, dehydrated vegetables or *Drahtverhau*. While her First Officer, Lieutenant-Commander Herzbruch, was able to assuage the stokers with promises of bread and bacon, the hunger strike encouraged Beckers and Köbis to establish a sailors' council (*Soldatenbund*) to coordinate future mass actions. Conditions on the flagship *Friedrich der Grosse* reached the danger point on 5 July, when in the course of coaling the men ate the next day's rations and were refused more bread. A hunger strike was organized under the leadership of Reichpietsch and Sachse; the officers gave in, serving up a meal of groat soup. Moreover, Captain Theodor Fuchs agreed to set up a *Menagekommission* at once.

With this action, the corner had been turned. The leaders on the other ships in the fleet after 5 July approached their superiors and asked for the creation of food supervisory committees. The *Prinzregent Luitpold* through yet another coaling strike obtained her food committee, headed by Beckers and Köbis. On the *Helgoland* the men refused to unload several tons of spoiled flour, and again the officers capitulated and granted the ratings their commission. The light cruiser *Pillau* gained her *Menagekommission* in the wake of a strike, following capricious cancellation of shore leaves. In similar fashion, almost all units in the fleet established food committees over the protests of their officers; what Admiral v. Capelle had freely granted on 20 June was thereafter bitterly taken in numerous food and coal strikes.

The hitherto purely military action took a political turn late in June, when several leaders of the enlisted men's movement visited the USPD's offices in Berlin to air their complaints. Sachse and Köbis in particular conversed with deputies Wilhelm Dittmann, Luise Zietz, Adolf Hoffmann, and others, promising recruitment for the party in the fleet – it was later estimated that about 5,000 sailors did, indeed, join the USPD in July and August 1917 – and support for the forthcoming Socialist Congress in Stockholm that would work for an end to the war.

But the sailors were disappointed by the cold shoulder that they received from Deputy Dittmann. The USPD, like other political parties, was busy debating the future of Chancellor v. Bethmann

Hollweg, the highly publicized Peace Resolution in the Reichstag denouncing all annexations and indemnities, and suffrage reform in Prussia. It could spare little time for two ratings from the fleet. And when General Ludendorff's new chancellor, Georg Michaelis, on 19 July 1917 accepted the Peace Resolution – albeit with the caveat "as I see it" – the missions of Köbis and Sachse appeared superfluous. All the sailors took back to the fleet from Berlin were a few application forms for membership of the USPD and some of that party's literature.

Purely military matters in the High Sea Fleet were once again to rekindle the spirit of rebellion. On 31 July, the stokers on the *Prinzregent Luitpold* had their recreational period and cinema cancelled and instead were ordered out for infantry drill. Beckers now spied his chance, and the head of the food supervisory committee ordered the third division of stokers not to turn out for the drill.

On 1 August, forty-seven stokers left the *Prinzregent Luitpold* rather than report to their superiors. After several hours of lingering on shore, the recalcitrants returned to their ship, fully expecting cancellation of the drill by the officers. But the mood of the latter had changed since June and July. Instead, Captain Karl v. Hornhardt ordered his officers to select eleven ringleaders from among the men, to degrade them in rank, and to place them under arrest for two to three weeks.

The mood in the High Sea Fleet turned ugly as news of this capricious action spread. That night, representatives from *Friedrich der Grosse, Kaiser, Kaiserin,* and *Pillau* met with those from the *Prinzregent Luitpold* in an empty railway car on the dock and decided to stage a walkout by the entire crew of the *Prinzregent Luitpold.* Mutiny was in the air.

Lieutenant-Commander Herzbruch was confronted by an unaccustomed sight early on the rainy morning of 2 August 1917 : the *Prinzregent Luitpold* was almost deserted; about 600 men had left ship and headed for the little village of Rüstersiel. This time, Herzbruch was determined not to yield to the enlisted men. He dispatched three executive and ten petty officers to search for the missing sailors. Police in Wilhelmshaven as well as naval shore patrols were called out. The *Prinzregent Luitpold* was placed under siege. The sympathy strike had misfired. Leaders of the enlisted men's movement faced charges of mutiny and political conspiracy. Similar actions on other ships, culminating in an unrelated wildcat coaling strike on the *Westfalen* fourteen days later, were also vigorously repressed. The officers' vacillation of June had turned by August to bitter retrenchment.

On 3 August, eighteen leaders of the walkout strike were assembled on the port-side deck of the *Prinzregent Luitpold*, and a machine-gun was trained on them. A tender came alongside; the men were taken ashore to face interrogation and possibly military charges. Captain v. Hornhardt the following day reported to the fleet "widespread agitation and recruitment" by the USPD as the root cause of the wildcat strike, thereby ensuring that any subsequent investigation and punitive action would revolve round political issues rather than war-weariness, mistreatment and deplorable food.

Admiral Scheer apparently did not share this dire evaluation at first, and preferred to view the unrest as the result of abuses that needed to be corrected. By 9 August, perhaps as a result of Hornhardt's report, the commander accepted the idea of "a connection between the movement and the Independent Social Democratic Party". A court-martial was hastily assembled to try the leaders of the walkout strike : they were charged with violation of Paragraphs 89 and 90, Article 6 of the Code of Military Justice, that is, with giving aid to a foreign power and with "treasonable incitement to rebellion". On 26 August the court-martial declared five leaders of the strike (Reichpietsch, Sachse, Köbis, Weber, and Beckers) guilty as charged and ordered the death sentence for them. Others found guilty received lesser sentences amounting to over 360 years of imprisonment.

Scheer, as Chief of the High Sea Fleet, was confronted with a decision : he could either sign or commute the death sentences, or he could refer the entire matter to the Kaiser as the final arbiter in all military matters. Scheer opted for the former course, and on 3 September confirmed the death sentences for Köbis and Reichpietsch, while commuting those of the other three sailors. Anxious since 14 August for "a few death sentences" in order to restore discipline in the fleet, Scheer ordered execution of the sentences within forty-eight hours. According to Admiral v. Capelle, this action denied the men any possible appeal to the Kaiser. At 7.03 a.m. on the morning of 5 September 1917, Köbis and Reichpietsch were shot by a twenty-man firing squad at Wahn, near Köln.

But the Navy's senior admirals were not content with "a few death sentences". Instead, they pressed for prosecution of the USPD deputies whom the sailors had contacted in Berlin. Admirals Scheer, Bachmann and Schmidt were especially vocal in their demands for the punishment of this left-wing party, and when on 9 October, in the course of a discussion of right-wing propaganda in the armed services, Admiral v. Capelle received word that one of the sailors had confessed to the existence of a plot against His Majesty, which involved the USPD, Chancellor Michaelis decided to pursue the case against the Independent Social Democrats in the Reichstag.

Michaelis could hardly have done worse. When he repeated his earlier pledge to treat all parties and philosophies objectively, "in so far as they do not pursue aims that threaten the existence of the German Empire", and stated that the USPD had clearly placed itself outside this category by its activity in the fleet, tumultuous scenes ensued in the Reichstag. Admiral v. Capelle, speaking for the Navy, was interrupted repeatedly by catcalls and interjections. The Reichstag deputies temporarily buried party differences to uphold the principle of parliamentary immunity and protection from government harassment. Friedrich Ebert for the Social Democratic Party delivered the most telling blow of the day : "We shall be glad of every day that the German people are freed from this government." It was a stunning blow for Capelle and the Navy.

Most senior *Seeoffiziere* were highly critical of Capelle – now that he had failed. Admiral Scheer noted that the entire affair in the Reichstag could have been avoided had the mutinies been reported at the time to the German people. Captain Karl Boy-Ed informed his chief, Admiral v. Holtzendorff, that Capelle had "operated extremely unpropitiously" by naming the USPD deputies involved with the sailors; further prosecution of the parliamentary delegates might reveal the "most painful fact" that the principal witnesses against them "have already been executed". Captain William Michaelis of the Navy Office advised Capelle to press the legal suit against the USPD. "I would have risked a *coup d'état*." In the end, Capelle was spared because Wilhelm was in no mood to change his state secretary. Such a step would have revived demands for Tirpitz's reappointment on the one hand, and charges that the ruler was yielding to civilian pressures on the other. Above all, there was no suitable successor in sight.

The unrest in June, the mutinies in August, and the parliamentary fiasco in October 1917 left the naval command in a precarious position. Harmony within the service had been severely strained, and its public image badly tarnished. Successful operations of some magnitude were needed to restore lost confidence and to rekindle the public's enthusiasm for the Navy. And the Kaiser's wounded pride needed a lift; during his most recent visit to the High Sea Fleet, shouts of "hunger" rather than the traditional "hurrah" had greeted him.

The Baltic offered the best prospects. Russian naval units for the greater part of the war had failed to leave their sheltered harbours, and the British Grand Fleet, stripped of its escort craft by the exigencies of the U-boat campaign, was in no position to venture into the Baltic Sea to assist its ally, or to risk an all-out encounter with the High Sea Fleet near the German coast in the North Sea. The Imperial Navy accordingly chose the islands of Oesel, Moon and Dagö in the Bay of Riga for attack. Army headquarters favoured the naval initiative because it expected thereby to relieve pressure on the left wing of its forces on the Eastern Front.

According to Walther Hubatsch, such a joint Army–Navy operation in the summer of 1915 might well have brought a speedy end to the war against Russia; in October 1917, following the collapse of Russia's army and on the eve of the Bolshevik revolution, it was out of all proportion to the risks involved. However, Vice-Admiral Albert Hopman, chief naval officer in the Baltic, appreciated the psychological value of the planned operation : "It brings a fresh breath of air into the fleet, whose spirit, as far as the ratings are concerned, is in even more dire straits than Your Excellency [Tirpitz] suggested some time ago." On the other hand, Hopman left no doubt that there was little military advantage to be gained by the undertaking; in fact, he had described it to Admiral Prince Heinrich as "nonsense". Lieutenant-Commander Johann Bernhard Mann, navigation officer of the Third Squadron which was to take part in the operation, also spied the reasons behind the undertaking : "All are nevertheless happy that we are finally to go into action."

The German sortie into the Bay of Riga, commanded by Vice-Admiral Ehrhardt Schmidt, was a classic case of overkill. The Third and Fourth Squadrons of the High Sea Fleet (10 battleships), the battle-cruiser *Moltke,* 8 light cruisers, 6 U-boats, and 50 torpedo-boats as well as small supporting craft between 11 and 19 October managed to cripple one of the four Russian battleships (*Slava*) in the Baltic, and to sink four enemy destroyers. Schmidt's task force landed 24,000 men of the Eighth Army Group on the islands. On the German side, the battleships *Grosser Kurfürst* and *Bayern* ploughed on to Russian mines; both ships managed to stay afloat and were towed to Kiel for repairs. A strike by Bolshevik sailors had hampered Russian minelaying operations, thereby saving the Germans possible further losses.

The naval raid gave Germany command over the Gulf of Riga, and brought the Reich within striking distance of the Russian naval bases at Reval, in the Gulf of Finland, and at Kronstadt. Moreover, it greatly embarrassed the provisional government now headed by Alexander Kerensky; the latter continued unsuccessfully to plead for British naval action in the Baltic. The earlier schemes of Admiral Fisher notwithstanding, the Admiralty in late 1917 realized that any action in the shallow, mine-infested waters was doomed to failure. Even a successful thrust by the Grand Fleet into the Baltic would be of no avail as the British ships could easily be trapped if the Germans sank ships to block the Greater and Lesser Belts. There remained no alternative but to continue submarine raids into the Baltic in order to interrupt German iron ore deliveries from Sweden; if need be, the British submarines could be scuttled in the Baltic if the German pursuit became too relentless.

Even the Germans realized that the seizure of the three islands had basically been a morale-booster. Captain Boy-Ed in the Admiralty Staff informed Prince Heinrich: "We are doing everything in our power to use the successful execution of the Oesel undertaking to restore fully the justified . . . confidence of the German people . . . in the Navy." And on 26 October, during an imperial audience, Admiral v. Holtzendorff emphasized the connection between the mutinies, Capelle's parliamentary defeat, and the Oesel operation by pointing out that the naval action had improved discipline and raised morale. "For this reason Your Majesty's order to seize the islands in the Bay of Riga was greeted with . . . particular pleasure by the big ships." Of lesser pleasure to the monarch were the events surrounding the erstwhile German Mediterranean Squadron.

Late in 1917, with mounting German Army successes in southern Russia, the Admiralty in London became concerned that the Germans might plan a concerted effort in the eastern *Mittelmeer*. A simultaneous sortie by the Austro-Hungarian Fleet from the Adriatic and a thrust from the Dardanelles by the former German battle-cruiser *Goeben* and the light cruiser *Breslau* seemed particularly dangerous. Instead, Vice-Admiral Hubert v. Rebeur-Paschwitz, Admiral Souchon's successor, emboldened by the Russian armistice on 15 December 1917, opted to offset the Turkish loss of Jerusalem by an operation against Mudros, hoping in the process to destroy Allied troop transports in the Aegean Sea bound for Salonika.

The two cruisers, escorted by four destroyers, passed through the Dardanelles early in the morning of 20 January 1918, bearing south-west. British destroyers guarding the Straits failed to notice the German-Turkish vessels. However, Rebeur-Paschwitz had been so careless as to forego a careful reconnaissance of British mines, and shortly after passing the Dardanelles, the *Goeben* struck one. Damage was only slight, and the German commander continued the operation, first destroying the British wireless station at Cape Kephalo.

Two hours later, while manoeuvring to escape from British bombers from Imbros, the *Breslau* ran onto a mine. Her steering went out of control, and her starboard turbine became inoperative. As the *Goeben* came to the rescue, she, too, ploughed onto a mine. The situation of the two vessels was precarious. Bombers were buzzing all around. More mines could clearly be seen in the waters. Two British destroyers were closing in for attack. Shortly after 9 a.m., the *Breslau* ran onto four mines and, bow high in the air, slipped beneath the waves.

Rebeur-Paschwitz at last decided to cancel the Mudros operation and to head for home. But his troubles were not over: within an hour of the loss of the light cruiser, the *Goeben* struck another mine. While damage was slight, she took on a fifteen-degree list to port. Despite the constant presence of British bombers, the battle-cruiser managed to reach the Dardanelles – only to run onto a sandbank at Nagara, where for six days she was subjected to ineffective British aerial attacks. The damage sustained by the *Goeben* was too extensive to be repaired at Constantinople and, after taking nominal possession of the surrendered Russian ports of Sevastopol and Novorossisk in the Black Sea in March 1918, she was laid up for practically the rest of the war. The loss of the *Breslau* and the damage to the *Goeben,* however, were quickly overshadowed in March by the end of the war against Russia and the successful German intervention in Finland.

Lenin had seized power in Petrograd in November 1917, following the total collapse of General Brusilov's last offensive in Galicia, and during the following month opened peace talks with the Germans. On 10 February 1918, Russo-German negotiations were broken off by Leon Trotsky's famous "no war, no peace" declaration. Wilhelm II, in turn, demanded that the Bolsheviks be "beaten to death", and on 18 February, Generals Max Hoffmann and Rüdiger von der Goltz launched Operation "Faustschlag". The Germans rapidly advanced against the disorganized Russian resistance and occupied Narva, Pskov and Kiev. Lenin, afraid that the Germans would next seize Petrograd, the "cradle of the revolution", agreed to terms on 23 February, and on 3 March the Bolsheviks signed the German treaty at Brest-Litovsk. Russia lost Poland, Courland and Lithuania. Estonia and Livonia nominally remained under Russian rule, but in fact were subjected to "German police power". The Ukraine and Finland were declared independent states.

But already on 19 January 1918, civil war had spread throughout Finland, thereby threatening the Russo-German negotiations at Brest-Litovsk. Both Hindenburg and Ludendorff favoured German intervention in Finland on the side of the White Army under General Carl Mannerheim. Wilhelm II endorsed the "police action" for the opportunity to crusade against Bolshevism, whose leaders must be "slaughtered" because they were "revolutionary", and for dynastic purposes as one of his sons might gain a crown in Finland.

Rear-Admiral v. Trotha, acting in his capacity as chief of staff of the High Sea Fleet, supported the Army's initiative. The admiral realized that much of the remaining Russian Baltic Sea Fleet, consisting of 4 battleships, 13 cruisers, 6 submarines, and 39 destroyers, had taken refuge in the ice-bound Finnish base on Sveaborg Island, just off downtown Helsingfors (Helsinki). Trotha left no doubt that he considered the Russian ships as "war booty", failure to seize which would entail "disgrace" for the Imperial Navy.

Already on 20 February 1918, a special naval task force of 3 battleships, 3 cruisers and 4 torpedo-boats had been formed under Rear-Admiral Hugo Meurer in Kiel. General von der Goltz's "Baltic Division" was transported to the Aaland Islands on 5 March, and from there to Hanko on 4 April. Eight days later, Helsinki fell to the Germans. About 400 sailors from Meurer's squadron took part in the street fighting against the Red Guards.

By April 30, Meurer was ready to leave Helsinki and to rejoin the High Sea Fleet in the North Sea. The battleship *Rheinland* had meanwhile (11 April) run upon rock formations in the Baltic Sea and was lost for the duration of the war.

This maritime operation, however, was of secondary importance. Trotha's eagerness to capture the Russian Baltic Sea Fleet did not reflect official Navy policy, as witnessed by the fact that the Germans between 21 April and 25 May 1918 permitted the Russian naval forces – which had remained neutral during the seizure of the Finnish capital – to return unmolested to Kronstadt. In particular, Admiral v. Holtzendorff refused to allow peripheral operations in the Baltic to distract him from the major objective of destroying Allied and American shipping in the North Sea and the Atlantic Ocean. Wilhelm II fully supported his Chief of the Admiralty Staff. As Holtzendorff noted on 8 April, "His Majesty orders reckless submarine warfare as the main objective in the future." On 31 May 1918, Meurer's task force was formally disbanded; on 15 June, the last three German cruisers left Finnish waters.

In April 1918 Admiral Scheer decided once more to take the entire High Sea Fleet out to sea. After the successful thrust of the light cruisers *Brummer* and *Bremse* into Norwegian waters, the British convoyed Scandinavian shipping and used heavy surface units to protect it. Therefore the German commander on 24 April chose to take the fleet north as far as Norway in order to intercept the convoys which, unknown to Scheer, were crossing the North Sea now at four-day intervals. According to the official German history of the war at sea, the sortie was also designed to ease the plight of the U-boats operating in the English Channel and thereby indirectly to aid Ludendorff's "Michael"' offensive in France. The fuel capacity of Scheer's light units militated against a stay of more than three days off Norway.

The High Sea Fleet left Schillig Roads early on 23 April 1918. Scheer planned to steam one day in the area west of Norway, with Admiral v. Hipper and the scouting forces about sixty miles ahead of the High Sea Fleet. Lady Luck seemed to be with the Germans this day: several British submarines stationed near Helgoland either did not see the fleet depart, or mistakenly took it for British units.

Later that afternoon Hipper was in position off Bergen, desperately searching for enemy convoys. Early on 24 April, fate intervened to disrupt the entire undertaking. At 6.10 a.m. the battle-cruiser *Moltke* lost her inner propeller and, before the turbine could be brought under control, a gear wheel outside the casing flew apart and punctured a condenser. The engine-room was in short order flooded. Both the starboard and the centre engines were knocked out of action. Worse yet, salt water entered the boilers, and within ninety minutes *Moltke* reported to Hipper that she was "out of control", her speed reduced to four knots.

Hipper dispatched the crippled battle-cruiser to the High Sea Fleet in order not to jeopardize the planned action against possible Scandinavian convoys; Admiral Hugo v. Waldeyer-Hartz, Hipper's biographer, claims that the commander well remembered having left the *Blücher* to her fate in January 1915 at the Dogger Bank, and was resolved not to lose the *Moltke* in similar fashion. Hipper, meanwhile, continued to search for convoys as far as sixty degrees north. Henry Newbolt accurately depicted Hipper's actions as "steaming into a no-man's sea, abandoned alike by merchantmen and men-of-war". The absence of British heavy ships is also partly explained by the Admiralty's need to cover the Zeebrugge–Oostende blocking operation, which had been carried out during the night of 22–23 April 1918.

Around noon on 24 April, just as Admiral Beatty was finally dashing out of the Firth of Forth, Scheer called off the entire operation rather than risk losses to the fleet as a consequence of the slow speed imposed by the impaired *Moltke*. The British submarine *E 42* had a final opportunity to sink the *Moltke*. About 7.00 p.m. on 25 April, the British craft hit the battle-cruiser's starboard engine-room with a torpedo. Almost 2,000 tons of sea water flooded into the engine-room, but the honeycomb internal protection saved *Moltke*; she managed to reach the Jade river under her own power.

Marder sums up the operation as follows : Scheer "had taken a serious risk in visiting more northerly waters than ever before in ignorance of the fact that the concentrated Grand Fleet lay at Rosyth, on his flank, and not, as he supposed, at Scapa". The sortie also marked the last time during the war that the two main fleets were out at sea at the same time; the next instance was 21 November 1918, under radically different circumstances.

The naval operations in the autumn of 1917 and the spring of 1918 at least relieved the past year's boredom and idleness. The Navy also took some steps towards remedying the conditions in the fleet which had prompted the men to rebel in the summer of 1917.

Patriotic instruction, or *Vaterländischer Unterricht,* constituted an attempt to educate the troops about the origins of the war and their role in that titanic confrontation. It was successful only in isolated cases; for the most part, officers were without experience in this line of work, as politics in the armed services had always been considered anathema in Prussia/Germany. Some executive officers attempted to organize hikes, games, theatre visits, and sport for their ratings, but the latter often felt uncomfortable in the unaccustomed presence of their military superiors. Others conducted patriotic instruction by reading historical novels, which generally put the men to sleep. Nor were public speeches by right-wing politicians, pastors and publishers welcomed by the enlisted men. Lieutenant-Commander Bogislav v. Selchow of the Admiralty Staff, the officer in charge of *Vaterländischer Unterricht,* judged the overall effort to be "extremely sad".

Yet by the summer of 1918, much of the confidence and enthusiasm generated by naval actions had been dissipated. The High Sea Fleet returned to its customary idleness. Discipline became once again rigid and formal, an end in itself. In many small ways the abuses of yesterday returned to the Navy. In general, a sullen resignation had taken hold of the men in the High Sea Fleet : they realized that their fate rested not with them, but with the outcome of the unrestricted submarine war and Ludendorff's offensive in France.

In March 1918, General Ludendorff launched Operation "Michael" in the West; sixty divisions were hurled against the Allied line Arras–St. Quentin–La Fère. Initial advances produced expectations of great land gains in the West. Admiral v. Holtzendorff beamed with optimism. He assured the Foreign Office that the U-boats could destroy enough enemy shipping to offset new construction and still bring the war to a successful conclusion. He now estimated that the undersea raiders could send about 650,000 tons of merchant shipping to the bottom per month; shipwrecks and other natural calamities would account for an additional monthly loss of 45,000 tons. He calculated further that the Allied and Associated Powers could build about 345,000 tons of shipping per month; therefore, the net reduction would reach nearly 350,000 tons. On the basis of these statistical gymnastics, one could project that by the middle of 1918 the Reich's enemies would have at their disposal only 10.5 million tons of merchant shipping to transport to Europe approximately 60 million tons of supplies as well as

American troops and their gear. Vice-Admiral Hopman, the German commander in the Black Sea, supported Holtzendorff's position, and in May 1918 reminded Wilhelm II "that our goals lie, now as before, in the West and along the [Atlantic] Ocean rather than in the East"; only the U-boats could "prevent world domination by the Anglo-Saxons".

However, not all military commanders shared this belief. General Wilhelm Groener, destined to replace Ludendorff as First Quartermaster-General, was far more prophetic in his diary: "Since we must count more and more on the arrival of American troops despite Tirpitz and the U-boats, the offensive [Michael] becomes a last attempt to speed an end to the war." Groener had hit the nail on the head. Despite Holtzendorff's claim that the United States could at best have 300,000 soldiers in Europe by the end of 1918, by November of that year the United States in fact maintained an army of 1.97 million men in France. In addition, the U-boats did not torpedo a single eastbound troop transport on the Atlantic; by June 1918, the Republic was safely shuttling 536,000 tons of supplies to France. Admiral William S. Benson sent virtually his entire destroyer force (68 units) as well as 121 so-called submarine-chasers to Europe to assist in the mounting anti-submarine effort. The United States Navy Dreadnoughts *Florida, Wyoming, New York, Texas,* and *Arkansas* under Rear-Admiral Hugh Rodman were attached to the Grand Fleet.

Out of desperation, German naval leaders in March 1918 again called for the expansion of the war zones to the eastern seaboard of the United States. Both Hindenburg and Ludendorff strongly endorsed this plan, hoping that the U-boats would thereby finally be able to intercept American troop transports and supply ships. The new Chancellor, Count v. Hertling, and State Secretary of the Foreign Office Richard Kühlmann, were of a different opinion, arguing that the few U-cruisers available for ocean duty were insufficient to alter the outcome of the submarine war. On 2 July 1918, Wilhelm II sided with his political leaders and refused to extend unrestricted submarine warfare into American waters. There were, in all, only seven raids according to prize rules by German undersea raiders in United States waters between 7 June 1918 and the end of the war, but their accomplishments were minimal. Approximately 110,000 tons of merchant shipping were destroyed during these forays.

The U-boats were by the summer of 1918 becoming an endangered species. Since November 1917, the waters between Dover and Calais had been effectively closed with new mines; the following year, the submarines stationed in Flanders lost twelve units off Dover and now reached the Atlantic in triple or quadruple the normal time by rounding the Orkney Islands. And this route also was becoming dangerous: between June and October 1918, the Allied and Associated Powers laid approximately 70,000 modern "horn" mines in the so-called "Northern Barrage" between Norway and Scotland. Worse yet, convoying in 1918 surpassed even Lloyd George's fondest dreams; the loss rate among convoys fell to 0.98 per cent, while that of the U-boats climbed to 7.4 per cent. Only in the Mediterranean did the undersea raiders continue to wreak havoc among Allied shipping. Until June 1918, the U-boats in the *Mittelmeer* sent an average of thirty-four ships per month to the bottom, a total of 800,000 tons between November 1917 and June 1918. Traffic in the Suez Canal at one time in 1917 was down to 40 per cent of peacetime, and the risk percentage remained almost double that in British waters.

The German and Austro–Hungarian submarine forces stationed at Pola and Cattaro in the Adriatic Sea remained a relatively small contingent throughout the war. The Reich maintained only 32 boats and Austria–Hungary 27 older units; German losses amounted to 16 boats, 11 during the final year of the war. The Central Powers thus maintained an aggregate force of about 50 vessels in the Adriatic Sea during most of 1917–18.

Inter-Allied wrangling assured the success of the U-boats. French, Italian, British, and Japanese naval leaders continued to act independently; in particular, France and Italy rejected an Anglo–American plan in May 1918 to appoint Admiral Jellicoe as admiralissimo for the Mediterranean. The projected massive blockade of the Otranto Straits remained on paper. Finally, the Italian Navy opted not to leave port and face the Austro–Hungarian Navy of Rear-Admiral Miklós Horthy de Nagybánya (three battleship divisions) because, as Admiral Thaon di Revel explained to his colleagues at the Naval Inter-Allied Conference in Rome, the currents, beaches, harbours, islands, channels, and anchorages all favoured the enemy. When the United States Assistant Secretary of the Navy, Franklin D. Roosevelt, visiting Italy, inquired why the Italians did not even put to sea for training exercises, the response was that it was superfluous because the Austrians also refrained from such activity. Roosevelt noted in his diary: "This is a naval classic which is hard to beat, but which perhaps should not be publicly repeated for a generation or two."

The Germans made one final attempt in the autumn of 1918 to overcome their difficulties at sea. "When a headquarters staff is no longer in a position to lead its forces in the proper sense of the word, it sets about reorganizing." Ernst v. Weizsäcker hit the mark with this caustic statement. On 11 August 1918, the triumvirate of Scheer, Trotha and Levetzow managed under threats of resignation (*à la* Bismarck and Tirpitz) to force Wilhelm II to streamline the naval hierarchy. Scheer became Chief of the Admiralty and head of the newly created Supreme Navy Command (*Seekriegsleitung*), Captain v. Levetzow was appointed his chief of staff, Hipper replaced Scheer as Chief of the High Sea Fleet, and Trotha stayed on temporarily as the High Sea Fleet's chief of staff in order to provide continuity and stability during the change of commanders. It was agreed, however, that Trotha would take over the Navy Cabinet as soon as Admiral v. Müller could be removed from office. The splintered command structure of the Imperial Navy, which had helped to maintain the fiction of Wilhelm's personal command and which perfectly suited Tirpitz's designs of someday becoming supreme naval commander, was at last abolished.

One of the first steps taken by the new leaders was an attempt to set up submarine production on a grand scale. As was mentioned earlier, the new *Seekriegsleitung* ordered 450 submarines as well as 2 battleships and 15 cruisers. Yet Scheer realized that the effort was largely a psychological ploy and that it stood little chance of success owing to shortage of raw materials, skilled workers and trained crews. In fact, the admiral termed it "a twelfth-hour attempt to save everything". This it failed to do.

Equally illusory was the triumvirate's endorsement of Holtzendorff's war-aims programme. It confirmed the earlier Atlantic position, including the retention of Flanders and a naval base either in Finland or at Murmansk – both designed to outflank the British Isles. The new naval paladins were willing to abandon demands for the Azores, for example, but only in return for compensation in the French and Portuguese colonies in West Africa. The Mediterranean concept still centred round a naval base at Valona, but was expanded to include the Albanian hinterland, Constantinople with the Dardanelles, and a *Stützpunkt* in the Gulf of Alexandretta. Admiral v. Tirpitz, in retirement in his official capacity as head of the Fatherland Party (1.25 million members), disseminated these views to the German public.

Central to all of these war aims was the desire to acquire naval bases on the eastern shores of the Atlantic – be it in Africa, the Faeroe Islands, Finland, or Murmansk – in order to challenge what German naval planners regarded as an Anglo–Saxon monopoly of western maritime arteries. Rear-Admiral Karl Hollweg of the Navy Office called for a future German surface fleet of 40 battleships, 40 light cruisers and 200 U-boats in order to break the Anglo–American "monopoly". Other naval officers, including Tirpitz, even spoke of the present struggle as the equivalent of the "Second Punic War" between Rome (Germany) and Carthage (Britain), believing that it was their duty to prepare the Reich to the utmost for the ultimate reckoning, the "Third Punic War". Although these war aims were utterly Utopian in the autumn of 1918, they were to be found again in the war-aims programme presented to Adolf Hitler by Admirals Rolf Carls, Kurt Fricke, Erich Raeder, Otto Schniewind, and Gerhard Wagner in the summer of 1940.

By mid-July 1918, Marshal Ferdinand Foch had managed to halt the German offensive around Reims. Emboldened by the monthly arrival of 300,000 (fresh) American doughboys, Foch launched a long-prepared strike against the German Marne salient. It was completely successful : on 8 August, French and Canadian troops broke through the German lines at the Somme. British tanks completed what Ludendorff termed "the black day of the German Army in the history of the war". By the first week of September, the Germans had been driven back to their positions prior to the "Michael" offensive, to the so-called Hindenburg Line. Moreover, Turkish armies in Palestine were trapped and rounded up by an Anglo–French force under Field-Marshal Edmund Allenby. And when Bulgaria withdrew from the war on 29 September, German military leaders lost their nerve and counselled the Kaiser to seek an armistice. Ludendorff repeated this call for an end to the war on 1 October, and two days later Prince Max v. Baden became the new chancellor. He at once appealed to President Woodrow Wilson for an armistice, and unrestricted submarine warfare came to an end on 16 October in accordance with the terms of Wilson's second note. On 26 October 1918, Ludendorff resigned and fled to Sweden. Four days later, Austria–Hungary as well as Turkey capitulated.

The U-boat campaign had failed, even though, in terms of personal courage, the officers and men in the submarine service achieved incredible results. Between 1914 and 1918, 104 U-boats destroyed 2,888 ships of 6,858,380 tons; 96 UB boats 1,456 ships of 2,289,704 tons; and 73 UC boats 2,042 ships of 2,789,910 tons. In addition, the undersea raiders sent to the bottom 10 battleships, 7 armoured cruisers, 2 large and 4 light cruisers, and 21 destroyers. But the cost ran high: 178 boats were lost to the enemy, and with them 4,744 officers and men.

German naval leaders, who as late as August 1918 had been planning amphibious operations against Kronstadt and Petrograd (Operation Schlussstein), proved surprisingly willing to cease the unrestricted submarine warfare. "The Navy", Scheer's planners lustily announced, "does not need an armistice." In fact, a new bold design had entered their heads: the fleet could be hurled against the combined British and American surface units stationed at Rosyth. Admiral v. Hipper concluded that "an honourable fleet engagement, even if it should become a death struggle", was preferable to an inglorious and inactive end to the High Sea Fleet. Rear-Admiral v. Trotha was equally adamant on this matter, arguing that a fleet encounter was needed "in order to go down with honour". And Admiral Scheer was not the man to stand in the way of such an adventurous undertaking. "It is impossible that the fleet . . . remains idle. It must be deployed." Scheer concluded that the "honour and existence of the Navy" demanded use of the fleet, even if "the course of events cannot thereby be significantly altered".

Hence, for reasons of honour and future naval building (*Zukunfts-flotte*), it was decided to launch the entire High Sea Fleet against the enemy in a suicide sortie. It is revealing that on 22 October 1918, Levetzow *verbally* passed on word of the projected sortie to Hipper. The new head of the Army, General Groener, was not brought into these discussions. Nor were the Kaiser or the chancellor informed of the planned operation; despite this, Germany's admirals at one point considered taking Wilhelm on board for the final naval assault. Scheer, however, simply did not think it "opportune" to inform political leaders of his designs.

On 24 October 1918, the Supreme Navy Command formally adopted Operations Plan No 19 (O-Befehl Nr 19). It called for one destroyer group to be sent to the Flanders coast and another to the mouth of the Thames, while the High Sea Fleet took battle station in the Hoofden, the North Sea between the Netherlands and Great Britain. Twenty-five U-boats were in position to intercept the British and American surface units in the North Sea. The Grand Fleet, the Germans argued, would rush out of its Scottish anchorages in order to attack the two destroyer "baits", which thereupon would draw the British and American fleets to Terschelling, a Dutch island in the North Sea, where the naval Armageddon would take place.

Execution of Operations Plan No 19 was set for 30 October 1918. With it German naval strategy in desperation returned not only to Tirpitz's dream of the *Entscheidungsschlacht* in the south-central North Sea, "between the Thames and Helgoland", but also to the conviction of Baudissin, Fischel and Wegener, among others, concerning the need for an offensive in the North Sea in order to force the approaches to the Atlantic Ocean.

XII

The Sun Sets

Scapa Flow 21 June 1919

Operations Plan No 19, seen in retrospect, was anything but fool-proof. In the first place, it is highly doubtful whether the Grand Fleet would have reacted to the advance of the two destroyer flotillas and the submarines in the prescribed manner; British naval leaders had ignored similar German sorties before. Secondly, the expectations which German admirals placed on the U-boats were not sound. By the end of October, only twenty-four submarines were in position and six were heading for their stations. While in the process of heading out to battle stations, seven U-boats were rendered *hors de combat* owing to mechanical breakdowns, and two were destroyed by the enemy. The weather was also against the submersibles: "Rain and hail showers, hazy, high seas and swell; dismal, stormy November weather. No visibility, no possible forward advance, no worthwhile targets for attack could be recognized in the haze." Finally, the Germans failed to appreciate that apart from Great Britain there was another major sea power involved in the war. In fact, German naval leaders throughout 1917–18 persisted in their claims that United States naval forces as a whole were not worthy of their consideration, and hence paid no attention to the five United States battleships attached to the Grand Fleet, to the three others stationed in Ireland, or to the entire capital-ship strength of thirty-nine units.

Of far greater ultimate effect was the deteriorating internal structure of the Imperial Navy. The naval reorganization of 11 August 1918, which had brought the triumvirate of Scheer, Trotha and Levetzow to the fore, had also caused apprehension concerning planned changes and discharges. Even Admiral v. Hipper noted: "I dread the next few days." Trotha spoke to

Levetzow of "insecurity" and "uneasiness" among commanders, and begged for the return of "at least a few leading figures" to the fleet. "We cannot discharge our duties . . . with only mediocre and bad *matériel*." On numerous surface vessels, both captain and first officer had recently been replaced. Nevertheless, when Levetzow asked Trotha on 16 October if he believed that naval personnel could be relied upon for a major sea battle, Trotha "answered without reservation in the affirmative". This miscalculation was to prove decisive within a fortnight.

The High Sea Fleet, according to Operations Plan No 19, was to assemble in Schillig Roads on the afternoon of 29 October. Two days before, the crews had already appeared anxious and excited. News had leaked out, especially from Hipper's eager staff, that a major battle with the British was in the offing. Men in both Kiel and Wilhelmshaven nervously spread the word of a "suicide sortie" planned by the executive officers to save their "honour" at the eleventh hour – a notion not without ample basis.

By the 29th, ratings from the battle-cruisers *Derfflinger* and *Von der Tann* failed to return to their posts from shore leave. Sailors assembled to demand peace and to cheer Woodrow Wilson. Insubordination quickly spread to the Third Squadron battleships *Kaiserin, König, Kronprinz Wilhelm*, and *Markgraf* as well as to *Thüringen* and *Helgoland* in the First Squadron. The *Baden*'s crew also seemed on the verge of revolt, and the battle-cruisers *Moltke* and *Seydlitz* were rendered inoperative because of rebellious sailors, as were the light cruisers *Pillau, Regensburg* and *Strassburg*. Only the men on the torpedo-boats and the U-boats remained calm and loyal to their officers.

The disturbances in the fleet on 29 October caught naval leaders off-guard and unprepared. Hipper initially cancelled sailing orders late in the evening of the 29th, but reactivated them later as he was unaware of the extent of the rebellion. Trotha at first agreed that the revolt was only temporary and that discipline could be restored shortly. But when disorder spread on 30 October to *Friedrich der Grosse* and *König Albert*, the game was up. Hipper now realized that Operations Plan No 19 had been stillborn. "What terrible days lie behind me. I had really not thought that I would return [from battle], and under what circumstances do I return now. Our men have rebelled."

One of Hipper's last acts as Chief of the High Sea Fleet was to disperse the rebellious ships, sending the First Squadron to the Elbe,

the Third to Kiel, where it surprised an utterly unprepared Admiral
Souchon, and the Fourth to Wilhelmshaven. He could hardly have
made a more grievous miscalculation. In the various ports along
both Baltic and North Sea shores, the sailors incited local uprisings
and there found mostly hospitable receptions. Sea battalion soldiers
refused to fire on them. Executive officers did not oppose them. A
mere four *Seeoffiziere* were wounded in their efforts on behalf of
the Kaiser.

Admiral v. Trotha quickly informed Scheer, on 2 November,
that the rebellion was a "Bolshevist movement", but one that was
directed against the government rather than against the officer
corps. One day later, Trotha met with Levetzow to co-ordinate their
stories concerning Operations Plan No 19. It was placed entirely in
a defensive light, with stress placed primarily upon the submarines
in the North Sea; the anticipated British advance from the north
was sold as an attack on the German fatherland. Trotha even
visited the offices of the Social Democratic newspaper *Vorwärts* to
make quite certain that this official line was properly played up.
Not yet knowing of the official line, the State Secretary of the Navy
Office, Vice-Admiral v. Mann, told the rebellious sailors of the
Third Squadron that the sortie against the British had been designed
to bring the U-boats home safely.

Admiral Scheer was not quite as inventive. He placed the entire
blame for the failure of the operation upon the Social Democrats,
and specifically upon the government's inability in the autumn of
1917 to suppress the USPD. Scheer wrote after the war: "It still
appears almost incomprehensible to me: this reversal from certain
victory to complete collapse, and [it is] especially degrading that
the revolution was planned without haste, and in thorough detail,
right under our eyes." At least the Navy's liaison officer at Army
headquarters, Lieutenant-Commander v. Weizsäcker, grasped the
meaning of the events in the fleet: "We do not even know the state
of mind within the naval hierarchy; this has been demonstrated
during the planned assault."

The royal family behaved no better. Grand Admiral Prince
Heinrich of Prussia fled from Kiel on 5 November driving a truck
that flew the red flag. After his getaway, he blamed developments on British "silver bullets", that is, money that had bought
the mutineers. But the greatest disappointment was reserved for
Wilhelm II. He had extended his special patronage to the Navy
since 1888, and now, shocked and embittered, had to witness the

"disloyal and ungrateful" manner in which his past efforts were being repaid. On 5 November he ordered Admiral v. Schröder, the "Lion of Flanders", to retake Kiel with several hundred battle-hardened troops. But Chancellor Prince Max v. Baden promptly termed this scheme "suicidal" and persuaded Wilhelm to desist from any further bloodshed. When Admiral Scheer informed the monarch on 9 November that the Navy could no longer be relied upon, Wilhelm sarcastically replied: "My dear admiral, the Navy has deserted me very nicely." The Supreme War Lord dismissed the "Victor of the Skagerrak" with the words: "I no longer have a Navy." It was the last time he saw his naval paladins. That same day, the last of the Hohenzollerns quietly crossed into exile in the Netherlands in his imperial cream-and-gold train.

By now much of Germany was in revolt. Many a city fell without opposition to the sailors who streamed to the various parts of the land, relieved that the long war was finally over. By 5 November, Lübeck and Travemünde had fallen to rebellious sailors. Hamburg fell the next day: the 12,000 employees at the gigantic Blohm & Voss shipyard stopped work at the behest of a dozen sailors, and the port's railway station surrendered to two or three armed rebels. The military commander of Bremen on 6 November surrendered the city without firing a shot. That same day, Cuxhaven also succumbed, as did Wilhelmshaven, without bloodshed. Thereafter, the sailors were in complete command. Köln's garrison of 45,000 soldiers allowed a band of sailors to rule the city on 7 November. Ten sailors from Wilhelmshaven likewise assumed power in Bielefeld. Even Hanover, the seat of the Tenth Army Command, fell to a group of sailors "on leave" from Kiel, who managed to empty the local prisons and arrest the commanding general. Everywhere long-standing personal oaths of loyalty to Wilhelm II given in happier times were forgotten or ignored.

A small band of executive officers attempted to organize some resistance early in November. Captain Karl v. Restorff of the Navy Cabinet suggested to Levetzow that rebellious ships be torpedoed. Restorff was willing to condone what he termed "large-scale blood-letting" because a rebel fleet "appeared to me less valuable afloat than at the bottom of the sea". State Secretary v. Mann also counselled that loyal submarines fire upon rebellious ships. On 5 November, Mann asked the cabinet in Berlin for permission to storm Kiel by land with Army units, and with submarines and torpedo-boats from sea. One day later, he requested an order to declare all ships flying the red emblem to be "pirates", and to organize *Seeoffizier* battalions to crush the uprising. To be sure, Scheer's office did order that red-flagged units were to be regarded as "hostile", but when Hipper's flagship hoisted the red banner on 9 November, the admiral quietly packed his bags and went ashore.

Incredibly, Trotha was still unwilling to accept the fleet's historic verdict. On 11 November, he and Hipper approached Bernhard Kuhnt, chairman of the executive committee of the naval "Council of Twenty-One" in Wilhelmshaven, to seek assistance in getting the High Sea Fleet ready for a last patriotic hurrah. Trotha brazenly informed Kuhnt that the British fleet was approaching the German coast: it was now the duty of all German sailors to rally to their country's defence. Only when Kuhnt refused to go along did Trotha finally concede that the war was over. Formally the end came on 28 November 1918, when Wilhelm II released all military and naval personnel from their oaths of allegiance.

There remained the disposition of the High Sea Fleet. During October 1918, the Allied and Associated Powers wrangled over who should get the spoils of battle, and during the Armistice deliberations it was finally decided between 8 and 11 November that 10 German battleships, 6 battle-cruisers, 8 light cruisers, 50 destroyers, and all U-boats were to be interned in neutral ports. The Reich would be allowed to retain the oldest models of 6 battleships, 6 cruisers and 24 destroyers altogether. Not surprisingly, the neutral nations declined to host the rebellious High Sea Fleet, and on 13 November the victors in Paris decided that the German surface units were to be interned at Scapa Flow and the U-boats at various other British ports.

These draconian stipulations (eventually Article 181 of the Treaty of Versailles) came as a shock even to the rebellious sailors. One of them, Seaman Richard Stumpf, described the preparations for surrender in Wilhelmshaven : "It is like a funeral. We shall not see them again. Impassively holding their sea-bags, the men who are being left behind stand at the pier. . . . I, too, feel disgusted to remain here any longer. I wish I had not been born a German." The ships were to be disarmed, to carry only enough fuel to reach England, and to be staffed with skeleton crews – about 400 men for the capital ships. Hipper initially wanted Levetzow to command the German ships intended for internment, but when State Secretary v. Mann refused to promote Levetzow to flag rank, the choice fell upon Vice-Admiral Ludwig v. Reuter.

The other naval stipulations imposed upon the vanquished were equally stern. Germany had to surrender control over Danzig. Helgoland was demilitarized. North Schleswig had to be turned over to Denmark. The numerous coastal batteries had to be dismantled. No new fortifications could be erected. All nations were given free access to the Kaiser-Wilhelm Canal. The major German rivers were internationalized. And the Reich was barred from building submarines, aircraft and large warships. It was a heavy blow that caused many to believe that they had been deceived by believing that President Wilson's celebrated Fourteen Points precluded such a victor's peace. The surrender of the High Sea Fleet thus became a symbol for the entire humiliation heaped upon the Germans at Paris.

Der Tag, as the Germans called it, was 21 November 1918. The world's second largest fleet was to be surrendered to the enemy. One of Reuter's junior officers caught the prevailing mood: "At 1.30 pm, the endless funeral procession was set in motion. In front the First Reconnaissance Squadron headed by the *Seydlitz*; then came the 9 battleships, then 7 light cruisers, and finally 50 torpedo-boats. In this manner the endless procession, over 50 km in length, slowly wallowed towards the North." The surface units, apart from the fifty torpedo-boats, included the Dreadnoughts *Baden* (a replacement for the *Mackensen*, still in dock), *Bayern, Grosser Kurfürst*, and *Kronprinz Wilhelm* of the Third Squadron; *Friedrich der Grosse, Kaiser, Kaiserin, König Albert*, and *Prinzregent Luitpold* of the Fourth Squadron; the battle-cruisers *Derfflinger, Hindenburg, Moltke, Seydlitz*, and *Von der Tann*; and the light cruisers *Bremse, Brummer, Cöln, Dresden, Emden, Frankfurt, Karlsruhe*, and *Nürnberg. König* was still in dock and came over later with the *Mackensen*. Admiral v. Reuter left Germany in brilliant sunshine, proudly flying the imperial war flag. The sight proved too much for Hipper: "My heart is breaking. Herewith my job as chief of the fleet comes to an inglorious end." A sailor on the *Nassau* sadly termed the surrender "the most shameful deed in all the history of the sea".

For the British, 21 November was a glorious day. Never before in the annals of naval history had such an armada capitulated so ignominiously. And the British were determined to put on a show. Two days earlier they had at Harwich quietly and without ceremony received the surrender of 176 German U-boats, but they now decided to greet the Germans in a style reminiscent of the great reviews at Spithead. In addition to the Grand Fleet bedecked in white ensigns, about 90,000 men in 370 warships assembled at the western edge of the North Sea to welcome Reuter's force. Nor could the Americans and French resist the temptation to be part of the spectacle. Yet Admiral Beatty knew in his heart of hearts that this was not a happy day for any sailor. "It was a pitiable sight, in fact I should say it was a horrible sight, to see these great ships . . . come in, led by a British light cruiser, with their old antagonists, the battle-cruisers, gazing at them."

The High Sea Fleet arrived at the Firth of Forth on 21 November and, after careful inspection, was escorted to Scapa Flow between 25 and 27 November 1918. Here all wireless equipment was removed from aboard and the heavy guns were rendered inoperable by the removal of their breech blocks. The German crews were now reduced to less than 200 officers and men for the capital ships and 20 for the torpedo-boats.

The internment was sheer misery for all concerned. Four years of frustration at home were now compounded by eight months of virtual imprisonment. In Scapa Flow, time stood still. The atmosphere of rebellion lingered on. Soldiers' councils dominated all the capital ships save the *Baden*. In time the vessels rusted, discipline dropped to deplorable levels, idleness gnawed at the nerves of the men. News from home arrived infrequently. Food from Germany came over twice a month; it was sufficient, but monotonous and of poor quality. The mail was censored at snail's pace. German newspapers, cigarettes, films, dental services, and so on, were barred from the ships. Visits on shore or between vessels were prohibited. Even swimming in the icy waters was banned. Only fishing remained to while away the dreary weeks. As one British sailor observed, the Germans were treated as "lepers". Admiral v. Reuter described the life of his officers on board ship as a "martyrdom", and informed Trotha that his officers were "vegetating under the most degrading and undignified conditions". Reuter denounced the majority of ratings as "revolutionary rabble", and informed home authorities that Spartacist propaganda was "tormenting the officers beyond endurance".

A break in the monotony of internment came on 31 May 1919, the third anniversary of the Battle of Jutland. Some of the German ships hoisted imperial war flags, while others raised red emblems to celebrate the occasion. Several battle-cruisers even fired off red and white Very lights. But thereafter the prevailing demoralization con-

tinued. The ships were not cleaned and began to smell. Beatty's
former verdict on Scapa Flow could well apply now to the Germans.
They were "Scapa weary, weary of seeing the same old damned
agony of grey grey grey, grey sky, grey sea, grey ships".

Above all, the fate of the fleet in Scapa Flow remained Reuter's
primary concern. His ships were low on fuel and the one possible
route of escape, the Holm Sound, was constantly guarded by British
destroyers. Moreover, Reuter's heavy guns were inoperative and
munitions unavailable. There remained no alternative but surrender
or scuttling. Back in November 1918, the naval command in
Germany had discussed contingency plans for scuttling the fleet in
the North Sea rather than surrender it to the victors. The idea was
dropped at the time because of fears of Allied reprisals. And despite
Article XXXI of the Armistice, which stated: "No destruction of
ships . . . to be permitted", the officers in Scapa frequently toyed
with this option during the dreary winter months. Admiral v.
Trotha made it known to Reuter that under no circumstances must
he permit the ships to be divided among the victors.

Reuter learned from a copy of *The Times* that the Armistice
would expire at noon on 21 June 1919, and hence four days prior
to this date had distributed scuttling orders to his officers. As if to
facilitate the German plans, Vice-Admiral Sir Sydney Fremantle
ordered the British naval forces guarding Scapa Flow out to sea for
routine exercises without informing Reuter that the Armistice had
been extended to 23 June by the Council of Four in Paris.

At 11.20 am on 21 June, Reuter gave the order to scuttle. Sea-
cocks and watertight doors were opened. That afternoon, 10 battleships, 5 battle-cruisers, 5 light cruisers, and 46 torpedo-boats slipped
beneath the waves or were beached before the disbelieving eyes of
the British harbour patrol. It was an unprecedented spectacle in
naval history: approximately 500,000 tons of warships, estimated
at a cost of 855,890,000 GM, disappeared into the sea flying the
imperial war flag. Reuter explained later that he was merely following the Kaiser's order of 1914 which had stated that no German
ships were to be surrendered to the British during the war. The
admiral assumed full responsibility for the order to scuttle, and
there is little doubt that he had decided on this course of action
before he left Germany. In return, the Allied and Associated Powers
demanded that Berlin hand over to them five light cruisers and
400,000 tons of docks, tugs, dredges, cranes, and the like.

But the sad spectacle at Scapa Flow did not end with the scuttling of the German surface vessels. The British harbour patrol panicked. In all, nine Germans were killed and twenty-one wounded by gunfire or bayonets. The 1,860 officers and men captured were taken to prisoner-of-war camps at Nigg, Oswestry and finally Donnington Hall. The harsh British reaction can be seen as a result of frustration and fury; they had been cheated at the last moment of the spoils of war. Admiral Scheer "rejoiced" over the events at Scapa Flow. "This last act is true to the best traditions of the German Navy." And once the initial shock had ebbed, British and American naval leaders were not disappointed that the German ships rested on the bottom of the sea; the First Sea Lord, Admiral Sir Rosslyn Wemyss, looked upon the scuttling "as a real blessing", while the French and Italians suspected British connivance in the matter in order to deprive them of their anticipated booty.

On 31 January 1920, the officers and men of the erstwhile High Sea Fleet returned to Germany, where they were accorded a triumphant reception. Masses thronged the shores, flags and banners were unfurled again, bands played, and an Army guard of honour greeted them as returning heroes. Admiral v. Trotha welcomed them upon their arrival and gave them a gala reception. War-weary and humiliated Germany at last had an opportunity to celebrate and rejoice. The fleet had redeemed itself, even if in defeat. War-time idleness and the stigma of revolution were forgotten or forgiven. The *Reichsmarine* now had its martyrs and a legend to see it through the sad days that lay ahead. The "luxury" fleet was gone for ever; its remaining officers could only attempt to maintain that force's heritage and tradition in the hope that some day a new patron would restore it to favour.

Appendixes

List of Tables

Table 1   *Major German Naval Commands to 1919*

Chief of the Admiralty

Lieutenant-General Albrecht v. Roon	April 1861 – December 1871
Lieutenant-General Albrecht v. Stosch	January 1872 – March 1883
Lieutenant-General Leo v. Caprivi	March 1883 – July 1888
Vice-Admiral Alexander v. Monts	July 1888 – January 1889
Vice-Admiral Max v.d. Goltz	January 1889 – March 1889

Chief of the High Command

Vice-Admiral Max v.d. Goltz	March 1889 – May 1895
Vice-Admiral Eduard v. Knorr	May 1895 – March 1899

Chief of the Admiralty Staff

Rear-Admiral Felix Bendemann	March 1899 – December 1899
Vice-Admiral Otto v. Diederichs	December 1899 – August 1902
Vice-Admiral Wilhelm Büchsel	August 1902 – January 1908
Vice-Admiral Friedrich v. Baudissin	January 1908 – Fall 1909
Admiral Max v. Fischel	Fall 1909 – March 1911
Vice-Admiral August v. Heeringen	March 1911 – February 1913
Admiral Hugo v. Pohl	April 1913 – February 1915
Vice-Admiral Gustav Bachmann	February 1915 – September 1915
Admiral Henning v. Holtzendorff	September 1915 – August 1918

Chief of the Supreme Navy Command

Admiral Reinhard Scheer	August 1918 – November 1918

Chief of the Navy Cabinet

Captain Gustav v. Senden-Bibran	April 1889 – March 1906
Rear-Admiral Georg Alexander v. Müller	April 1906 – November 1918

State Secretary of the Navy Office

Rear-Admiral Eduard Heussner	March 1889 – April 1890
Rear-Admiral Friedrich Hollmann	April 1890 – June 1897

Rear-Admiral Alfred v. Tirpitz	June 1897 – March 1916
Admiral Eduard v. Capelle	March 1916 – October 1918
Vice-Admiral Paul Behncke	October 1918
Vice-Admiral Ernst Ritter v. Mann Edler v. Tiechler	October 1918 – February 1919

Chief of the First Squadron
Admiral Hans v. Koester   1900

Chief of the Active Battle Fleet
Admiral Hans v. Koester   June 1903

Chief of the High Sea Fleet

Admiral Heinrich Prinz v. Preussen	Autumn 1906 – Autumn 1909
Vice-Admiral Henning v. Holtzendorff	Autumn 1909 – April 1913
Vice-Admiral Friedrich v. Ingenohl	April 1913 – February 1915
Admiral Hugo v. Pohl	February 1915 – January 1916
Vice-Admiral Reinhard Scheer	January 1916 – August 1918
Vice-Admiral Franz Ritter v. Hipper	August 1918 – November 1918

Table 2 German Pre-Dreadnought Battleships 1890–1900

Classes and Dates	Displacement (t)	Length (m)	Beam (m)	Draft (m)	Horsepower Output	Armament (cm)	Best Speed	Range	Coal (normal and maximum loads)	Officers	Ratings	Cost (GM)
1890–1894												
Brandenburg	10,097 to 11,894	116	19.5	7.9	9,820 to 10,242	6–28cm	16 kn	4,500sm/ 10kn	640t — 1,050t	38	530	15,832,000 to 16,054,000
Kurfürst Friedrich Wilhelm						8–10.5						
Weissenburg						8–8.8						
Wörth						6–45cm torpedo tubes						
1895–1902												
Kaiser Friedrich III	11,097 to 11,894	125	20.4	8.3	13,000	4–24cm	18	1,500sm/ 16kn	650t — 1,070t	39	612	20,301,000 to 21,472,000
Kaiser Wilhelm II						18–15cm						
Kaiser Wilhelm der Grosse						12–8.8						
Kaiser Karl der Grosse						5–45cm torpedo tubes						
Kaiser Barbarossa												

Table 3   German Large Cruisers 1896–1908

Classes and Dates	Displacement (t)	Length (m)	Beam (m)	Draft (m)	Horsepower Output	Armament (cm)	Best Speed	Range	Coal (normal and maximum loads)	Officers	Ratings	Cost (GM)
1896–1899												
Hertha	5,660	111	17.6	6.9	10,312	2–21cm	18	2,810sm/	500t	31	446	10,270,000
Victoria	to			to	to	6–15cm	kn	15kn	—			to
Louise	6,705			7.3	10,792	10–8.8			950t			11,094,000
Vineta						3–45cm						
Freya						torpedo						
Hansa						tubes						

German Armoured Cruisers 1896–1902

Classes and Dates	Displacement (t)	Length (m)	Beam (m)	Draft (m)	Horsepower Output	Armament (cm)	Best Speed	Range	Coal (normal and maximum loads)	Officers	Ratings	Cost (GM)
1896–1900												
Fürst	10,690	127	20.4	8.5	13,500	4–24cm	18	3,230sm/	1,000t	36	585	18,945,000
Bismarck	to				to	12–15cm	kn	12kn	—			
	11,461				13,810	10–8.8			1,700t			
						6–45cm						
						torpedo						
						tubes						

Classes and Dates	Displacement (t)	Length (m)	Beam (m)	Draft (m)	Horsepower Output	Armament (cm)	Best Speed	Range	Coal (normal and maximum loads)	Officers	Ratings	Cost (GM)
1898–1902 Prinz Heinrich Prinz Adalbert Friedrich Carl Roon Yorck	9,806 to 10,266	127	20.2	8.0	15,000 to 20,625	2–24cm 10–15cm 10–8.8cm 4–45cm torpedo tubes	20 kn	2,980sm / 18kn	750t — 1,600t	35	532	15,345,000 to 16,588,000

Table 4 German Light Cruisers 1897–1904

Classes and Dates	Displacement (t)	Length (m)	Beam (m)	Draft (m)	Horsepower Output	Armament (cm)	Best Speed	Range	Coal (normal and maximum loads)	Officers	Ratings	Cost (GM)
1897–1904 Gazelle	2,643 to 3,180	108	12.1	5.4	6,000 to 9,318	10–10.5cm 3–45cm torpedo tubes	20 to 22	1,600sm / 19kn	300t — 560t	14	243	4,487,000 to 4,858,000

Table 5   Major Stages of German Naval Building

Ship Formation and/or Class	Navy Bill 10 April 1898	Navy Bill 14 June 1900	Novelle 1906	Novelle 1912
Fleet flagship	1	2	2	1
Battleships	16	32	32	40
	2 squadrons	4 squadrons	4 squadrons	5 squadrons
Armoured cruisers (coast-defence-ships)	8	—	—	—
Battle fleet cruisers				
Large	6	8	8	12
Light	16	24	24	30
Overseas cruisers				
Large	3	3	8	8
Light	10	10	10	10
Material reserve				
Battleships	2	4	4	—
Large cruisers	3	3	4	—
Light cruisers	4	4	4	—

Table 6   German Pre-Dreadnought Battleships 1899–1908

Classes and Dates	Displacement (t)	Length (m)	Beam (m)	Draft (m)	Horsepower Output	Armament (cm)	Best Speed	Range	Coal (normal and maximum loads)		Officers	Ratings	Cost (GM)
1899–1904 Wittelsbach Wettin Zähringen Schwaben Mecklenburg	11,774 to 12,789	126.8	22.8	8.0	14,000 to 15,530	4–25cm 18–15cm 12–8.8cm 6–45cm torpedo tubes	18 kn	3,150sm/ 16kn	650t 1,800t		33	650	21,678,000 to 22,740,000
1901–1906 Braunschweig Elsass Hessen Preussen Lothringen	13,208 to 14,394	127.7	25.6	8.2	16,000 to 18,374	4–28cm 14–17cm 18–8.8cm 6–45cm torpedo tubes	18 kn	3,400sm/ 16kn	850t 1,665t		35	708	23,801,000 to 24,373,000
1903–1908 Deutschland Hannover Pommern Schlesien Schleswig- Holstein	13,191 to 14,218	127.6	22.2	8.3	16,000 to 23,456	4–28cm 14–17cm 20–8.8cm 6–45cm torpedo tubes	18 kn	3,470sm/ 16kn	690t 1,720t		31	565	24,253,000 to 24,972,000

Table 7 German Armoured Cruisers 1904–1909

Classes and Dates	Displacement (t)	Length (m)	Beam (m)	Draft (m)	Horsepower Output	Armament (cm)	Best Speed	Range	Coal (normal and maximum loads)	Officers	Ratings	Cost (GM)
1904–1908 Scharnhorst Gneisenau	11,616 to 12,985	144.6	21.6	8.4	26,000 to 30,396	8–21cm 6–15cm 18–8.8cm 4–45cm torpedo tubes	24 kn	4,800sm/14kn	800t 2,000t	38	726	19,243,000 to 20,319,000
1907–1909 Blücher	15,842 to 17,500	161.8	24.5	8.8	34,000 to 43,886	12–21cm 8–15cm 16–8.8cm 4–45cm torpedo tubes	25 kn	3,520sm/18kn	900t 2,400t	41	812	28,532,000

Table 8 *German Light Cruisers 1902–1908*

Classes and Dates	Displacement (t)	Length (m)	Beam (m)	Draft (m)	Horsepower Output	Armament (cm)	Best Speed	Range	Coal (normal and maximum loads)	Officers	Ratings	Cost (GM)
1902–1907 Bremen	3,278 to 3,821	111.1	13.3	5.6	11,220 to 14,403	10–10.5cm 2–45cm torpedo tubes	23 kn	4,270sm/ 12kn	400t 860t	14	274	4,545,000 to 5,436,000
1905–1908 Nürnberg	3,390 to 4,002	117.4	13.3	5.4	12,000 to 21,670	10–10.5cm (8–5.2cm) 2–45cm torpedo tubes	24 kn	4,100sm/ 12kn	400t 880t	14	308	5,407,000 to 6,398,000

Table 9 German and British Battleship Comparisons to 1914

Nassau Launched: 7 March 1908		*Dreadnought* Launched: 10 February 1906
18,870t	Displacement :	17,900t
20kn	Best Speed :	21kn
1,008	Complement :	656
6–45cm	Torpedo Tubes :	5–45cm
12–28cm	Armament :	10–30.5cm
12–15cm	:	22–7.6cm
16–8.8cm	:	
30cm	Water Line Armour Belt :	27.9cm

Kaiser Launched: 22 March 1911		*King George V* Launched: 9 October 1911
24,700t	Displacement :	27,000t
22kn	Best Speed :	22kn
1,088	Complement :	900
5–50cm	Torpedo Tubes :	3–53cm
10–30.5cm	Armament :	10–34.3cm
14–15cm	:	16–10.2cm
12–8.8cm	:	4–4.7cm
35cm	Water Line Armour Belt :	30.5cm

Table 10 *German and British Battle-Cruiser Comparisons*
to 1910

	Von der Tann Launched : 20 March 1909			*Invincible* Launched : 13 April 1907
Displacement	:	19,400t	:	17,250t
Best Speed	:	27kn	:	25kn
Complement	:	911	:	730
Torpedo Tubes	:	4–45cm	:	5–45cm
Armament	:	8–28cm	:	8–30.5cm
	:	10–15cm	:	16–10.2cm
	:	16–8.8cm		
Water Line	:	25cm	:	15.2cm
Armour Belt				

Table 11 *German Light Cruisers 1907–1911*

Classes and Dates	Displacement (t)	Length (m)	Beam (m)	Draft (m)	Horsepower Output	Armament (cm)	Best Speed	Range	Coal (normal and maximum loads)	Officers	Ratings	Cost (GM)
1907–1909 Dresden Emden	3,664 to 4,268	118.3	13.5	5.5	13,500 to 18,880	10–10.5cm 2–45cm torpedo tubes	24 kn 25 kn	3,600sm/ 14kn	400t 860t	18	343	7,460,000 to 5,960,000
1907–1911 Kolberg Augsburg Cöln Mainz	4,362 to 4,915	130.5	14.0	5.6	19,000 to 31,033	12–10.5cm 4–5.2cm 2–45cm torpedo tubes 100 mines	26 kn	3,630sm/ 14kn	400t 1,010t	18	349	7,593,000 to 8,777,000

Table 12 German Dreadnought Battleships 1907–1913

Classes and Dates	Displacement (t)	Length (m)	Beam (m)	Draft (m)	Horsepower Output	Armament (cm)	Best Speed	Range	Coal (normal and maximum loads)	Officers	Ratings	Cost (GM)
1907–1910 Nassau Westfalen Rheinland Posen	18,873 to 20,535	146.1	26.9	8.8	22,000 to 28,117	12–28cm 12–15cm 16–8.8cm 6–45cm torpedo tubes	20 kn	8,300sm/ 12kn 2,800sm/ 19kn	950t 3,000t (later 160cbm oil)	40	968	36,916,000 to 37,615,000
1908–1912 Helgoland Ostfriesland Oldenburg Thüringen	22,808 to 24,700	167.2	28.5	8.9	28,000 to 35,550	12–30.5cm 14–15cm 14–8.8cm 6–50cm torpedo tubes	21 kn	3,600sm/ 18kn 2,700sm/ 20kn	900t 3,200t (later 197cbm oil)	42	1,071	43,579,000 to 46,314,000
1909–1913 Kaiser Friedrich der Grosse Kaiserin Prinzregent Luitpold König Albert	24,724 to 27,000	172.4	29.0	9.1	31,000 to 55,187	10–30.5cm 14–15cm 8–8.8cm 5–50cm torpedo tubes	22 kn	3,900sm/ 18kn 2,400sm/ 21kn	1,000t 3,600t (later 200cbm oil)	41	1,043	44,997,000 to 46,374,000

Table 13 German Dreadnought Battle–Cruisers 1908–1913

Classes and Dates	Displacement (t)	Length (m)	Beam (m)	Draft (m)	Horsepower Output	Armament (cm)	Best Speed	Range	Coal (normal and maximum loads)	Officers	Ratings	Cost (GM)
1908–1910 Von der Tann	19,370 to 21,300	171.7	26.6	9.2	42,000 to 79,007	8–28cm 10–15cm 16–8.8cm 4–45cm torpedo tubes	27 kn	4,400sm/ 14kn	1,000t 2,800t	41	882	36,523,000
1909–1912 Moltke Goeben	22,979 to 25,400	186.5	29.5	9.2	52,000 to 85,782	10–28cm 12–15cm 12–8.8cm 4–50cm torpedo tubes	28 kn	4,210sm/ 14kn	1,000t 3,100t	43	1,010	42,603,000 to 41,564,000
1911–1913 Seydlitz	24,988 to 28,550	200.6	28.5	9.3	67,000 to 89,738	10–28cm 12–15cm 12–8.8cm 4–50cm torpedo tubes	29 kn	4,200sm/ 14kn	1,000t 3,600t	43	1,025	44,685,000

Table 14 German Light Cruisers 1910–1915

Classes and Dates	Displacement (t)	Length (m)	Beam (m)	Draft (m)	Horsepower Output	Armament (cm)	Best Speed	Range	Coal (normal and maximum loads)	Officers	Ratings	Cost (GM)
1910–1912 Magdeburg Breslau Stralsund Strassburg	4,570 to 5,587	138.7	13.4	6.0	25,000 to 35,515	12–10.5cm 2–50cm torpedo tubes 120 mines	27 to 28 kn	5,820sm/12kn 900sm/25kn	450t 1,200t 106cbm oil	18	336	7,302,000 to 8,058,000
1911–1914 Karlsruhe	4,900 to 6,191	142.2	13.7	5.4	26,000 to 37,885	12–10.5cm 2–50cm torpedo tubes 120 mines	28 kn	5,000sm/12kn 900sm/25kn	400t 1,300t 70–260 cbm oil	18	355	8,126,000
1912–1915 Rostock Graudenz	4,912 to 6,382	142.7	13.8	6.1	26,000 to 43,628	12–10.5cm 2–50cm torpedo tubes 120 mines	28 kn	5,500sm/12kn 1,000sm/25kn	380t 1,280t 100–375 cbm oil	21	364	8,124,000 to 8,800,000

Table 15 *Major German Battleship And Battle–Cruiser (BC) Yards to 1918*

	Yard	Ships
1.	A.G. Vulcan Hamburg	*Friedrich der Grosse, Grosser Kurfürst*
2.	A.G. Vulcan Stettin	*Rheinland*
3.	A.G. Weser Bremen	*Westfalen, Thüringen, Markgraf*
4.	Blohm & Voss Hamburg	*Von der Tann* (BC), *Moltke* (BC), *Goeben* (BC), *Seydlitz* (BC), *Derfflinger* (BC)
5.	Friedrich Krupp "Germania" Kiel	*Posen, Prinzregent Luitpold, Kronprinz*
6.	Friedrich Schichau Danzig	*Oldenburg, König Albert, Baden, Lützow* (BC)
7.	Howaldtswerke Kiel	*Helgoland, Kaiserin, Bayern*
8.	Kaiserliche Werft Kiel	*Kaiser*
9.	Kaiserliche Werft Wilhelmshaven	*Nassau, Ostfriesland, König, Hindenburg* (BC)

Table 16 German Dreadnought Battleships 1911–1916

Classes and Dates	Displacement (t)	Length (m)	Beam (m)	Draft (m)	Horsepower Output	Armament (cm)	Best Speed	Range	Coal (normal and maximum loads)	Officers	Ratings	Cost (GM)
1911–1914												
König Grosser Kurfürst Markgraf Kronprinz	25,796 to 28,600	175.4	29.5	9.2	31,000 to 46,200	10–30.5cm 14–15cm 6–8.8cm 5–50cm torpedo tubes	21 kn	8,000sm/ 12kn 4,000sm/ 18kn	1,000t/ 3,600t 700cbm oil	41	1,095	45,000,000
1913–1916												
Bayern Baden	28,600 to 32,200	180.0	30.0	9.4	35,000 to 56,275	8–38cm 16–15cm 4–8.8cm 5–60cm torpedo tubes	22 kn	8,000sm/ 12kn 4,000sm/ 18kn	900t/ 3,400t 200–600 cbm oil	42	1,129	49,000,000 to 50,000,000

Table 17 Comparative World Naval Budgets 1899–1914

Country	Naval Budget 1899	Naval Budget 1905–1906	Naval Budget 1913–1914
Great Britain	498,000,000 GM	681,100,000 GM	944,700,000 GM
France	235,000,000 GM	254,900,000 GM	369,000,000 GM
United States	198,000,000 GM	421,400,000 GM	590,700,000 GM
Russia	186,000,000 GM	252,000,000 GM	497,300,000 GM
Germany	133,000,000 GM	233,400,000 GM	467,300,000 GM
Italy		101,800,000 GM	205,300,000 GM
Japan			202,800,000 GM

Table 18 *German Dreadnought Battle-Cruisers 1912–1917*

Classes and Dates	Displacement (t)	Length (m)	Beam (m)	Draft (m)	Horsepower Output	Armament (cm)	Best Speed	Range	Coal (normal and maximum loads)	Cost (GM)
1912–1914 Derfflinger	26,600 to 31,200	210.4	29.0	9.6	63,000 to 76,600	8–30.5cm 12–15cm 8–8.8cm 4–50cm torpedo tubes	26 kn	5,300sm/ 14kn	750t 3,700t 250 to 1,000cbm oil	56,000,000
1912–1915 Lützow	26,741	210.4	29.0	9.6	63,000 to 80,988	8–30.5cm 14–15cm 8–8.8cm 4–60cm torpedo tubes	26 kn	5,300sm/ 14kn	750t 3,700t 250 to 1,000cbm oil	58,000,000
1913–1917 Hindenburg	26,947 to 31,500	212.8	29.0	9.6	72,000 to 95,777	8–30.5cm 14–15cm 8–8.8cm	27 kn	5,300sm/ 14kn	750t 3,700t 250 to 1,000cbm oil	59,000,000

Table 19 *German Light Cruisers 1912–1915*

Classes and Dates	Displacement (t)	Length (m)	Beam (m)	Draft (m)	Horsepower Output	Armament (cm)	Best Speed	Range	Coal (normal and maximum loads)	Officers	Ratings	Cost (GM)
1912–1915 Regensburg Pillau Elbing	4,390 to 6,382	135·3	13·6	6·0	30,000	8–15cm 4–5.2cm 2–50cm torpedo tubes 120 mines	28 kn	4,300sm/12kn	80t 620t 250–580 cbm oil	21	421	8,800,000 (?)
1913–1915 Wiesbaden Frankfurt	5,180 to 6,601	145·3	13·9	6·1	31,000	8–15cm 4–5.2cm 4–50cm torpedo tubes 120 mines	28 kn	4,800sm/12kn 1,200sm/25kn	350t 1,280t 150–470 cbm oil	17	457	8,800,000 (?)

Table 20 German and British Destroyers to 1914

Torpedo-Boats S 13–24 1911–1913			Destroyers Acasta, Achates 1912–1913
564t	Displacement :	950t	
30kn	Best Speed :	30kn	
73	Complement :	100	
4–50cm	Torpedo Tubes :	2–53cm	
2–8.8cm	Armament :	3–10.2cm	

Table 21 Bismarck's Colonial Empire (1909 figures)

Colony and Date of Acquisition	Area (1,000 square km)	Population (1,000)	German Residents	German Colonial Troops	German Subsidy (1,000 GM)	Disposition on 28 June 1919
German South-West Africa August 1884	835.1	120	6,215	2,430	17,125	Union of South Africa
Togoland July 1884	87.2	1,000	239	—	250	France/ Great Britain
Cameroons July 1884	495.6	3,000	971	163	2,267	France/ Great Britain
German East Africa February 1885	995.0	10,000	2,014	269	3,579	Great Britain/ Belgium
New Guinea May 1885; December 1886	240.0	300	482	—	916	Australia

Table 22 *Wilhelm II's Colonial Empire (1909 figures)*

Colony and Date of Acquisition	Area (1,000 square km)	Population (1,000)	German Residents	German Colonial Troops	German Subsidy (1,000 GM)	Disposition on 28 June 1919
Marshall Islands October 1885						Japan
Nauru Island April 1888	2.476	56	191	—	350	Great Britain
Caroline, Palau, Mariana Islands June 1899						Japan
Kiaochow March 1898	0.501	33	1,412	2,374	8,545	Japan
Samoa December 1899	2.572	37	262	—	250	New Zealand

Table 23 *Kiaochow's Annual Subsidies*

Year	Regular Navy Administration	Reich subsidy (non-recurring expenses)
1898	—	5,256,000 GM
1899	—	8,500,000 GM
1900	39,300 GM	9,780,000 GM
1901	51,100 GM	10,750,000 GM
1902	56,000 GM	12,044,000 GM
1903	71,800 GM	12,353,000 GM
1904	90,000 GM	12,583,000 GM
1905	97,100 GM	14,660,000 GM
1906	106,100 GM	13,150,000 GM
1907	111,800 GM	11,735,000 GM
1908	115,400 GM	9,740,000 GM
1909	142,400 GM	8,545,000 GM
Total	881,000 GM	115,340,000 GM

Table 24 German–British Officer Rank Equivalents

German Navy	German Army	Royal Navy	Engineers Germany	Engineers Britain	Torpedo-Engineers Germany	Corps of Medical Officers German Navy	Corps of Medical Officers Royal Navy
Grossadmiral	Generalfeldmarschall	Admiral of the Fleet	—	—	—	—	—
Admiral	General der Inf. Art. Kav.	Admiral	—	—	—	—	—
Vizeadmiral	Generalleutnant	Vice-Admiral	—	Engineer Vice-Admiral	—	—	—
Konteradmiral	Generalmajor	Rear-Admiral	—	Engineer Rear-Admiral	—	Marine-Generalstabsarzt	Inspector General of Hospitals and Fleets
—	—	Commodore	—	—	—	—	—
Kapitän zur See	Oberst	Captain	—	Engineer Captain	—	Marine-Generalarzt	Deputy Inspector General of Hospitals and Fleets

Fregattenkapitän	Oberstleutnant	—	Marine-Chef Ingenieur	Engineer Captain (less than 8 years)	—	Marine-Generaloberarzt	—
Korvettenkapitän	Major	Commander	Marine-Oberstabsingenieur	Engineer Commander	Torpedo-Oberstabsingenieur	Marine-Oberstabsarzt	Fleet Surgeon
Kapitänleutnant	Hauptmann, Rittmeister	Lieutenant-Commander	Marine-Stabsingenieur	Engineer Lieutenant	Torpedo-Stabsingenieur	Marine-Stabsarzt	Staff Surgeon
Oberleutnant z. See	Oberleutnant	Lieutenant	Marine-Oberingenieur	Engineer Lieutenant (less than 8 years)	Torpedo-Oberingenieur	Marine-Oberassistenzarzt	Surgeon
Leutnant z. See	Leutnant	Sub-Lieutenant	Marine-Ingenieur	Engineer Sub-Lieutenant	Torpedo-Ingenieur	Marine-Assistenzarzt	—
Fähnrich z. See	Fahnenjunker	Midshipman	—	Engineer Cadet	—	Unterarzt	—

Table 25 *German Naval Uniform Insignia (Executive officers)*

Rank	Epaulettes	Stars	Shoulder straps	Stars	Sleeve stripes (gold) [Imperial Crown above]
I. FLAGGOFFIZIERE Grossadmiral	Anchor and Imperial Eagle. Imperial Crown near collar buttons.	[2 silver batons]	Woven tress of two gold and one silver-black-red cord	[2 silver batons]	1–5.2cm; 4–1.4cm
Admiral	Thick, loose, brilliant gold bullions (fringes)	2 silver		2 silver	1–5.2cm; 3–1.4cm
Vizeadmiral		1 silver		1 silver	1–5.2cm; 2–1.4cm
Konteradmiral		—		—	1–5.2cm; 1–1.4cm
II. STABSOFFIZIERE Kapitän z. See	Anchor. Thick, loose, dull gold bullions (fringes)	2 gold	Woven tress of silver-black-red cords	2 gold	4–1.4cm
Fregattenkapitän		1 gold		1 gold	4–1.4cm
Korvettenkapitän		—		—	3–1.4cm
III. SUBALTERN-OFFIZIERE Kapitänleutnant	Anchor. Thin, loose gold fringes	2 gold	Flat silver-black-red cords	2 gold	2–1.4cm
Oberleutnant z. See		—		1 gold	1–1.4cm
Leutnant z. See	Anchor. No gold fringes	—		—	1–0.7cm
Fähnrich z. See	None	—	Thin silver with black and red threads	—	3 buttons on each sleeve
Seekadett	None	—	None	—	3 buttons on each sleeve

Table 26 *German Dreadnought Building Not Completed 1916–1918*

A. Battleships

Class	Ships	Displacement (t)	Armament (cm)	Best Speed (kn)	Date Launched	Work Remaining	Cost (GM)
Bayern	Sachsen	32,500	8–38cm 16–15cm 8–8.8cm	22 kn	Nov. 1916	9 months	49,000,000
	Württemberg				June 1916	12 months	50,000,000

B. Battle-cruisers

Class	Ships	Displacement (t)	Armament (cm)	Best Speed (kn)	Date Launched	Work Remaining	Cost (GM)
Mackensen	Mackensen	35,300	8–35cm 14–15cm 8–8.8cm	27 kn	1917 to 1920		66,000,000
	Prinz Eitel Friedrich						
	Graf Spee						
	Fürst Bismarck				No		
"Ersatz Yorck"	"Ersatz Yorck"	38,000	8–38cm 12–15cm 8–8.8.cm	27 kn	No		75,000,000
	"Ersatz Gneisenau"				No		
	"Ersatz Scharnhorst"				No		

Table 27 German Light Cruisers 1915–1918

Classes and Dates	Displacement (t)	Length (m)	Beam (m)	Draft (m)	Horsepower Output	Armament (cm)	Best Speed	Range	Coal (normal and maximum loads) oil	Officers	Ratings	Cost (GM)
1915–1916												
Brummer Bremse	4,385 to 5,856	140.4	13.2	6.0	33,000 to 47,748	4–15cm 2–8.8cm 2–50cm torpedo tubes 400 mines	28 kn	5,300sm/12kn 1,400sm/25kn	300t 600t 500–1,000 cbm oil	16	293	8,800,000 (?)
1914–1917												
Königsberg II Emden II Karlsruhe II Nürnberg II	5,440 to 7,125	151.4	14.3	6.3	31,000 to 55,700	8–15cm 2–8.8cm 4–50cm torpedo tubes 200 mines	27 to 28 kn	4,850sm/12kn 1,200sm/27kn	350t 1,340t 300–1,000 cbm oil	17	458	(?)

| 1915–1918 Cöln II Dresden II | 5,620 to 7,486 | 155.5 | 14.3 | 6.4 | 31,000 to 49,428 | 8–15cm 3–8.8cm 4–60cm torpedo tubes 200 mines | 28 to 29 kn | 5,000sm/12kn 1,200sm/25kn | 300t 1,100t 200– 1,050 cbm oil | 17 542 | (?) |

Started 1915–1916 but not completed:
Wiesbaden, Magdeburg, Leipzig, Rostock, Frauenlob, "Ersatz Cöln",
"Ersatz Emden", "Ersatz Karlsruhe" ("A")

Table 28 Sample German Submarine Construction 1904–1918

Type Boat Date	Displacement (t)	Best Speed Surface/Submerged (kn)	Range	Torpedo Tubes Mines	Horse-power Output	Armament (cm)	Crew	Cost (1,000 GM)
U1 1904–1906	238	10.8/8.7	1,400sm/10kn	1/—	400	—	22	1,905
U30 1912–1914	675	16.7/9.8	7,900sm/8kn	4/—	2,000	1 or 2 8.8cm	35	2,980
U70 1912–1914	791	16.8/9.0	6,500sm/8kn	4 or 5/—	2,300	1 or 2 8.8cm	36	3,510
U139/141 1913–1915	1,930	15.8/7.6	17,750sm/8kn	6/—	3,500	2–15cm 2–8.8cm	62	10,817
U151/157 1916–1918	1,512	12.4/5.2	2,500sm/5.5kn	2/—	800	2–15cm 2–8.8cm	56	5,741
UB I (UB 10) 1916–1917	127	7.45/6.2	1,500sm/5kn	2/—	60	—	14	711
UB II (UB 40) 1914–1915	274	9.1/5.7	8,150sm/5kn	2/—	270	1–8.8cm	23	1,152
UB III (UB 90) 1915–1916 1917–1918	510	13.0/7.4	7,120sm/6kn	5/—	1,100	1–10.5cm	34	3,654

UC I (UC 10) 1914–1915	168	6.2/5.2	780sm/5kn	—/12	90	—	14	(?)
UC II (UC 20) 1915–1916	417	11.6/7.0	9,430sm/7kn	3/18	500	1–10.5cm	26	1,729
(UC 60) 1916–1917	415	11.6/7.3	9,450sm/7kn	3/18	600	1–10.5cm	26	1,935
UC III (UC 90) 1917–1918	491	11.5/6.6	10,000sm/7kn	3/14	600	1–8.8cm	32	3,303

Table 29   *German Submarine Strength 1915–1918*

War Year	Fleet Boats "U"	Coastal Boats "UB"	Mine-Boats "UC"	Total	Lost	Net Gain
1915	15	22	15	52	19	33
1916	32	25	51	108	22	86
1917	32	42	13	87	63	24
1918	25	47	16	88	69	19
TOTAL	104	136	95	335	173	162

Reference Literature

The German Navy Archive (*Marinearchiv*) in Freiburg, West Germany, at the Federal Military Archive (*Bundesarchiv-Militärarchiv*) forms the documentary basis for this work. Originally in Berlin as an integral part of the High Command, the Navy Archive was moved early in November 1944, because of heavy Allied air raids, to Tambach Castle near Coburg in Bavaria. It was stored in the swimming pool there and was, by order of Admiral Karlgeorg Schuster, chief of the Navy History Office, to be destroyed rather than surrendered if Germany lost the war. About 200 litres of petrol and several cords of wood were gathered for this purpose, but in the severe winter of 1944-5 the staff used the combustible material for heat rather than archival destruction. By 7 May 1945, Washington knew of the capture of these vital records, and over the next two years 3,900 reels of microfilm copies of the material were made in London. The records were returned – excluding the submarine logs, which are still held in Great Britain – between 1959 and 1965 in eight large shipments totalling 110 tons. I have throughout this work used the original documents in Freiburg, but have spared the reader from the cumbersome academic apparatus known as footnoting; scholars wishing to ascertain exact references are welcome to contact me. I prefer simply to list some of the major categories of records perused:

1. "Bundesarchiv-Militärarchiv" (Freiburg i. Br.)
   Admiralität (RM 1), also Marine Ministerium
   Admiralsteb der Marine (RM 5)
   Inspektion des Bildungswesens der Marine
   Kommando der Hochseestreitkräfte (RM 47)
   Marine-Kabinett (RM 2)
   Marinestation der Nordsee (RM 33)
   Marinestation der Ostee (RM 31)
   Oberbefehlshaber der Osteestreitkräfte (RM 28)
   Reichs-Marine-Amt (RM 3)
   Seekriegsleitung
   "Dienstliche Nachlässe" (Official Personal Papers)
   F 7580/85 Behncke
   F 7589/90 Hollweg
   F 7591/93 Knorr
   F 7605   Tirpitz

F 7610/15a Vanselow
F 7631/35 Dähnhardt
F 7635d Capelle
IM 46/2 Bachmann (Personalakte)
"Nachlässe" (Personal Papers)
N 156 (Souchon)
N 159 (Müller)
N 161 (Keyserlingk)
N 162 (Hipper)
N 164 (Michaelis)
N 165 (Groos)
N 168 (Büchsel)
N 170 (Capelle)
N 173 (Behncke)
N 225 (Eschenburg)
N 239 (Levetzow)
N 253 (Tirpitz)
2. "Bundesarchiv" (Koblenz)
Logbücher Bogislav v. Selchow
R.I. Reichsinstitut für Geschichte des neuen Deutschland :
Berichte v. Holtzendorff an Ballin, 16 vols
Nachlass Bülow
Nachlass Gothein
Nachlass Hohenlohe-Schillingsfürst
3. "Hauptstaatsarchiv" (Stuttgart)
Nachlass Haussmann
E 130. I. Staatsministerium, vols 860/64. "Niederschriften über Sitzungen von Reichstagausschüssen 1915–1918"
4. Private Archival Source. "The Papers of Ernst v. Weizsäcker, 1900–1918", Professor L. E. Hill, University of British Columbia, Canada

In addition, a number of basic reference works were frequently consulted without exact citation, primarily for statistical or technical data. These included :
1. Naval Annuals
Brassey's Naval Annual (London, 1887 ff.)
Deutscher Schiffskalender für Kriegsmarine und Handelsmarine (Berlin, 1887 ff.)
The Naval Pocket Book (London, 1896 ff.)
Jane's All the World Fighting Ships (London, 1898 ff.)
Weyer's Taschenbuch der deutschen Kriegsflotte (Berlin, 1898 ff.)
Nauticus. Jahrbuch für Deutschlands Seeinteressen (Berlin, 1900 ff.)
The Fleet Annual and Naval Year Book (London, 1906 ff.)
Taschenbuch der Luftflotten (München, 1914 ff.)

2. Naval Journals
 Journal of the Royal United Services Institution (London, 1857 ff.)
 Marine-Rundschau (Berlin, 1890 ff.)
 Militärgeschichtliche Mitteilungen (Freiburg, 1967 ff.)
 United States Naval Institute Proceedings (Annapolis, 1875 ff.)
3. Naval Handbooks
 Siegfried Breyer, *Schlachtschiffe und Schlachtkreuzer 1905–1970* (München, 1970).
 Friedrich Forstmeier, *Deutsche Grosskampfschiffe 1915–1918. Die Entwicklung der Typenfrage im Ersten Weltkrieg* (München, 1970)
 Erich Gröner, *Die deutschen Kriegsschiffe, 1815–1945* (München, 1966–8), 2 vols
 Günter Kroschel and August-Ludwig Evers, *Die deutsche Flotte 1848–1945* (Wilhelmshaven, 1962)
 Naval History Division, Washington, D.C. *Dictionary of American Naval Fighting Ships* (Washington, 1959 ff.), 5 vols to date
 O. Parkes, *British Battleships, 1860–1950* (London, 1956)
 Rangliste der Kaiserlich Deutschen Marine (Berlin, 1871 ff.)
 Ehrenrangliste der Kaiserlichen Marine 1914–1918 (Berlin, 1930)
 Albert Röhr, *Handbuch der deutschen Marinegeschichte* (Oldenburg, 1963)

Finally, mention should be made of the "official" histories of the Great War:
1. Sir Julian S. Corbett and Sir Henry Newbolt, *History of the Great War. Naval Operations* (London, 1920–31), 5 vols
2. Germany, Ministry of Marine, *Der Krieg zur See, 1914–1918* (Berlin, 1920–66). This series consists of seven sets:
 Der Krieg in der Nordsee (1920–65), 7 vols
 Der Handelskrieg mit U-Booten (1932–66), 5 vols
 Der Krieg in den türkischen Gewässern (1928, 1938), 2 vols
 Der Kreuzerkrieg in den ausländischen Gewässern (1922–37), 3 vols
 Der Krieg in der Ostsee (1922–64), 3 vols
 Die Kämpfe der kaiserlichen Marine in den deutschen Kolonien (1935)
 Die Überwasserstreitkräfte und ihre Technik (1930)

Among the voluminous literature dealing with the modern German Navy, the following titles are singled out for special mention:

Constantin v. Altrock, *Vom Sterben des deutschen Offizierkorps* (Berlin, 1922)

Detlef Bald, *Deutsch-Ostafrika 1900–1914* (München, 1970)

Hermann Bauer, *Reichsleitung und U-bootseinsatz* (Lippoldsberg, 1956)

Winfried Baumgart, *Deutschland im Zeitalter des Imperialismus (1890–1914)* (Frankfurt, 1972)

Volker R. Berghahn, *Der Tirpitz-Plan. Genesis und Verfall einer innenpolitischen Krisenstrategie unter Wilhelm II.* (Düsseldorf, 1971)

Rüstung und Machtpolitik. Zur Anatomie des "Kalten Krieges" vor 1914 (Düsseldorf, 1973)

"Zu den Zielen des deutschen Flottenbaus unter Wilhelm II.", *Historische Zeitschrift,* 210 (February 1970), 34–100

"Der Tirpitz-Plan und die Krisis des preussisch–deutschen Herrschaftssystems", *Marine und Marinepolitik 1871–1914* (Düsseldorf, 1972), 89–115. Edited by Herbert Schottelius and Wilhelm Deist

Volker R. Berghahn and Wilhelm Deist, "Kaiserliche Marine und Kriegsausbruch 1914. Neue Dokumente zur Juli-Krise", *Militärgeschichtliche Mitteilungen,* 1/1970, 37–58

Gerhard Bidlingmaier, *Seegeltung in der deutschen Geschichte. Ein Seekriegsgeschichtliches Handbuch* (Darmstadt, 1967)

Helmut Bley, *South-West Africa under German Rule 1894–1914* (Evanston, Ill., 1971)

Werner Bräckow, *Die Geschichte des deutschen Marine-Ingenieuroffizierkorps* (Oldenburg and Hamburg 1974)

Bund der Deckoffiziere, *Deckoffiziere der Deutschen Marine. Ihre Geschichte 1848–1933* (Berlin, 1933)

Andrew R. Carlson, *German Foreign Policy, 1890–1914, and Colonial Policy to 1914* (Metuchen, NJ, 1970)

Wilhelm Deist, "Die Politik der Seekriegsleitung und die Rebellion der Flotte Ende Oktober 1918", *Vierteljahrshefte für Zeitgeschichte,* XIV (October 1966), 341–368

Quellen zur Geschichte des Parlamentarismus und der politischen Parteien. Zweite Reihe. Militär und Innenpolitik im Weltkrieg 1914–1918 (Düsseldorf, 1970), 2 vols

Karl Demeter, *Das Deutsche Offizierkorps in Gesellschaft und Staat 1650–1945* (Frankfurt, 1965)

Wahrhold Drascher, "Zur Soziologie des deutschen Seeoffizierkorps", *Wehrwissenschaftliche Rundschau,* XII, 555–569

Franz Carl Endres, "Soziologische Struktur und ihr entsprechende Ideologien des deutschen Offizierkorps vor dem Weltkriege", *Archiv für Sozialwissenschaft und Sozialpolitik,* LXVIII, 282–319

Karl Dietrich Erdmann, *Kurt Riezler. Tagebücher, Aufsätze, Dokumente* (Göttingen, 1972)

Elisabeth Fehrenbach, *Wandlungen des deutschen Kaisergedankens 1871–1918* (München, 1969)

Korv.-Kap. Ferber, *Organisation und Dienstbetrieb der Kaiserlich deutschen Marine* (Berlin, 1901)

D. K. Fieldhouse, *The Colonial Empires. A Comparative Survey from the Eighteenth Century* (New York, 1965)

Fritz Fischer, *Griff nach der Weltmacht. Die Kriegszielpolitik des kaiserlichen Deutschland 1914/18* (Düsseldorf, 1964)

Friedrich Forstmeier, "Der Tirpitzsche Flottenbau im Urteil der Historiker", *Marine und Marinepolitik*, 34–53

"SMS Emden. Small Protected Cruiser 1906–1914", *Profile Warship* 25 (Windsor, 1972)

"Probleme der Erziehung und Ausbildung in der Kaiserlichen Marine in Abhängigkeit von geistiger Situation und sozialer Struktur", *Marine-Rundschau*, LXIII, 189–198

Albert Gayer, *Die deutschen U-Boote in ihrer Kriegführung 1914–1918* (Berlin, 1920–30), 3 vols

Carl-Axel Gemzell, *Organization, Conflict, and Innovation. A Study of German Naval Strategic Planning, 1888–1940* (Lund, 1973)

R. H. Gibson and Maurice Prendergast, *The German Submarine War, 1914 to 1918* (London, 1931)

Robert M. Grant, *U-Boats Destroyed. The Effect of Anti-Submarine Warfare, 1914–1918* (London, 1964)

Peter Gray and Owen Thetford, *German Aircraft of the First World War* (London, 1962)

Handbuch zur deutschen Militärgeschichte 1648–1939, V, *Organisationsgeschichte der Luftwaffe von den Anfängen bis 1918* (Frankfurt, 1968), 288–291

Karin Hausen, *Deutsche Kolonialherrschaft in Afrika* (Zürich, 1970)

Holger H. Herwig, *The German Naval Officer Corps. A Social and Political History 1890–1918* (Oxford, 1973)

Politics of Frustration: The United States in German Naval Planning 1889–1941 (Boston, 1976)

"Admirals *versus* Generals: The War Aims of the Imperial German Navy 1914–1918", *Central European History*, V (September 1972), 208–233

"Soziale Herkunft und wissenschaftliche Vorbildung des Seeoffiziers der Kaiserlichen Marine vor 1914", *Militärgeschichtliche Mitteilungen*, 2/1971, 81–111

"Zur Soziologie des kaiserlichen Seeoffizierkorps vor 1914", *Marine und Marinepolitik*, 73–88

"German Policy in the Eastern Baltic Sea in 1918: Expansion or Anti-Bolshevik Crusade?", *Slavic Review*, XXXII (June 1973), 339–357

Holger H. Herwig and David F. Trask, "The Failure of Imperial Germany's Undersea Offensive Against World Shipping, February

1917–October 1918", *The Historian,* XXXIII (August 1971), 619–632

Bodo Herzog, *60 Jahre Deutsche Uboote 1906–1966* (München, 1968)
Die deutschen Uboote 1906–1945 (München, 1959)
Bodo Herzog and Günter Schomaekers, *Ritter der Tiefe – Graue Wölfe. Die erfolgreichsten U-Boot-Kommandanten der Welt des Ersten und Zweiten Weltkrieges* (München, 1965)
Vice-Admiral Sir Arthur Hezlet, *Aircraft and Sea Power* (New York, 1970)
Daniel Horn, *The German Naval Mutinies of World War I* (New Brunswick, NJ, 1969)
Edmund Glaise von Horstenau and Rudolf Kiszling, *Österreich-Ungarns Letzter Krieg, 1914–1918*, VI, *Das Kriegsjahr 1917* (Vienna, 1936)
Walther Hubatsch, *Kaiserliche Marine. Aufgaben und Leistungen* (München, 1975)
Die Ära Tirpitz. Studien zur deutschen Marinepolitik 1890–1918 (Göttingen, 1955)
Der Admiralstab und die obersten Marinebehörden in Deutschland 1848–1945 (Frankfurt, 1958)
"Finnland in der deutschen Ostseepolitik 1917/18", *Ostdeutsche Wissenschaft,* II (1956), 55 ff
John, Earl of Jellicoe, *The Grand Fleet 1914–1916* (London, 1919)
H. A. Jones, *The War in the Air* (Oxford, 1928–37), 6 vols
Paul Kässner, *Zur Geschichte der Deckoffizierbewegung des Deckoffizierbundes und des Bundes der Deckoffiziere* (Altona, 1932)
P. Kemp, "Balance of Naval Power August 1914", *Warships of the First World War* (London, 1973)
Paul M. Kennedy, "Mahan versus Mackinder. Two Interpretations of British Sea Power", *Militärgeschichtliche Mitteilungen,* 2/1974, 39–66
"German World Policy and the Alliance Negotiations with England, 1897–1900", *Journal of Modern History,* 45 (December 1973), 608–623
"Tirpitz, England and the Second Navy Law of 1900 : A Strategical Critique", *Militärgeschichtliche Mitteilungen,* 2/1970, 33–57
"Imperial Cable Communication and Strategy, 1870–1914", *The English Historical Review,* LXXXVI (October 1971), 740–752
"The Development of German Naval Operations Plans against England, 1896–1914", *The English Historical Review,* LXXXXIX (January 1974), 48–76
"The End of the High Sea Fleet", *Warships of the First World War* (London, 1973)
John Killen, *A History of Marine Aviation 1911–68* (London, 1969)

Kapitän z.S. a.D. von Kühlwetter, "The Personnel of the German Navy", *Brassey's Naval Annual 1913*, 132–150

Victor Lavarrenz, *Deutschlands Kriegsflotte* (Erfurt and Leipzig, 1906)

H. M. LeFleming, *Warships of World War I* (London, 1960)

Wm. Roger Louis, *Great Britain and Germany's Lost Colonies 1914–1919* (Oxford, 1967)

Erich Ludendorff, *Meine Kriegserinnerungen, 1914–1918* (Berlin, 1919)

Kriegführung und Politik (Berlin, 1922)

Urkunden der Obersten Heeresleitung über Ihre Tätigkeit 1916–18 (Berlin, 1922)

Eberhard von Mantey, *Deutsche Marinegeschichte* (Charlottenburg, 1926)

Arthur J. Marder, *The Anatomy of British Sea Power. A History of British Naval Policy in the Pre-Dreadnought Era, 1880–1905* (New York, 1940)

From the Dreadnought to Scapa Flow. The Royal Navy in the Fisher Era, 1904–1919 (London 1961–70), 5 vols

Marine und Marinepolitik im Kaiserlichen Deutschland 1871–1914 (Düsseldorf, 1972). Edited by Herbert Schottelius and Wilhelm Deist

Edgar Graf von Matuschka, "Organisationsgeschichte des Heeres 1890–1918", *Handbuch zur deutschen Militärgeschichte 1648–1939*, V (Frankfurt, 1968), 247 ff

Heinrich Otto Meisner, *Denkwürdigkeiten des General-Feldmarschalls Alfred Grafen von Waldersee* (Berlin, 1922–3), 3 vols

Andreas H. Michelsen, *Der U-Bootskrieg 1914–1918* (Leipzig, 1925)

Militärgeschichtliches Forschungsamt, *Die Militärluftfahrt bis zum Beginn des Weltkrieges 1914* (Frankfurt, 1965)

Georg Alexander von Müller, *Der Kaiser . . . Aufzeichnungen des Chefs des Marinekabinetts Georg Alexander v. Müller über die Ära Wilhelms II.* (Göttingen, 1965). Edited by Walter Görlitz

Regierte der Kaiser? Kriegstagebücher, Aufzeichnungen und Briefe des Chefs des Marinekabinetts Admiral Georg Alexander v. Müller 1914–1918 (Göttingen, 1959). Edited by Walter Görlitz

Kurt Naudé, *Der Kampf um den uneingeschränkten U-Boot-Krieg 1914 bis 1917. Ein Beitrag zu dem Problem "Politik und Kriegführung"* (Hamburg, 1941)

Alfred Niemann, *Revolution von oben – Umsturz von unten. Entwicklung und Verlauf der Staatsumwälzung in Deutschland 1914–1918* (Berlin, 1927)

Organisatorische Bestimmungen für das Personal des Soldatenstandes der Kaiserlichen Marine (Berlin, 1906)

Peter Padfield, *The Battleship Era* (London, 1972)

Gerhard Papke, "Anciennität und Beförderung nach Leistung", *Beiträge zur Militär- und Kriegsgeschichte* (Stuttgart, 1962)

Karl Peter, "Seeoffizieranwärter-Ausbildung in Preussen/Deutschland, 1848–1945," MS, Militärgeschichtliches Forschungsamt, Freiburg, Germany, n.d.

Vice-Admiral von Reuter, *Scapa Flow. Das Grab der Deutschen Flotte* (Leipzig, 1921)

John C. G. Röhl, *1914 : Delusion or Design? The Testimony of Two German Diplomats* (London, 1973)

"Admiral von Müller and the Approach of War, 1911–1914", *The Historical Journal,* 12 (1969), 656–667

Jürgen Rohwer, "Kriegsschiffbau und Flottengesetze um die Jahrhundertwende", *Marine und Marinepolitik,* 211–235

Friedrich Ruge, "SMS Seydlitz. Grosser Kreuzer 1913–1919", *Profile Warship 14* (Windsor, 1972)

"Die Verwendung der Mine im Seekrieg 1914 bis 1918. Ihre Erfolge und Misserfolge", *Marine-Rundschau,* 32 (June 1927), 258–300

Scapa Flow 1919. Das Ende der Deutschen Flotte (Oldenburg and Hamburg, 1969)

Reinhard Scheer, *Germany's High Sea Fleet in the World War* (London, 1920)

Wiegand Schmidt-Richberg, "Die Regierungszeit Wilhelms II.", *Handbuch zur deutschen Militärgeschichte,* V (Frankfurt, 1968)

John E. Schrecker, *Imperialism and Chinese Nationalism. Germany in Shantung* (Cambridge, Mass., 1971)

Hans Hugo Sokol, *Österreich-Ungarns Seekrieg, 1914–1918,* III, IV (Vienna, 1933)

Arno Spindler, *Wie es zu dem Entschluss zum uneingeschränkten U-Boots-Krieg 1917 gekommen ist* (Göttingen, n.d.)

Bernd Stegemann, *Die deutsche Marinepolitik 1916–1918* (Berlin, 1970)

Jonathan Steinberg, "The Kaiser's Navy and German Society", *Past and present,* XXVIII (1964), 102–110

"The Copenhagen Complex", *Journal of Contemporary History,* I (1966), 23–46

"Diplomatie als Wille und Vorstellung : Die Berliner Mission Lord Haldanes im Februar 1912", *Marine und Marinepolitik,* 263–281

Yesterday's Deterrent. Tirpitz and the Birth of the German Battle Fleet (London, 1965)

The Submarine Library, General Dynamics Corp., Electric-Boat Division, *Submarine Data* (New London, Groton, Conn., 1965)

James E. Sutton, "The Imperial German Navy 1910–1914", unpublished dissertation, Indiana University, 1953

A. J. P. Taylor, *Germany's First Bid for Colonies 1884–1885. A Move in Bismarck's European Policy* (London, 1928)

Mary Evelyn Townsend, *The Rise and Fall of Germany's Colonial Empire 1884–1918* (New York, 1966)

Ulrich Trumpener, "The Escape of the Goeben and Breslau : A Reassessment", *Canadian Journal of History,* VI (1971), 171–186

Ekkhard Verchau, "Von Jachmann über Stosch und Caprivi zu den Anfängen der Ära Tirpitz", *Marine und Marinepolitik,* 54–72

Hugo v. Waldeyer-Hartz, *Admiral von Hipper. Das Lebensbild eines deutschen Flottenführers* (Leipzig, 1930)

Ernst v. Weizsäcker, *Erinnerungen* (München, 1950)

R. Werner, *Das Buch von der Deutschen Flotte* (Bielefeld and Leipzig, 1893)

Peter-Christian Witt, *Die Finanzpolitik des Deutschen Reiches von 1903 bis 1913* (Lübeck and Hamburg, 1970)

"Reichsfinanzen und Rüstungspolitik 1898–1914", *Marine und Marinepolitik,* 146–177

Josef Zienert, *Unsere Marineuniformen. Ihre geschichtliche Entstehung seit den ersten Anfängen und ihre zeitgemässe Weiterentwicklung von 1816 bis 1969* (Hamburg, 1970)

Index